T0319983

Environmental Politics and Deliberative Democracy

Examining the Promise of New Modes of Governance

Edited by

Karin Bäckstrand

Associate Professor in Political Science, Lund University, Sweden

Jamil Khan

Assistant Professor, Environmental and Energy Systems Studies, Lund University, Sweden

Annica Kronsell

Associate Professor in Political Science, Lund University, Sweden

Eva Lövbrand

Assistant Professor, Centre for Climate Science and Policy Research, Linköping University, Sweden

Edward Elgar

Cheltenham, UK • Northampton, MA, USA

Published by
Edward Elgar Publishing Limited
The Lypiatts
15 Lansdown Road
Cheltenham
Glos GL50 2JA
UK

Edward Elgar Publishing, Inc.
William Pratt House
9 Dewey Court
Northampton
Massachusetts 01060
USA

A catalogue record for this book is available from the British Library

Library of Congress Control Number: 2009941251

ISBN 978 1 84844 954 1

Typeset by Cambrian Typesetters, Camberley, Surrey
Printed on FSC approved paper
Printed and bound in Great Britain by Marston Book Services Ltd, Oxfordshire

Contents

Figures and tables

FIGURE

TABLES

Contributors

Karin Bäckstrand is Associate Professor at the Department of Political Science at Lund University, with a background in international relations and environmental politics. Her research revolves around global environmental politics, the role of scientific expertise in environmental decision-making and global climate change policies. Bäckstrand coordinates the GreenGovern project, a cross-faculty research project where the legitimacy and effectiveness of 'new' modes of environmental governance are examined in the domains of climate, forestry and food safety. She is also leading a new research programme, The Politics and Policy of Carbon Capture and Storage, financed by the Swedish Foundation for Strategic Environmental Research. Bäckstrand's research has been published in *Global Environmental Politics*, *European Journal of International Relations*, *European Environment* and *Environmental Politics* as well as in chapters in book volumes on climate politics and environmental policy.

Beatrice Bengtsson is a PhD candidate at the Research Policy Institute at Lund University, Sweden. She holds an MA in urban development and planning and a BA in social policy and welfare studies. Bengtsson is currently involved in the GreenGovern project on the legitimacy and effectiveness of 'new' modes of European governance, particularly with regard to genetically modified organisms. Her dissertation deals with stakeholder dialogue in the EU food safety domain.

Lovisa Hagberg works as Senior Policy Adviser at World Wildlife Fund Sweden and has until recently been a Lecturer at the Department of Political Science at Lund University, Sweden. She holds a PhD in political science from Umeå University. Her research is concerned with the organization of environmental politics in space and time, green political theory and globalization. Hagberg has also held posts at the Swedish Forest Agency working with strategic forest policy issues and the implementation of the EU Water Framework Directive in European forestry.

Roger Hildingsson is a PhD candidate at the Department of Political Science at Lund University, Sweden. He has an academic background in environmental politics, law and economics and holds an MA in political science. Besides the GreenGovern project, he is currently involved in research projects on European climate governance and renewable energy policy and on governance for transitions towards low-carbon energy and transport systems to meet long-term climate policy objectives. Hildingsson also has experience in the practice of sustainability governance working in public administration and NGOs in Sweden.

Gustav Holmberg is a Lecturer at the Research Policy Institute at Lund University, Sweden. He holds a PhD in the history of science and ideas from Lund University. His research focuses on the relationship between science, politics and media; the history of food technologies; the development of modern astrophysics; and twentieth-century technological futurology. Holmberg's work has been published in academic journals such as *Annals of Science*.

Jamil Khan is Assistant Professor at the Department of Environmental and Energy Systems Studies at Lund University, Sweden. He holds an MA in political science and a PhD in environmental and energy systems studies. His PhD thesis from 2004 dealt with the issue of local politics of renewable energy. Khan's current research interests lie in the fields of environmental governance, policy and implementation studies, renewable energy, sustainable transport, urban climate governance and green political theory. He has published in journals such as *Environmental Planning and Management* and *Local Environment* and has contributed with book chapters. He has also been a peer-reviewer of articles in various scientific journals including the above-mentioned.

Mikael Klintman is Associate Professor and Senior Lecturer in Social Studies of Environment, Science and Risk at the Research Policy Institute, Lund University, Sweden. His research areas include environmental and health-related governance, ethical and political consumerism, and the sociology of consumption. He is currently conducting research on the relationship between soft and hard regulation surrounding health-related, environmental and ethical product claims on an international scale, within the sectors of organic and genetically modified food, electricity, mutual funds, cotton, tourism, medicines and green chemistry. Klintman's work has been published in journals such as *Journal of Consumer Policy, International Journal of Consumer Studies* and *Agriculture and Human Values* as well as in academic books on eco-standards, labelling and political consumerism.

Annica Kronsell is Associate Professor at the Department of Political Science at Lund University, Sweden. She has a background in international relations,

EU studies, environmental politics and feminist theory. Her current research centres particularly on various aspects of governance. She leads a cross-faculty research project on governance for low-carbon futures in the energy and transport sector. In the GreenGovern project she studies 'new' governance modes at the European level in the area of sustainable development. Kronsell is a participating partner in Lund University Centre of Excellence for Integration of Social and Natural Dimensions of Sustainability. She has contributed to textbooks on international relations, several chapters on Swedish environmental politics, multi-level governance and on gender and security studies in books published by Routledge and Cambridge University Press. Her research has been published in journals such as *European Journal of Public Policy*, *Environmental Politics*, *International Feminist Journal of Politics* and *Cooperation and Conflict*.

Eva Lövbrand is Assistant Professor at the Centre for Climate Science and Policy Research at Linköping University, Sweden. She has a background in environmental politics and environmental studies from the universities of Kalmar and Lund. Her doctoral thesis focused on the science–policy interplay in the Kyoto negotiations on land use change and forestry. Since then Lövbrand's research has revolved around the role of science and expertise in environmental politics as well as efforts to link science and democracy. She has also studied the marketization of climate governance and explored the techniques of government that enable and legitimize the international trade in carbon credits. Her work has been published in journals such as *Review of International Studies*, *Global Environmental Politics*, *Environmental Science and Policy*, *Global Environmenal Change* and *Climatic Change*.

Peter Schlyter is Senior Lecturer and Director of Environmental Studies at the Department of Physical Geography and Quaternary Geology at Stockholm University. He holds a PhD in physical geography and a licentiate of engineering in energy and environmental systems studies from Lund University, Sweden. He has researched on environmental impacts of potential future energy systems, remote sensing methods for forest decline surveys, air pollution, soils and tree vitality, and climate change impacts on forestry. Schlyter has been an expert for the Swedish Forest Agency, regional authorities and a member of government inquiries. His work has been published in journals such as *Geografiska Annaler*, *Theoretical and Applied Climatology*, *Climate Research*, *Geographical and Environmental Modelling* and *Forest Policy and Economics*.

Ingrid Stjernquist is Senior Lecturer at the Department of Physical Geography and Quaternary Geology at Stockholm University, Sweden. She holds a PhD in plant ecology from Lund University, Sweden. Her research is focused on sustainable forestry, air pollution deposition and nutrient imbalance in the soil, the impacts of climate change and extreme weather situations on boreal and nemoral forests as well as modelling the plant/soil relationship today and under climate change. She has also researched environmental impacts of renewable energy resources. She is an expert with the Swedish Forest Agency and a member of the Regional Forest Stakeholder Advisory Board. Stjernquist's work has been published in journals such as *Forest Ecology and Management*, *Plant and Soil*, *Climate Change*, *Environmental Pollution*, *Journal of Sustainable Forestry* and *Forest Policy and Economics*.

Johannes Stripple is Senior Researcher at the Department of Political Science, Lund University, Sweden. He holds a licentiate of philosophy in environmental science at Kalmar University, Sweden, and a PhD in political science from Lund University. Stripple has investigated concepts central to international climate policy such as security, territory and authority. His current work focuses on climate policy in the EU, theorizations of carbon markets, the privatization of climate governance, subjectivity and carbon emissions, and Earth System governmentality. His work has been published in journals such as *International Environmental Agreements: Politics, Law and Economics*, *Review of International Studies*, *Global Environmental Change*, *Global Governance* and *European Environment*.

Abbreviations

Anon.	Anonymous
AWG-KP	Ad Hoc Working Group on Further Commitments
BSE	bovine spongiform encephalopathy
CCP	Cities for Climate Protection
CD	(European) Commission Decision
CDM	Clean Development Mechanism
CER	Certified Emission Reduction
CIS	common implementation strategy
CO_2	carbon dioxide
COP	Conference of the parties
COP/MOP	Conference of the parties/meeting of the parties
CSD	(UN) Commission on Sustainable Development
CSR	corporate social responsibility
DG	Directorate General (of the European Commission)
DG SANCO	Directorate General for Health and Consumer Protection
DNA	Designated National Authority
DNV	Det Norske Veritas
DOE	Designated Operational Entities
Ds.	Swedish Governmental PM ('Departementsserien')
EB	Executive Board (of the CDM)
EC	European Commission
ECJ	European Court of Justice
EEB	European Environmental Bureau
EFSA	European Food Safety Authority
EIA	environmental impact assessment
EOC	Environmental Objectives Council
EP	European Parliament
EPA	(Swedish) Environmental Protection Agency
EQO	environmental quality objective
EU-ETS	EU Emissions Trading System
FFW	LIFE Forests for Water project (funded by the EU LIFE fund)
GHG	greenhouse gas
GM	genetically modified
GMO	genetically modified organism
HFI	Home Research Institute

IETA	International Emission Trading Agency
IOs	international organizations
IPCC	Intergovernmental Panel on Climate Change
IR	international relations
IVA	Academy of Engineering Sciences
IWRM	Integrated Water Resources Management
JPOI	Johannesburg Plan of Implementation
KF	(Swedish) Cooperative Federation
KLIMP	Climate Investment Programme
KTH	Royal Institute of Technology
LA21	Local Agenda 21
LDC	least developed countries
LIP	local investment programme for ecological sustainability
MB	Swedish Environmental Code
MS	Member State
NGO	non-governmental organization
OECD	Organisation for Economic Co-operation and Development
OEEC	Organisation for European Economic Co-operation
PDD	project design document
PPP	public–private partnerships
Prop.	Swedish governmental bill ('Proposition')
R&D	research and development
RBMP	River Basin Management Plan
SCFCAH	Standing Committee on the Food Chain and Animal Health
SD	Social Democrats
SDG	Stakeholder Dialogue Group (DG SANCO)
SEK	Swedish krona
SFS	Statute book of Swedish law ('Svensk författningssamling')
SIK	Swedish Institute for Food Preservation Research
SNLT	Sectoral no-lose target
SOU	Swedish governmental inquiry ('Statens offentliga utredningar')
SSNC	Swedish Society for Nature Conservation
STS	science and technology studies
SUV	sports utility vehicle
UNCED	United Nations Conference on Environment and Development (Rio 1992)
UNDP	United Nations Development Programme
UNEP	United Nations Environment Programme
UNFCCC	United Nations Framework Convention on Climate Change
WFD	Water Framework Directive (2000/60/EC)
WHO	World Health Organization

WSSD   World Summit on Sustainable Development (Johannesburg 2002)
WWF   World Wildlife Fund

Preface and acknowledgements

This book reflects the cumulated insights and research results from a three-year multi-disciplinary research project – GreenGovern – 'Participation, Deliberation and Sustainability. Governance beyond Rhetoric in the Domains of Climate, Forestry and Food Safety'. The project was coordinated by Karin Bäckstrand at the Department of Political Science at Lund University in Sweden and funded by Formas, the Swedish Research Council on Environment, Agricultural Sciences and Spatial Planning (2006–2009). The aim of the project was to critically evaluate how new mechanisms for participation of citizens, stakeholders and organizations have gained ground in different areas of environmental and sustainability governance, more particularly climate change, forestry and food safety. The ambition of the research was to critically examine the rhetoric around new modes of governance that has emerged in the policy debate, and it asked if new modes of deliberative and market-based governance can effectively address what social science perceives as the main problems of sustainability governance: the implementation and legitimacy deficits. Can democratic legitimacy, participation and accountability be secured while at the same time assuring environmental performance and effective policies?

The idea to pull together a multi-disciplinary project on the legitimacy and effectiveness of new modes of environmental governance was first initiated in the creative and innovative atmosphere of the environmental seminar group at the Department of Political Science. The ideas were developed further in the autumn of 2004 with the help of a planning grant from the Lund University Vice Chancellor's Office and the Lund University Centre for Sustainability Studies (LUCSUS). In the spring of 2005, a group of 10 researchers at the Department of Political Science, the Research Policy Institute at Lund University, the Environmental and Energy Systems Studies at Lund Institute of Technology, and the Department of Physical Geography at Stockholm University brainstormed on research topics, theoretical approaches and empirical case studies. From this multi-disciplinary dialogue between political scientists, historians of science, ecologists, engineers, science and technology scholars, physical geographers and environmental scientists a research application emerged, which was granted the largest funding for cross-disciplinary research by Formas in the autumn of 2005. Our deepest gratitude is extended to Formas. The generous project funding enabled us to critically examine and reflect upon how environmental politics can be rendered more effective and legitimate during a time frame of three years.

This book would not have come about without the sustained multi-disciplinary dialogue enabled by the GreenGovern project. The process of the project – a stimulating intellectual journey, dialogue and conversation between participating scholars – was as important as the outcomes. The work conducted in GreenGovern has been inspired by deliberative ideas. Ideas and arguments have been probed, tested and contested during the entire project. The annual project workshops in 2006, 2007 and 2008 at the seaside villages of Vitemölle and Kivik on the Swedish east coast Österlen have provided an environment for academic conversations and reflections, solitude and great fun. Our monthly literature seminars in Lund on various topics such as deliberative democracy, legitimacy, governance and environmental effectiveness have been lively and very helpful in gaining a common understanding of key concepts, theoretical frameworks and empirical fields of studies informing the project and the book.

The disciplinary and methodological diversity in the backgrounds of the project participants has been a great strength, as has the mix between theoretical inquiries and empirical work. In GreenGovern we have discussed literature in environmental politics, forest ecology, governance studies, history of science, consumer politics, EU studies, international relations and social constructivism. We have not always agreed: the debates have been heated but always very stimulating. The combined competence of researchers in different empirical fields: forest certification, climate governance, food safety, biodiversity and water governance informed discussions of a more philosophical kind on the nature of deliberative democracy and communicative action. It was very fruitful to confront abstract theoretical notions with the concrete reality of environmental problems.

Two workshops were arranged in the spring of 2008 with a broader academic audience, policy practitioners and stakeholders. We extend our deep thanks to Ingrid Stjernquist and Peter Schlyter for hosting the Forest Governance workshop at the Department of Physical Geography at Stockholm University in April 2008. We are likewise very grateful to Eva Lövbrand, Joakim Nordquist, Jamil Khan and Johannes Stripple for successfully co-organizing the Climate Governance workshop at Lund University in May 2008. Through the years the project has benefited from the constructive comments and reflections of many colleagues in Lund and beyond: Rasmus Karlsson, Åsa Knaggård, Gunhildur Magnusdottir, Emma Paulsson, Lennart Olsson and Linn Takeuchi-Waldegren. We also wish to thank our colleagues in the international research community who have, at various stages of the project, provided valuable input and encouragement. We extend our gratitude to Marie Appelstrand, Per Angelstam, Frank Biermann, Michael Böcher, Harriet

Bulkeley, Ken Conca, Katarina Eckerberg, Lars Gulbrandsen, David Humphreys, Erik Hysing, Lisa Holmgren, Carina Keskitalo, Dainela Kleinschmit, Per Larsson, Anna Lawrence, Diane Liverman, James Meadowcroft, Matthew Paterson, Philipp Pattberg, Roger Pielke, Tapio Rantala, Gunilla Reischl, Charlotte Streck, Harro van Asselt and Fariborz Zelli.

Effective project administration is a precondition for creative and cumulative knowledge building, empirical inquiry and theoretical synthesis. Roger Hildingsson has made our lives easier through his effective work as GreenGovern's project assistant along with his constructive substantial input to the project. We are also very grateful to Rasmus Karlsson who set up GreenGovern's intranet, our virtual meeting place which saved our inboxes from collapsing from all versions of draft papers by the project participants. We also express our gratitude to Stefan Alenius, who was very helpful in all matters relating to administration of the project at the Department of Political Science.

The idea of writing a book synthesizing the cumulated insights on the effectiveness and legitimacy of new modes of environmental governance was there from the inception of the GreenGovern project. This book builds on the contributions of GreenGovern's participating scholars at three universities in Sweden. Of the 14 researchers, 11 are based at Lund University or Lund Institute of Technology: Karin Bäckstrand, Roger Hildingsson, Annica Kronsell, Lovisa Hagberg, Johannes Stripple (Department of Political Science), Beatrice Bengtsson, Gustav Holmberg, Mikael Klintman (Research Policy Institute), Jamil Khan, Lars J. Nilsson, Joakim Nordquist (Environment and Energy System Studies). Two researchers – Peter Schlyter and Ingrid Stjernquist – are affiliated with the Department of Physical Geography and Quaternary Geology at Stockholm University. Finally. Eva Lövbrand works at the Centre for Climate Science and Policy Research at Linköping University. Many of the project participants divided their time between GreenGovern and other projects with overlapping themes. The ADAM project (EU), ClimateColl (The Swedish Energy Agency), IMPACT (Mistra), LETS (Swedish Environmental Protection Agency), the SPARC project (the US National Science Foundation, University of Colorado) and the Transdemos programme (Bank of Sweden), enabled fruitful conversations to take place across projects on common concepts and topics.

However, more concrete ideas of book structure, themes and chapters took form during the spring of 2008 through a series of seminars. In GreenGovern's workshop in Vitemölle in September 2008, the first draft chapters of the book were discussed. In this context we would like to express our gratitude to James Meadowcroft, who was invited to the workshop as an external commentator on the book project. James's sharp, constructive and helpful input was instrumental in moving the book forward. We are also very grateful to Felicity Plester at Edward Elgar for assisting in the publication of this book with professionalism, speedy and helpful response and enthusiasm. Furthermore, we are grateful to several anonymous reviewers who challenged us to push the boundaries of the book to achieve greater theoretical and empirical synthesis. Finally, this book would not have been possible without the collective input, support and help from colleagues and friends. However, we take full responsibility for any errors or omissions remaining in the book.

PART I

Theorizing the promise of new modes of governance

1. The promise of new modes of environmental governance

Karin Bäckstrand, Jamil Khan, Annica Kronsell and Eva Lövbrand

In August 2008 the European Commission invited European Union (EU) citizens and stakeholders from industry, trade unions, consumer organizations, environmental NGOs and academia to comment on the design of a future climate treaty beyond 2012. The consultation covered both normative and technical issues and was organized in the form of an online questionnaire distributed via the European Commission's webpage.[1] This attempt to engage public and private actors in a debate over European climate policy exemplifies a governance trend that extends well beyond the EU. We call this trend 'the deliberative turn', which we take to mean an increased attention in environmental politics to procedural qualities such as participation, dialogue, transparency and accountability. Although the deliberative turn may be more rhetorical than practical, we argue that it is epitomized by the recent proliferation of 'new' modes of environmental governance. During the past decades environmental policies on local, national, EU and global levels have become associated with the rise of less hierarchical and more collaborative governance arrangements (Koehnig-Archibugi and Zürn, 2006; Smismans, 2006). Stakeholder dialogues, citizen juries, network governance, public–private partnerships and voluntary standards are some examples of the deliberative, participatory and market-oriented strategies that have gained ground in policy areas such as food safety, forestry and climate change (for example Meadowcroft, 2004; Bäckstrand, 2006, 2008; Lövbrand et al., 2009; Pattberg, 2007).

In this book we approach this governance trend as an empirical phenomenon, analysed in literature on environmental and sustainability governance and manifested in debates, strategies and policies related to the practice of environmental politics. While typically associated with less hierarchical and 'softer' forms of steering, we argue that new modes of environmental governance also harbour a normative agenda to open up politics and make environmental decision-making more inclusive, transparent, accountable and reflexive, while at the same time effective and performance-oriented. Linked to deliberative ideals of democracy articulated by democracy, governance and policy scholars, the deliberative turn thus denotes the range of more or less explicit attempts to democratize environmental politics and simultaneously foster more effective environmental policies. Although far from all new modes of environmental governance involve actual practices of deliberation, we suggest that they rest upon an underlying assumption that broad participation by public and private actors in collective decision-making will bring about both more legitimate and effective policy outcomes. We call this normative assumption 'the promise' of new modes of environmental governance, as indicated by the sub-title of the book.

The promise of new modes of environmental governance has been articulated among political theorists, governance scholars and policy practitioners, who in recent years have attached much hope to new governance arrangements that increase the participation and deliberation across market, government and civil society sectors. In this book we trace and scrutinize this promise by linking literature on democratic theory, green political theory and scholarly work on governance and environmental policy. We argue that this literature tends to reproduce the assumption that 'softer' and more decentralized forms of steering will strengthen both the democratic quality and performance of environmental policies compared to 'old' forms of hierarchical governance (legislation, regulation and traditional command and control). At the same time we note that to date there is little scholarly work that has examined the theoretical and empirical foundations of this assumption. This book takes a step in that direction by linking the normative aspirations associated with environmental governance to policy practice.

Through eight case studies we compare how deliberative ideals have informed forestry, climate, water and food safety policy from the local to the global level through the employment of various modes of governance. The case studies represent a rich set of examples of common pool resources (for example forestry and water) and common sink problems (for example climate change) and, hence, cover both pollution abatement and the management of natural resources. Moreover, the book broadens the study of environmental policy by offering empirical examples of 'governance of sustainable development' (Jordan, 2008; Lafferty, 2004; Meadowcroft, 2008). These include the governance of genetically modified food, local Agenda 21, global summitry for sustainable development and the interplay between climate change and the sustainable development agenda. Accordingly, the book investigates how theoretical ideals of deliberative democracy have informed new modes of governance such as networks, public–private partnerships and multi-stakeholder dialogues employed in different policy domains. Through our eight case studies we address the main research question of this book; *can new modes of governance ensure effective environmental policy performance as well as deliberative and participatory quality?*

The remainder of this introduction provides the context for the book by discussing what meaning we attach to the deliberative turn and new modes of environmental governance. In the first section we begin by tracing how deliberative democratic ideals play out in academic inquiry and in environmental policy practice. The second section places the book in the broader governance debate and clarifies how we relate to the various scholarly definitions of new modes of environmental governance.

In the third section we move on to our specific 'unit of analysis': new modes of environmental governance. In reviewing the multifaceted scholarly debate around new modes of governance, we clarify our distinct approach, which is based on a critical inquiry on the governance rationalities and forms underpinning new modes. In the fourth section, we examine the expectations tied to new governance modes found in the literature (what promise do they hold?), and the fifth section highlights some of the pitfalls of new modes of governance as pointed out by critics. The final section presents the outline of the book.

DELIBERATIVE DEMOCRATIC IDEALS IN THEORY AND PRACTICE

Since the deliberative model of democracy gained renewed attention in democratic theory in the 1990s (for example Fishkin and Laslett, 2006; Gutmann and Thompson, 2004; Bohman and Regh, 1997), it has been advanced as a supplement to aggregate democracy, and, ultimately as a means to deepen or 'democratize' democracy. At the heart of the deliberative ideal is the notion that members of the public should be included and engaged on equal terms in collective decision-making. While there are differences between the liberal and critical tradition, deliberative models of democracy have in common that they promote values of public justification and political equality (Baber and Bartlett, 2005; Meadowcroft, 2004, p. 184). Through open and reasoned argument, free from manipulation and the exercise of power, better and more legitimate decisions will arise.

Although deliberative theory mostly draws attention to democratic procedures, green political thinkers have in recent years linked deliberative democratic ideals to environmental outcomes. The notion that public participation in environmental policy-making will increase the democratic legitimacy *and* performance of green regulation is a recurrent theme within contemporary green political theorizing (Baber and Bartlett, 2005; Meadowcroft, 2004; Smith, 2003; Dryzek, 2000). As argued in further depth by Lövbrand and Khan in Chapter 3 (this volume), many green political scholars expect that deliberative processes will foster critical self-awareness of the ecological grounds which support our lives. Through free and inclusive reason-giving on questions of common purpose, reflective citizens will bridge the dual goals of strong democracy and demanding environmentalism (Baber and Bartlett, 2005, p. 12). As a consequence, deliberative democracy has become a central component of the notion of ecological democracy (Arias-Maldonado, 2007; Mitchell, 2006).

Concerned with the relationship between democratic procedure and environmental outcomes, green political theory offers interesting links to debates about environmental governance that are increasingly dominated by questions of how to secure democratic legitimacy and policy effectiveness. In theoretical and policy debates alike, the pressing nature of the environmental challenge has drawn attention to the classic dilemma of democracy versus effectiveness, procedure versus outcome. The promise associated with new modes of environmental governance implies that less hierarchical and more collaborative forms of steering will resolve this dilemma. As outlined above, governance arrangements that build upon inclusive participation by public and private actors in collective decision-making are typically expected to bring about both more legitimate and effective policy outcomes. Since green political theory harbours a similar promise, we find this theoretical field particularly useful to our study. However, the chapters in this book also draw upon deliberative ideals found in other academic fields.

In recent years, theories of deliberative democracy have, for instance, informed debates on transnational democracy beyond the nation-state (Glasbergen et al., 2007, Koehnig-Archibugi and Zürn, 2006; Risse, 2004). Moreover, notions of global stakeholder democracy have gained ground (Bäckstrand, 2006; MacDonald, 2008). The global public sphere has been advanced as a viable model for counteracting the democratic deficit and enhancing the legitimacy of international governance arrangements and institutions (Beisheim and Dingwerth, 2008; Dingwerth, 2007; Börzel and Risse, 2005; Steffek, 2003). In the International Relations (IR) literature on the legitimacy of global governance, the procedural legitimacy of new forms of public–private interaction in the environmental domain is examined through the concepts of accountability, inclusiveness and deliberation (Dingwerth, 2007). A recurring argument also in this literature is that procedural values, such as public accountability, transparency, representation and participation of societal stakeholders, will strengthen the performance of environmental agreements (Mason, 2005).

Deliberative democratic ideals have also gained currency in studies of science and technology. Concepts such as 'citizen science' (Irwin, 1995; Fischer, 2005), 'the democratization of science' (Leach et al., 2007) and 'civic epistemology' (Jasanoff, 2005) all reflect the idea that citizens should be invited to critically scrutinize scientific and technological decisions that affect their lives (Hagendijk and Irwin, 2006). These reflective and participatory versions of science resonate with Ulrich Beck's concept of reflexive modernization. Risk society, with its associated global hazards, requires a wider process of public accountability, reflection, scrutiny and dissent (Beck, 1992). The uncertain and post-normal nature of controversies such as genetically modified organisms, nuclear waste and climate change can only be managed if the perspectives and insights from citizen and stakeholder groups are taken into account (Pellizzoni, 2003, see also Chapter 6, this volume). Hence, also in this literature there is an underlying assumption that deliberative democratic procedures will enhance policy performance.

Beyond the scholarly interest in deliberative forms of governance, this book also draws attention to policy debates where deliberative ideals have surfaced. In contemporary environmental policy practice it is often argued that inclusive and participatory decision-making will enhance public acceptance for policy decisions, while at the same time strengthening the knowledge base for implementation. Hence, policy innovations that increase the participation of and deliberation among citizens and societal stakeholders have in recent years been promoted in multilateral, national and local contexts. This trend can be exemplified with the United Nations Conference on Environment and Development (UNCED) in Rio de Janeiro in 1992, where the multi-stakeholder model for subsequent environmental mega-summits was initiated (Green and Chambers, 2006). Agenda 21, which was adopted in Rio, states that '[o]ne of the fundamental prerequisites for the achievement of sustainable development is broad public participation in decision-making' (UNCED, 1992, Ch. 23.2).

Participatory modes of governance became institutionalized in the years after the Rio meeting and were further reinforced by the World Summit on Sustainable Development (WSSD) in Johannesburg 2002 (Bäckstrand, 2006). The summit outcome exemplifies this trend with almost 400 partnerships for sustainable development and detailed procedures for including civil society, business and governments in stakeholder forums and dialogues (Martens, 2007). In the same spirit and with a similar logic, the UNCED also initiated a process geared toward deliberative governance through Agenda 21. Through the development of local Agenda 21 strategies, stakeholders were encouraged to engage in policy making on environment and sustainable development (see Chapter 8, this volume). Albeit a diversity of policy contexts, the message is similar. Deliberation among societal groups is claimed to produce more legitimate and effective environmental policies as affected stakeholders are included and granted ownership of environmental problems (Nanz and Steffek, 2004).

Also in the European Union (EU), the rise of new modes of governance can be interpreted as a response to the legitimacy deficit and crisis of governance.

New instruments have been advanced to counter this deficit, to strengthen policy performance and to improve public accountability (Knill and Liefferink, 2007; Schout and Jordan, 2005; Skogstad, 2003). The EU Commission's White Paper on governance in 2001 precipitated a call for participatory governance mechanisms, mirrored in the consultation procedures on the European sustainable development strategy, climate and environmentally related policies, as well as in a broader concern with stakeholder participation, both in the initiation and implementation of EU policies. The open method of coordination exemplifies what Eberlein and Kerwer (2004, p. 6) call 'deliberative supranationalism'.

So far we have only offered a few examples of how deliberative ideals have informed theoretical inquiry and policy practice in recent years. Although far from pre-emptive, these examples form the starting point for our examination of the deliberative turn and the promise of new modes of environmental governance. Through our eight in-depth case studies, we aim to extend and deepen the understanding of this governance trend. As outlined in further detail below, this book scrutinizes how the expectations tied to global public–private partnerships (Chapters 4 and 5, this volume), stakeholder participation in the EU (Chapters 6 and 7), deliberative innovations within public administrations (Chapters 8 and 10), and network governance (Chapters 9 and 11) hold out in practice. However, before turning to our cases, we will first place the book in the broader scholarly debate on environmental governance and new modes of governance.

ENVIRONMENTAL GOVERNANCE

The 'governance' concept is broad and denotes the totality of instruments and mechanisms available to collectively steer a society (Lafferty, 2004; Peters, 2005). Although governance is extensively discussed among scholars, there are, as Carter (2007, pp. 174–9) suggests, certain characteristics distinguishing the environment as a problem for governance. Environmental governance often concerns problems related to public goods, either as common resources or as common sinks. Environmental problems also vary with regard to their temporal and spatial effects. They are often transboundary, cross-sectoral and complex, and are consequently associated with a high degree of scientific uncertainty and risk (Meadowcroft, 2008). The characteristics associated with environmental problems partly explain why environmental governance tends to be global or transnational in design, why oftentimes environmental governance calls for the engagement of many sectors and multiple public and private actors, and why a future-looking and global perspective is relevant and precautionary action necessary. With this in mind, it is also possible to imagine why environmental governance has been fraught with implementation and legitimacy deficits (see Figure 1.1 below). This is the backdrop for calls for new and better governance mechanisms.

Initially, the concept of governance in scholarly work was used as a complement to government. By adopting the concept of governance we avoid making a sharp distinction between what goes on within states and what happens outside states. However, in recent years the locus of political authority has been of central concern to most governance scholars. In reviewing the literature, we have identified three governance approaches: empirical, normative and critical. The bulk of the expanding governance scholarship is empirical or normative, or a combination of both (Jordan, 2008, p. 24). A brief summary of the three governance approaches follows.

Empirical Governance

The empirical approach conceives of governance as a contemporary phenomenon connected to globalization. With a multitude of actors at multiple levels of authority, politics moves from and between governments to private actors, and in the process also dissolves or reshuffles levels of authority (Rosenau and Czempiel, 1992; Young, 1999; Scholte, 2002). A diverse set of actors such as companies, social movements, local authorities, environmental administrations, global and supranational bodies are involved in governance processes. A general insight is that governance is becoming less hierarchical and beyond the control of states. Through globalization and transnationalization, political, administrative and jurisdictional levels have become interrelated and interdependent.

The notion of shifting sites for politics has been explored particularly in relation to EU governance, but is also used more generally (for example Winter, 2006; Kohler-Koch and Eising, 1999; Hooghe and Marks, 2000; Bache and Flinders, 2004). Connections between local and global activities were highlighted early by environmental politics scholars (for example Hempel, 1996). Lundqvist (2004, p. 19) adds a normative twist to this observation when he argues that collective environmental management 'requires a multi-level governance approach'. This is because multi-level governance does not predetermine the level of authority but provides opportunities for delegation of competences, responsibility and authority to, for example, ecosystem-based entities. Multi-level EU dynamics have led to environmental policy innovations but also to compliance deficits (Andersen and Liefferink, 1997; Börzel, 1999, 2002; Jordan and Liefferink, 2004; Liefferink and Jordan, 2005; Knill and Lenschow, 2005).

Research on state governance also recognizes that the pressures from global actors and transnational policy processes have changed and challenged state governance (Pierre and Peters, 2000). There are similarities in these various items of literature in their focus on the role of non-state actors, networks and the fragmentation of authority and in the way they view the changing nature of the state. In Part III of this book we return to the transformed role of the state and hierarchical forms of governing in view of the deliberative turn. We offer several cases of Swedish state governance (Chapter 8–10, this volume) that challenge the conventional notion that the involvement of non-state actors in rule-making automatically leads to reduced state power and authority.

Normative Governance

The normative governance approach has an explicit prescriptive agenda, and often advances proposals for effective and legitimate governance (McCrew, 2002). Closely linked to the new modes of governance literature, it informs 'the promise' in its aim to improve and contribute to 'good governance'. New modes of governance are often framed as an alternative to the inadequacies of 'old' modes of governance. In line with Treib et al. (2007) we argue that the distinction between old and new modes of governance does not hold in practice. In light of historical analyses such as Holmberg's examination of food technology deliberations in the mid-twentieth century (Chapter 9, this volume), new modes do not seem all that 'new'. However, closely associated with novel governance arrangements are aspirations to increase accountability, performance and legitimacy (Keohane, 2003; Weiss, 2005). The quest for good environmental governance is about 'improving and reforming the functioning of democratic institutions, including the 'deepening' of democracy and exploring more active and creative roles for non-state actors' (Weiss, 2005, p. 76). Hence, 'good' environmental governance is closely associated with procedural and substantive ideals such as openness, participation, accountability, coherence and effectiveness (Bernstein, 2005).

Good governance debates primarily take place within policy circles of institutions such as the EU, the Organisation for Economic Co-operation and Development (OECD) and the World Bank. The call for larger societal participation in governance processes is a response to the perceived legitimacy crisis and democratic deficit of global and regional institutions in an era of globalization. The limits of hierarchical and top-down governance arrangements have been increasingly recognized in these debates. Consequently much faith is put in 'new modes of governance' that deal with transnational problems and emerge in different shapes: public–private partnerships, networks and market mechanisms. The normative governance approach seems most relevant and interesting to the policy community. However, concepts in the academic debate, such as legitimacy and accountability, diffuse to policy circles and vice versa. We therefore argue that the rhetorical promise of new modes of governance, which is subject to critical scrutiny in the book, has emerged in close interaction between academic scholars and policy makers in the normative debate on good governance.

Critical Governance

There is a range of critical governance approaches. For example, neo-gramscian scholars have conceived of governance as a structuring process connected with conditions of globalization and late capitalism. Accordingly, governance is both a disciplining order and one that gives rise to resistance, where key actors such as NGOs and social movements both resist and provide alternatives to the existing world order (Cox, 1986). Hereby, governance is integral to processes of globalization and the dominance of a neoliberal order where economic and political processes are interdependent (Murphy, 2005; Gill, 2005; Petersen, 2003; Paterson, 2007). The role of the state is seen as complicit with the governing order of neoliberalism (Paterson, 2000) and 'sites of power' are assumed to shift from the political to the economic sphere. Governments as well as international organizations are highly implicated in this order of marketization.

Governmentality studies represent another approach with critical potential. Inspired by Foucault, governmentality scholars are also interested in the processes of ordering enabled by neoliberal forms of government (Barry et al., 1996; Lemke, 2002; Miller and Rose, 2008). However, rather than interpreting neoliberalism as an ideology that erodes state authority, governmentality scholars approach it as a new rationality and technique of government that shifts the responsibility for social risks (for example illness, unemployment, greenhouse gas emissions) from the state to free and economic-rational individuals (Burchell, 1996; Shamir, 2008). Through indirect means of intervention such as standards, codes of conduct, benchmarks and audits, social actors are given responsibility for their actions and are hereby 'governed at a distance' (Rose and Miller, 1992). In this process, the state is 'degovernmentalized' and operates as facilitator, mediator and partner rather than a distinct centre of calculation. While interested in historical transformations of statehood, governmentality scholars do not, however, ask who has power and authority in environmental governance. In focus instead are the practices and ways of thinking that enable rule in the first place and hereby shape the conduct of individuals.

In this book we do not side with a specific governance approach. However, our ambition to scrutinize the promise of new modes of environmental governance gives the book a critical twist. The analytical framework presented by Kronsell and Bäckstrand (Chapter 2, this volume) is based on forms and rationalities of governance, and hereby draws attention to patterns of behaviour and conduct in governance. In that sense it is inspired by governmentality scholars' ambition to problematize 'what is given to us as necessary to think and do' (Burchell, 1996, p. 32). Lövbrand's and Khan's analysis of deliberative ideals in green political theory (Chapter 3, this volume), in turn engages with the neo-gramscian critique of market environmentalism and the limited prospects for public deliberation in an age of economic globalization. The authors in Part II and III are all informed by these critical perspectives in their analyses of various modes of environmental governance. However, writing from different disciplinary vantage points, they do not advance a shared critical standpoint. Instead the book follows, in a more general sense, what Dalby (2007, p. 103) takes to be the role of critique in scholarly work: namely 'challenging the taken for granted categories in scholarly and political discourse.' Most importantly, our approach is critical-empirical because the critique has a rigorous empirical foundation, and this is its strength.

WHAT ARE NEW MODES OF GOVERNANCE?

In the environmental and sustainability governance literature, new modes are seen as examples of deliberative and collaborative governance (van Zeijl-Rozema et al., 2008). These governance modes are claimed to be functional, to handle the complex, cross-sectoral, multi-scale and long-term temporal aspects of modern environmental problems (Jordan, 2008; Biermann, 2007). Uncertainty and risk requires participation of a multiplicity of actors across spheres of government, civil society and market (Meadowcroft, 2007; Lafferty, 2004). The legitimacy and democratic quality of new modes of governance are increasingly receiving attention in scholarly research across different environmental policy domains (Meadowcroft, 2007; Nölke and Graz, 2007; Pattberg, 2007).

The literature on new modes of governance is expansive, and scholars in this field have in recent years been busy pinning down definitions. Treib et al. (2007) argue that new modes of governance are primarily found in the span between public authority and societal self-regulation. They are related to a trend towards less hierarchical governance, manifested inside states where governments cede control of the policy process to become managers of a complexity of governance relations (Pierre and Peters, 2000). This shift is also marked by a loss of state control in the international system, exemplified by processes of multi-level governance (for example Hooghe and Marks, 2000; Kohler-Koch and Eising, 1999) and global governance (for example Rosenau and Czempiel, 1992; Scholte, 2002; Weiss, 2005). As a consequence, governance today relies on a mix of hierarchical and non-hierarchical forms of steering, and builds upon collaboration between government, market and civil society actors (Boström and Klintman, 2008; Koehnig-Archibugi and Zürn, 2006). 'Reflexive governance' (Voss et al., 2006), 'network governance' (Benner et al., 2003), 'collaborative governance' (Glasbergen, 1998), 'market governance' (O'Neill, 2007), 'deliberative governance', and 'private governance' (Pattberg, 2007) are some of the concepts used to depict this trend.

Börzel and Risse (2005, p. 196) argue that new modes of governance rely primarily on non-hierarchical steering, such as positive incentives, bargaining and non-manipulative persuasion. This can be contrasted with 'old' modes of governance based on hierarchical steering, such as top-down regulation and enforcement and threat of sanctions. Compared to the traditional interventionist state, the state in new modes of governance takes on roles as facilitator of public–private policy networks. However, as will be argued in this book, the novelty of 'new' modes of governance can be questioned, as they operate in the shadow of the hierarchy with background conditions of state authority, intervention, steering and control. Public–private partnerships (see Chapter 5, this volume) can be conceived of as prime examples of new modes of governance as they rely on non-hierarchical steering and a mix of public and private actors. They can be distinguished from new modes that rest solely on private actor participation and self-regulation. Work on private authority (Cutler et al., 1999; Hall and Biersteker, 2002) and non-state market-driven governance systems (Cashore et al., 2004) focus on collaboration between non-state actors from the profit and non-profit sector.

The term 'governance for sustainable development' epitomizes the complex interaction between government, market actors, NGOs and international organizations in the quest for long-term goals of sustainability (Jordan, 2008; Meadowcroft, 2008). Along similar lines, Biermann (2007, p. 329) has advanced the concept 'Earth System governance' to denote the hundreds of international regimes, international bureaucracies, transnational activist groups, expert networks and national agencies that have been set up to secure a sustainable steering of human society. Within this field new modes are often defined as 'new environmental regulation', which combines participatory mechanisms, market instruments and public–private collaboration (Fiorini, 2006). Examples here are local Agenda 21 deliberations, multi-stakeholder panels on sustainable development, forest certification schemes and green labelling of consumer goods. The 'essence' of these new modes of environmental governance is that they display a combination of market-based and deliberative elements and a mix of public and private forms of steering (Fiorini, 2006; Pattberg, 2007).

Rather than advancing yet another definition of what new modes of governance are (and are not), this book is more concerned with the functional and normative context in which new modes are embedded. By analysing different modes of governance according to their forms (hierarchy, market, network) and their rationalities (administrative, economic and deliberative), we seek to assess how processes of steering play out in view of the deliberative turn. According to this framework, further elaborated by Kronsell and Bäckstrand in Chapter 2 (this volume), governance forms are not automatically informed by *a* rationality, but can rest upon a variety of governance rationalities that may vary over time. Following this line of arguing, seemingly new ways of steering do not necessarily take form in contrast to 'the old', but rather in relation to old governance forms or on a continuum. We agree with Börzel and Risse (2005, p. 197) that 'the distinction between hierarchical and non-hierarchical steering is primarily an analytical one'. In other words, new modes of governance occur in the context of hierarchical steering as governments and states often rely on networks of private actors for effective policy implementation. When studying new modes of governance from the vantage point of forms and rationalities, we are thus able to move the analysis beyond a strict old versus new distinction. The demarcation between public and private, which has preoccupied governance scholars in the past, also becomes less important. Instead of asking who governs in which sites, our framework draws attention to the 'hardware' and 'software' that informs contemporary rule-making in the environmental domain.

As will be shown in the book, the deliberative turn does not represent a clear-cut or definite governance trend. Our eight cases suggest that different forms and rationalities currently inform environmental governance. However, by comparing our eight cases we do observe that deliberative rationality now seems to be relevant to all forms of governance: hierarchy, markets and networks. We also note that market-oriented and deliberative steering mechanisms can be based on conflicting governance rationalities, yet they all seem to be designed with the ambition to simultaneously solve environmental problems and improve the legitimacy of environmental policies.

To reiterate, in this book we are not primarily interested in providing a particular definition of new modes of governance. Instead we want to explore how forms and rationalities of governance play out in contemporary environmental politics. Beyond our analysis of governance forms typically associated with new modes (for example public–private partnerships, networks, stakeholder deliberations), this book also examines how hierarchy has been influenced by the deliberative turn. This latter question is addressed in the Swedish context in Chapters 8 and 10 (this volume). Pure market and civil society governance is, however, beyond the scope of this book.

WHAT PROMISE DOES NEW MODES OF GOVERNANCE HOLD?

We argue that the broad mix of governance arrangements in the environmental domain, albeit diverse and different, is tied to the deliberative turn through a shared promise. In the following we examine this promise in further detail. Environmental politics and sustainable development has emerged as an experimental arena for new modes of governance. The attraction of such governance arrangements lies in their promise to counteract the prevailing 'governance', 'legitimacy' and 'implementation' deficits (see Figure 1.1). As suggested by Haas (2004), these three deficits constitute enduring challenges to governance arrangements in the environmental and sustainability domain. The governance deficit is a result of the cross-sectoral, fragmented and transnational nature of many environmental problems. Divided into different compartments and handled by different institutions, environmental challenges are often marginalized in national and world politics. Moreover, there is a chronic implementation deficit. High-level rhetoric and aspirations to environmental and sustainable development goals seldom translate into organizational practice, regulation, policies and implementation. Finally, the legitimacy deficit stems from the declining confidence among citizens that the state and governmental actors are able to manage the environmental crisis by themselves.

The rise of new modes of environmental governance can be interpreted as a response to the trilemma illustrated by Figure 1.1. Collaborative, flexible and soft forms of governance that include civil society and business in policy deliberations are advanced as a way to enhance the legitimacy of environmental policies and thus counteract the governance and implementation deficits. Hence, the promise of new modes of governance lies in the connection between

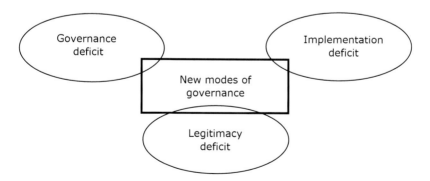

Figure 1.1   The promise of new modes of governance

legitimate democratic processes (input) and effective environmental policies (output). Central to the promise, which is illustrated in Figure 1.1, is that new modes are advanced as win–win policy tools that can respond to the governance, implementation and legitimacy deficits simultaneously.

When addressing our main research question – whether new modes of governance ensure effective environmental policy performance as well as deliberative and participatory quality – we adopt a normative conception of legitimacy that stipulates criteria for procedural qualities and effectiveness. Democratic or procedural legitimacy, which rests on values of participation and accountability, is only one source of legitimacy that is closely associated with domestic models of electoral democracy. When evaluating if the promise is fulfilled, we also include effectiveness and policy performance as central normative criteria. We argue that such performance-oriented criteria are particularly relevant when assessing non-electoral, non-territorial and transnational governance arrangements beyond the nation-state. Hence, drawing upon Scharpf's (1999; 2006) analysis of sources of legitimacy in the European Union, this book organizes the legitimacy of new modes of environmental governance according to an input (procedural) and output (problem-solving capacity) dimension. The dual legitimacy framework, further elaborated in Chapter 2, is based on (deliberative) democratic ideals of participation, transparency, dialogue and accountability as well as performance criteria such as institutional and environmental effectiveness.

CRITICS OF THE DELIBERATIVE IDEAL AND THE PROMISE OF NEW MODES

The promise that new modes of governance will deliver effective and legitimate policies and strengthen practical experiments with deliberative democracy should not be embraced uncritically. We are not the first to argue this. Despite the recent celebration of participatory and deliberative governance arrangements among scholars and practitioners alike, the scholarly literature also includes a range of sceptical voices. Below we highlight three central lines of critique that can be linked to the empirical and critical governance traditions outlined above. Whereas the first critical perspective questions the empirical foundation of the promise of new modes of environmental governance, the latter two target the deliberative ideal by raising questions about power and politics. Since all three strands of critique constitute a major challenge to the deliberative turn and its prospects of delivering more legitimate and effective environmental policies, they are essential to our study. Hence, in the concluding Chapter 12 we will revisit each line of critique in light of our empirical case studies and thereby assess their relevance and significance.

The empirically founded critique, to which we turn first, targets the main research question of this book. Do new governance arrangements ensure effective environmental policy performance as well as deliberative and participatory quality? To date and mainly limited to public–private partnerships, scholars have noted that there is poor or, at best, mixed evidence that this dual promise holds true in practice (Börzel and Risse, 2005; Benner et al., 2003). This critique resonates with debates in green political theory that question whether deliberative models of democracy indeed will generate green outcomes and effective environmental policies (cf. Smith, 2003; Wissenburg, 1998). Deliberative democratic processes may be emancipatory, lead to more informed choices, and increase the legitimacy of policies. However, on a principal level, many scholars have questioned the assumed link between public deliberations and enhanced environmental policy performance, as discussed further by Lövbrand and Khan (Chapter 3, this volume). Due to a lack of systematic studies, there is very thin empirical evidence for such a link (Baber and Bartlett, 2005; Smith, 2003). Accordingly, it has been argued that the environmental effectiveness of participatory innovations is assumed rather than validated.

This critique functions as a central starting point for this book. Our study emerges as a direct response to the lack of critical–empirical studies of the promise of new modes of environmental governance. And, as will become evident, we too find the link between legitimacy and environmental effectiveness, process and outcome, weak. Hence, the empirically founded critique remains valid. Secondly, the book also engages with the more structural critique against deliberative governance arrangements advanced by critical political economists. In this literature new modes of governance are placed within the dominant norm complex of 'liberal environmentalism' (Bernstein, 2001), 'ecological modernization' (Hajer, 1995) and 'embedded liberalism' (Ruggie, 1982; Steffek, 2007). This norm complex views environmental protection as compatible with the institutions of liberal democracy and market economy. Thus, the promise of new modes of governance is embedded in new public management, market environmentalism, privatization and deregulation.

The recurrent line of critique holds that market forces have colonized deliberative governance procedures and reinforced power asymmetries and inequalities (O'Neill, 2007). Under such structural conditions, any attempt to promote legitimate and effective environmental policies through means of public deliberation is bound to fail. In Chapter 3 (this volume), Lövbrand and Khan discuss how green political theorists have responded to this challenge. While some green scholars approach the market place as a potential site of citizen reflection and the practice of ecological virtue (Barry, 2006; Boström and Klintman, 2008), Chapter 3 returns to the importance of grounding this theoretical aspiration in empirical studies of environmental policy practice. As such it paves the way for the case studies to come. However, the structural concerns advanced by political economists do raise questions of a more ontological kind that tap into the third line of critique discussed here.

This third critical perspective primarily targets the deliberative conception of politics, which is claimed to underestimate the degree of conflict and antagonism in political life (Mouffe, 2000). Group-based or stakeholder deliberations often deviate from Habermas' ideal understanding of 'communicative rationality', which typically takes place in the public sphere, free from governmental interference and manipulation (Habermas, 1987; 1996). From the perspective of politics as antagonism, any attempt to foster inclusive participation and deliberation on equal grounds is naive and even dangerously utopian. In contrast to the ideal of a vital, autonomous civil society involved in unconstrained dialogue free from distortion, scholars attuned to the politics of difference have suggested that so-called deliberative governance arrangements often collapse into interest group politics underpinned by large asymmetries of power and voice (Young, 1996). Some groups, such as business actors or scientific experts, may have privileged access in terms of material and ideational resources, while others, such as indigenous people or grassroots movements are less likely to influence the process. From this vantage point the deliberative turn may indeed emerge as a 'new tyranny of participation' (Leach et al., 2007).

In our case studies we return to this fundamental critique and note that most participatory governance arrangements indeed are geared towards established stakeholder groups. Citizens and less organized groups are rather absent from the decision process. This trend can be seen in such different cases as global public–private partnerships (Chapter 5, this volume), stakeholder consultations in EU food governance (Chapter 6, this volume) and local network governance for climate mitigation (Chapter 11, this volume). This finding severely challenges the deliberative ideal in environmental governance. If we accept the claim that politics is entrenched by conflicting ideological and material perspectives, the promise of new modes of environmental governance suddenly appears less promising. Some environmental issue areas, such as the spread of genetically modified food or climate change, may indeed harbour such deep-seated value conflicts that they simply cannot be resolved through deliberative procedures. Disagreement and conflict may be the only possible outcome (Van de Kerkhof, 2006). In this book we do not take sides in the ontological battle between deliberative democrats and difference democrats. However, we do let our empirical findings speak to this debate. Hence, the fundamental questions raised here will resurface in our concluding Chapter 12.

OUTLINE OF THE BOOK

As we have argued above, there are today high expectations attached to new modes of governance that increase participation and deliberation across market, government and civil society sectors. The general idea is that governance arrangements that encourage broad participation by public and private actors in collective decision-making will foster more legitimate and effective environmental policies. We have proposed that this promise is tied to a normative ideal found in deliberative democratic theory. As a consequence, this book argues that there is a deliberative turn in environmental politics. Although the promise embedded in this deliberative turn has been subject to extensive scholarly critique, we have found that it is in need of further empirical investigation. The central aim of this book is therefore to critically scrutinize the theoretical promise of new modes of environmental governance by linking it to policy practice. To reiterate the main research question of the book: can new modes of governance generate more effective and legitimate policies simultaneously?

This book is organized in three parts, with a conclusion. Part I traces the deliberative turn and the promise of new modes of environmental governance in scholarly work on deliberative democracy, green political thought and governance studies. In Chapter 2, Kronsell and Bäckstrand analyse the emergence of new modes of governance according to organizational forms (hierarchy, markets and networks) and rationalities (administrative, market and deliberative) of governance. They also outline a framework for assessing the legitimacy of new modes of governance by distinguishing between input legitimacy (the quality of the decision-making process) and output legitimacy (the problem-solving capacity or effectiveness). In Chapter 3, Lövbrand and Khan examine how deliberative democratic ideals have informed green political thought. The chapter is organized around three principal tensions that challenge the viability of deliberative environmental governance: (i) means versus ends in green deliberative politics; (ii) participation versus representation in environmental decision-making; and (iii) the scope of deliberation in a time of market environmentalism. In sum, Part I arrives at a theoretical framework that places new modes of environmental governance in the context of deliberative democracy, forms and rationalities of governance and notions of legitimacy.

Part II and Part III are based on eight empirical case studies that scrutinize the legitimacy and environmental performance of different public–private governance arrangements. The four chapters in Part II take stock of new modes of governance, employed in European, UN and global contexts. Chapters 4 and 5 look at global public–private partnerships (PPP) and analyse both their effectiveness and to what extent they have embraced the deliberative ideal. Stripple

(Chapter 4) makes a critical examination of the Kyoto Protocol's Clean Development Mechanism (CDM) and finds that even though it is made up of non-hierarchic governance forms (networks and market relations) it is still firmly based on an administrative rationality by which a carbon market has been constructed through regulation, calculation and monitoring. In Chapter 5, Bäckstrand compares the legitimacy and effectiveness of two types of global environmental PPPs; the WSSD 'Johannesburg' partnerships and the projects under the CDM. The assessment of legitimacy and effectiveness shows mixed results, and Bäckstrand concludes that neither of the two types of partnership signifies a clear move towards deliberative multilateralism. While the CDM consolidates the rise of market environmentalism, the Johannesburg partnerships seem to signify a continued power of intergovernmental organizations and a global environmental bureaucracy.

Chapters 6 and 7 shift focus to the EU level and ask what lessons can be learned from recent institutional innovations in environmental governance in the EU. In Chapter 6, Bengtsson and Klintman examine the deliberative qualities of stakeholder consultations in the governance of Genetically Modified Organisms (GMO) and food safety in the EU. It is found that there has been a deliberative turn of sorts in EU food governance but that it does not live up to ideal accounts of deliberative democracy. The authors further find that stakeholder consultation is mainly about low-stake issues, while high-stake issues are kept outside the realm of public deliberation. In Chapter 7 on participatory modes of EU water governance, Hagberg analyses how processes for stakeholder participation and deliberation in water resource management have been developed and implemented in the different EU member states. The chapter draws particular attention to the implementation of the Water Framework Directive (WFD) in the forestry sector. Hagberg finds that the promise to bridge differences in problem perception and interests among stakeholders is compromised when employed in a context of regulation that limits the scope for innovative deliberative outcomes.

Part III offers examples of governance arrangements at the national and local levels. The chapters' empirical focus is mainly on the Swedish context. Since Sweden has had a pioneering role in environmental governance, and deliberative processes have a long tradition in Swedish policy making, we approach Sweden as an interesting test case for the deliberative turn and the promise of new modes of environmental governance. In Chapter 8, Hildingsson reviews Swedish sustainability reforms during the last 20 years to evaluate the deliberative quality of Swedish environmental governance. The ambition is to examine whether innovations in Swedish environmental governance encapsulate the deliberative turn also within hierarchical steering. It is found that while there has been a clear move towards more reflexive state governance and an improved implementation capacity, this does not seem to be accompanied by an increased focus on participation and deliberation. The question thus arises as to whether reflexive governance is possible without deliberative governance. In Chapter 9, Holmberg adopts a historical perspective on the Swedish governance of food technology during the 1940s and 1950s. Based on the assumption that governance of science and technology is not exclusively a matter for government, but involves a much wider range of actors, this chapter analyses technological governance and policy processes during the emergence of the modern Scandinavian welfare state. The chapter problematizes the newness of 'new' modes of governance and explores the role of public–private networks and boundary organizations, in the case of frozen food technologies.

In Chapter 10, Schlyter and Stjernquist evaluate and provide the historical context for deliberative and participatory innovations in Swedish forest politics and legislation from the early twentieth century. A core argument is that the deliberative turn in Swedish forestry governance reflects steering challenges as well as competing sectoral claims, rather than an increased interest in deliberative decision-making per se. Their historical outlook instead points to a 'deliberative return'. In Chapter 11, Khan analyses the adoption of new modes of governance within cities as a response to the challenge of climate change. It is argued that climate governance in cities can be seen as an example of local network governance, which is analysed with regard to input and output legitimacy. While network governance, on the one hand, can be seen as a way to strengthen environmental performance without compromising democratic legitimacy, it can, on the other hand, also be interpreted as a way for local elites to obtain control over an important policy issue.

Finally, in the concluding Chapter 12 (Part IV), the editors revisit the research questions posed in this chapter and summarize the theoretical and empirical implications for the study of environmental politics and deliberative democracy.

NOTE

1. See website http://ec.europa.eu/environment/consultations_en.htm, accessed 14 April 2009.

REFERENCES

Andersen, Mikael S. and Duncan Liefferink (eds) (1997), *European Environmental Policy: The Pioneers*, Manchester: Manchester University Press.
Arias-Maldonado, Manuel (2007), 'An imaginary solution? The green defence of deliberative democracy', *Environmental Values*, **16**, 233–52.
Baber, Walter and Robert Bartlett (2005), *Deliberative Environmental Politics: Democracy and Ecological Rationality*, Cambridge, MA: The MIT Press.

Bache, Ian and Matthew Flinders (eds) (2004), *Multi-level Governance*, Oxford: Oxford University Press.

Bäckstrand, Karin (2006), 'Democratising global governance? Stakeholder democracy after the World Summit on Sustainable Development', *European Journal of International Relations*, **12**(14), 467–98.

Bäckstrand, Karin (2008), 'Accountability of networked climate governance: the rise of transnational climate partnerships', *Global Environmental Politics*, **8**(3), 74–102.

Barry, Andrew, Thomas Osborne and Nicolas Rose (eds) (1996), *Foucault and Political Reason. Liberalism: Neo-Liberalism and Rationalities of Government*, Chicago, IL: The University of Chicago Press.

Barry, John (2006), 'Resistance is fertile: from environmental to sustainability citizenship', in Andrew Dobson and Derek Bell (eds), *Environmental Citizenship*, Cambridge, MA and London: The MIT Press, pp. 21–48.

Beck, Ulrich (1992), *The Risk Society*, London: Sage Publications.

Beisheim, Marianne and Klaus Dingwerth (2008), 'Procedural legitimacy and private transnational governance: are the good ones doing better?', Research Center (SFB) 700, SFB Governance Working Paper no. 14, June, Berlin.

Benner, Thorsten, Wolfgang Reinicke and Jan Martin Witte (2004), 'Multisectoral networks in global governance: towards a pluralistic system of accountability', *Government and Opposition*, **29**(2), 191–208.

Benner, Thorsten, Charlotte Streck and Jan Martin Witte (eds) (2003), *Progress or Peril? Networks and Partnerships in Global Environmental Governance: The Post-Johannesburg Agenda*, Berlin and Washington, DC: Global Public Policy Institute.

Bernstein, Steven (2001), *The Compromise of Liberal Environmentalism*, Cambridge: Cambridge University Press.

Bernstein, Steven (2005), 'Legitimacy in global environmental governance', *Journal of International Law and International Relations*, **1**(1–2), 139–66.

Biermann, Frank (2007), 'Earth system governance as a crosscutting theme of global change research', *Global Environmental Change*, **17**, 326–37.

Bocking, Stephen (2006), *Nature's Experts: Science, Politics and the Environment*, New Brunswick, NJ and London: Rutger University Press.

Bohman, James and William Regh (eds) (1997), *Deliberative Democracy: Essays on Reasons and Politics*, Cambridge, MA: The MIT Press.

Börzel, Tanja (1999), 'Toward convergence in Europe?', *Journal of Common Market Studies*, **39**(4), 573–96.

Börzel, Tanja (2002), 'Pace-setting, foot-dragging, and fence-sitting: member state responses to Europeanization', *Journal of Common Market Studies*, **40**(2), 193–214.

Börzel, Tanja and Thomas Risse (2005), 'Public–private partnerships: effective and legitimate tools for transnational governance?', in Edgar Grande and Louis W. Pauly (eds), *Complex Sovereignty: Reconstituting Political Authority in the Twenty-First Century*, Toronto, ON: University of Toronto Press.

Boström, Magnus and Mikael Klintman (2008), *Eco Standards, Product Labelling and Green Consumerism*, London: Palgrave.

Bull, Benedicte and Desmond McNeill (2006), *Development Issues in Global Governance: Public–Private Partnerships and Market Multilateralism*, London: Routledge.

Burchell, Graham (1996), 'Liberal government and techniques of the self', in Andrew Barry, Thomas Osborne and Nicolas Rose (eds), *Foucault and Political Reason: Liberalism, Neo-Liberalism and Rationalities of Government*, Chicago, IL: The University of Chicago Press.

Carter, Neil (2007), *The Politics of the Environment: Ideas, Activism, Policy*, 2nd edn, Cambridge: Cambridge University Press.

Cashore, Benjamin, Graeme Auld and Deanna Newson (2004), *Governing through Markets. Forest Certification and the Emergence of Non-State Authority*, New Haven, CT: Yale University Press.

Commission of the European Communities (2001), *European Governance. A White Paper*, COM (2001) 428 Final, Brussels: European Commission.

Commission on Global Governance (2005), 'A new world', in Rorden Wilkinson (ed.), *The Global Governance Reader*, London: Routledge, pp. 26–44, originally published (1995) in *Our Global Neighbourhood*, Oxford: Oxford University Press.

Cox, Robert (1986), 'Social forces, states and world orders: beyond international relations theory', in Robert Keohane (ed.), *Neorealism and its Critics*, New York: Columbia University Press, pp. 204–54.

Cutler, Claire, Tony Porter and Virginia Haufler (eds) (1999), *Private Authority and International Affairs*, New York: State University of New York Press.

Cutler, Claire, Virginia Haufler and Tony Porter (eds) (2009), *Private Authority and International Affairs*, New York: SUNY Press.

Dalby, Simon (2007), 'Anthropocene geopolitics: globalisation, empire, environment and critique', *Geography Compass*, **1**(1), 103–18.

DeBardeleben, Joan and Achim Hurrelmann (2007), *Democratic Dilemmas of Multilevel Governance: Legitimacy, Representation and Accountability in the European Union*, Basingstoke and New York: Palgrave Macmillan.

Dingwerth, Klaus (2007), *The New Transnationalism: Transnational Governance and Democratic Legitimacy*, Basingstoke: Palgrave Macmillan.

Dryzek, John (2000), *Deliberative Democracy and Beyond: Liberals, Critics, Contestations*, Oxford: Oxford University Press.

Durant, Robert, Daniel Fiorini and Rosemary O'Leary (eds) (2004), *Environmental Governance Reconsidered: Challenges, Choices and Opportunities*, Cambridge, MA: The MIT Press.

Eberlein, Burkard and Dieter Kerwer (2004), 'New governance in the European Union: a theoretical perspective', *Journal of Common Market Studies*, **42**(1), 121–42.

Fiorini, Daniel (2006), *The New Environmental Regulation*, Cambridge, MA: The MIT Press.

Fischer, Frank (2005), *Citizens, Experts and the Environment: The Politics of Local Knowledge*, Durham, NC and London: Duke University Press.

Fishkin, James S. and Peter Laslett (eds) (2006), *Debating Deliberative Democracy*, Malden, MA, Oxford and Melbourne, VIC: Blackwell Publishing.

Gill, Stephen (2005), 'New constitutionalism, democratisation and global political economy', in Rorden Wilkinson (ed.), *The Global Governance Reader*, London: Routledge, pp. 174–86, originally published (1998) in *Pacific Review*, **10**(1).

Glasbergen, Pieter (ed.) (1998), *Public–Private Agreements as a Policy Strategy*, Dordrecht: Kluwer Academic Press.

Glasbergen, Pieter, Frank Biermann and Arthur Mol (eds) (2007), *Partnerships, Governance and Sustainable Development: Reflections on Theory and Practice*, Cheltenham, UK and Northampton, MA, USA: Edward Elgar.

Goldman, Michael (2001), 'Constructing an environmental state: eco-governmentality and other transnational practices of a "green" World Bank', *Social Problems*, **48**(4), 499–523.

Green, Jessica and Bradnee Chambers (2006), *The Politics of Participation in Sustainable Development Governance*, Tokyo, New York and Paris: United Nations University Press.

Gutmann, Amy and Dennis Thompson (2004), *Why Deliberative Democracy?*, Princeton, NJ: Princeton University Press.

Haas, Peter M. (2004), 'Addressing the global governance deficit', *Global Environmental Politics*, **4**(4), 1–15.

Habermas, Jürgen (1987), *The Theory of Communicative Action, Vol. 2, Life World and System*, Boston, MA: Beacon Press.

Habermas, Jürgen (1996), *Between Facts and Norms: Contribution to a Discourse Theory of Law and Democracy*, Cambridge, MA: MIT Press.

Hagendijk, Rob and Alan Irwin (2006), 'Public deliberation and governance: Engaging with science and technology in contemporary Europe', *Minerva*, **44**, 167–84.

Hajer, Maarten (1995), *The Politics of Environmental Discourse: Ecological Modernization and the Policy Process*, New York: Oxford University Press.

Hall, Rodney B. and Thomas J. Biersteker (eds) (2002), *The Emergence of Private Authority in Global Governance*, Cambridge: Cambridge University Press.

Hempel, Lamont (1996), *Environmental Governance: The Global Challenge*, Washington, DC: Island Press.

Hooghe, Liesbet and Gary Marks (2000), *Multi-level Governance and European Integration: Governance in Europe*, Lanham, MD: Rowman & Littlefield.

Irwin, Alan (1995), *Citizen Science: A Study of People, Expertise, and Sustainable Development*, London: Routledge.

Jasanoff, Sheila (2005), *Designs on Nature: Science and Democracy in Europe and the United States*, Princeton, NJ: Princeton University Press.

Jordan, Andrew (2008), 'The governance of sustainable development: taking stock and looking forwards', *Environment and Planning C: Government and Policy*, **26**, 17–33.

Jordan, Andrew and Duncan Liefferink (eds) (2004), *Environmental Policy in Europe: The Europeanization of National Environmental Policy*, London: Routledge.

Keohane, Robert O. (2003), 'Global governance and accountability', in David Held and Mathias Koehning-Archibugi (eds), *Taming Globalization: Frontiers of Governance*, Cambridge, UK: Polity Press, pp. 130–59.

Knill, Christoph and Andrea Lenschow (2005), 'Compliance, communication and competition: patterns of EU environmental policy making and their impact on policy convergence', *European Environment*, **15**, 114–28.

Knill, Christoph and Duncan Liefferink (2007), *Environmental Politics in the European Union*, Manchester and New York: Manchester University Press.

Koehnig-Archibugi, Mathias and Michael Zürn (eds) (2006), *New Modes of Governance in the Global System: Exploring Publicness, Delegation and Inclusiveness*, London: Macmillan.

Kohler-Koch, Beate and Rainer Eising (eds) (1999), *The Transformation of Governance in the European Union*, London: Routledge.

Lafferty, William M. (ed.) (2004), *Governance for Sustainable Development: The Challenge of Adapting Form to Function*, Cheltenham, UK and Northampton, MA, USA: Edward Elgar.

Leach, Melissa, Ian Scoones and Brian Wynne (eds) (2007), *Science and Citizens: Globalization and the Challenges of Engagement*, London: Zed Books.

Lemke, Thomas (2002), 'Foucault, governmentality and critique', *Rethinking Marxism*, **14**(3), 49–64.

Liefferink, Duncan and Andrew Jordan (2005), 'An "ever closer union" of national policy? The convergence of national environmental policy in the European Union', *European Environment*, **15**, 102–13.

Lövbrand, Eva, Joakim Nordquist and Teresia Rindefjäll (2009), 'Closing the legitimacy gap in global environmental governance: lessons from the emerging CDM market', *Global Environmental Politics*, **9**(2), 74–100.

Lundqvist, Lennart J. (2004), *Sweden and Ecological Governance: Straddling the Fence*, Manchester: Manchester University Press.

MacDonald, Terry (2008), *Global Stakeholder Democracy: Power and Representation Beyond Liberal States*, Oxford: Oxford University Press.

McGrew, Anthony (2002), 'From global governance to good governance: theories and prospects of democratizing the global polity', in Morten Ougaard and Richard Higgot (eds), *Towards a Global Polity*, London and New York: Routledge, pp. 207–26.

Martens, Jens (2007), 'Multi-stakeholder partnerships: future models of multilateralism?', Friedrich-Ebert Stiftung occasional paper no. 29, January 2007, Berlin.

Mason, Michael (2005), *The New Accountability: Environmental Responsibility Across Borders*, London: Earthscan.

Meadowcroft, James (2004), 'Deliberative democracy', in Robert Durant, Daniel Fiorini and Rosemary O'Leary (eds), *Environmental Governance Reconsidered: Challenges, Choices and Opportunities*, Cambridge, MA: MIT Press, pp. 183–217.

Meadowcroft, James (2007), 'Democracy and accountability: the challenge for cross-sectoral partnerships', in Pieter Glasbergen, Frank Biermann and Arthur Mol (eds), *Partnerships, Governance and Sustainable Development: Reflections on Theory and Practice*, Cheltenham, UK and Northampton, MA, USA: Edward Elgar, pp. 194–212.

Meadowcroft, James (2008), 'Who is in charge here? Governance for sustainable development in a complex world', *Journal of Environmental Policy and Planning*, **9**(3–4), 299–314.

Miller, Peter and Nicolas Rose (2008), *Governing the Present*, Cambridge: Polity Press.

Mitchell, Ross E. (2006), 'Green politics or environmental blues? Analyzing ecological democracy', *Public Understanding of Science*, **15**, 459–80.

Mouffe, Chantal (2000), *The Democratic Paradox*, London: Verso.

Murphy, Craig (2005), 'Global governance: poorly done and poorly understood', in Rorden Wilkinson (ed.), *The Global Governance Reader*, London and New York: Routledge, pp. 90–104, originally published (2000) in *International Affairs*, **76**(4).

Nanz, Patricia and Jens Steffek (2004), 'Global governance, participation and the public sphere', *Government and Opposition*, **39**(2), 314–34.

Nölke, Andreas and Jean-Christophe Graz (2007), 'Limits to the legitimacy of transnational private governance', paper presented at the conference 'Pathways to legitimacy. The future of regional and global governance', University of Warwick, 17–19 September.

O'Neill, John (2007), *Markets, Deliberation and the Environment*, London and New York: Routledge.

Paterson, Matthew (2000), *Understanding Global Environmental Politics: Domination, Accumulation, Resistance*, Basingstoke: Macmillan.

Paterson, Matthew (2007), *Automobile Politics: Ecology and Cultural Political Economy*, Cambridge: Cambridge University Press.

Pattberg, Philip H. (2007), *Private Institutions and Global Governance: The New Politics of Environmental Sustainability*, Cheltenham, UK and Northampton, MA, USA: Edward Elgar.

Pellizzoni, Luigi (2003), 'Uncertainty and participatory democracy', *Environmental Values*, **12**, 195–224.

Peters, Guy B. (2005), *Institutional Theory in Political Science: The 'New Institutionalism'*, London: Continuum.

Petersen, Spike V. (2003), *A Critical Rewriting of Global Political Economy*, London and New York: Routledge.

Pierre, Jon and Guy Peters (2000), *Governance, Politics and the State*, New York: St. Martin's Press.

Risse, Tomas (2004), 'Global governance and communicative action', *Government and Opposition*, **39**(2), 288–313.

Rose, Nicolas and Peter Miller (1992), 'Political power beyond the state: problematics of government', *The British Journal of Sociology*, **43**(2), 173–205.

Rosenau, James and E. Czempiel (eds) (1992), *Governance without Government: Order and Change in World Politics*, Cambridge: Cambridge University Press.

Ruggie, John G. (1982), 'International regimes, transactions and change: embedded liberalism in the postwar economic order', *International Organization*, **26**(2), 379–415.

Scharpf, Fritz W. (2006), *Problem Solving Effectiveness and Democratic Accountability in the European Union*, Political Science Series, Vienna: Institute for Advanced Studies.

Scharpf, Fritz W. (1999), *Governing in Europe: Effective and Democratic?*, Oxford: Oxford University Press.

Scholte, Jan Aart (2002), 'Civil society and democracy in global governance', *Global Governance*, **8**(3), 281–304.

Schout, Adriaan and Andrew Jordan (2005), 'Coordinated European governance: self-organizing or centrally steered?', *Public Adminstration*, **83**(1), 201–20.

Shamir, Ronen (2008), 'The age of responsibilization: on market-embedded morality', *Economy and Society*, **37**(1), 1–19.

Skogstad, Grace (2003), 'Legitimacy and/or policy effectiveness? Networked governance and GMO regulation in the European Union', *Journal of European Public Policy*, **10**(3), 321–38.

Smismans, Stijns (2006), 'New modes of governance and the participatory myth', European Governance Papers EUROGOV no. N-06-01.

Smith, Graham (2003), *Deliberative Democracy and the Environment*, London and New York: Routledge.

Steffek, Jens (2003), 'The legitimation of international environmental governance', *European Journal of International Relations*, **9**(2), 249–76.

Steffek, Jens (2007), *Embedded Liberalism and its Critics: Justifying Global Governance in the American Century*, New York: Macmillan.

Treib, Oliver, Holger Bähr and Gerdna Falkner (2007), 'Modes of governance: towards a conceptual clarification', *Journal of European Environmental Policy*, **14**(1), 1–20.

United Nations Conference on Environment and Development (UNCED) (1992), Agenda 21, Geneva.

Van der Kerkhof, Marleen (2006), 'Making a difference: on the constraints of consensus building and relevance of deliberation stakeholder dialogues', *Policy Sciences*, **39**, 279–99.

Van Zeijl-Rozema, Annemarie, Ron Cörvers, René Kemp and Pim Martens (2008), 'Governance for sustainable development: a framework', *Sustainable Development*, **16**, 410–21.

Voss, Jan Peter, Dierk Bauknecht and René Kemp (eds) (2006), *Reflexive Governance for Sustainable Development*, Cheltenham, UK and Northampton, MA, USA: Edward Elgar Publishing.

Weiss, Thomas G. (2005), 'Governance, good governance and global governance: conceptual and actual challenges', in Rorden Wilkinson (ed.), *The Global Governance Reader*, London and New York: Routledge, pp. 68–88, originally published (2000) in *Third World Quarterly*, **21**(5).

Whitehead, Mark (2008), 'Cold monsters and ecological Leviathans: reflections on the relationships between states and the environment', *Geography Compass*, **2**(2), 414–32.

Winter, Gerd (ed.) (2006), *Multilevel Governance of Global Environmental Change*, Cambridge: Cambridge University Press.

Wissenburg, Marcel (1998), *Green Liberalism. The Free and the Green Society*, London: UCL Press.

Young, Marion Iris (1996), 'Communication and the other: beyond deliberative democracy' in Seyla Benhabib (ed.), *Democracy and Difference: Contesting the Boundaries of the Political*, Princeton, NJ: Princeton University Press, pp. 120–35.

Young, Oran (1999), *The Effectiveness of International Environmental Regimes: Causal Connections and Behavioral Mechanisms*, Cambridge, MA: MIT Press.

2. Rationalities and forms of governance: a framework for analysing the legitimacy of new modes of governance

Annica Kronsell and Karin Bäckstrand

INTRODUCTION

The overarching aim of this chapter is to bring conceptual clarity in the terminology related to new modes of governance in the context of the deliberative turn. As argued previously, environmental governance has been influenced by ideals of deliberative democracy. This has led to an increased use of deliberative rationality in governance processes and in the choice of modes of governance. The extent to which ideas of democracy and deliberative rationality have turned into governance practice varies between different contexts, states and international organizations. This chapter provides a framework for analysing the promise of new modes of environmental governance in terms of legitimacy and effectiveness that will be employed in the chapters to follow. Two questions are addressed: how is the deliberative turn in environmental governance reflected in the forms and rationalities of environmental governance? How can the legitimacy and effectiveness of various modes of governance be conceptualized?

First, the chapter develops a theoretical framework that explores the emergence of new modes of governance according to two dimensions: organizational forms and rationalities. The governance forms of hierarchy, markets and networks are analysed as well as the rationality, or logic, underpinning governance modes (administrative, economic and deliberative rationality). The rationality of governance revolves around how the behaviour and way of thinking of different actors can change, what the optimal forms of steering (governance) are, and what type of steering is most appropriate to induce change. We categorize governance modes explored in the empirical chapters, such as public–private partnerships, multi-stakeholder dialogues, networks, certification and voluntary standards, in the conceptual framework. The final section turns to the question of legitimacy and proposes that new modes of governance can be evaluated by distinguishing between input legitimacy (the quality of the decision-making process) and output legitimacy (the problem-solving capacity or effectiveness). For this purpose we develop specific criteria that can be used to evaluate legitimacy empirically.

FORMS AND RATIONALITIES OF GOVERNANCE

The aim of this section is to explore the emergence of new modes of governance according to the logic behind governance conduct through two dimensions: organizational forms (hierarchy, market, networks) and rationalities (administrative, economic, deliberative). The two dimensions, forms and rationalities, are linked together in Table 2.1. Subsequent empirical chapters will examine how form and rationality relate to specific modes of governance in the environmental field explored in the eight case studies.

Governance Forms

A focus on governance forms relates to the organization, or the 'hardware' of governance. Hierarchy, markets and networks are three forms highlighted in political science and relevant for environmental governance (Jordan, 2008, pp. 19, 23). The hierarchical form operates through administrative orders and sets of rules. Hierarchy is normally associated with the authority exercised by states, governments and bureaucracies in relationship to societal actors. Hierarchy also describes an organizational form, with chains of delegation, which can be used internally within a firm, or a government agency (Thompson et al., 1991, p. 9). Hierarchy is a governance form, often labelled as 'old' mode in the governance literature. Old modes of government, based on command and control regulations are often pitted against new modes of governance usually referring to market-based, voluntary and informational instruments. The stylized presentation of 'old' versus 'new' is confusing and of little analytical value, and thus is not part of our conceptual framework. Treib et al. (2007, p. 2) argue convincingly that 'some modes of governance may have been historically relatively new in some empirical contexts' and hence, they are labelled new while 'the same governing modes may turn out to be long-established practice in other areas'. As we will see, the rise of new modes of governance is in many instances based on the continued operation of traditional regulatory policies. Thus, in Table 2.1 hierarchy remains an important governance form.

While hierarchy is a governance form (operating with a set of rules), it relies on the fact that rulers may be appointed and dismissed through democratic means. The ultimate authority remains in the hands of democratically elected governments with the power to delegate. Delegation of power is also possible to supranational institutions, to local governments and to other actors. The role of governments and international economic institutions in correcting and saving the markets during the financial crisis initiated late in 2008 serves as a poignant reminder of the co-dependency of governance forms and the relevance of hierarchy.

The market is a self-organizing governance form. The critical governance literature argued that it is becoming the most dominant form of governance (Murphy, 2005; Gill, 2005; Petersen, 2003). The market is often contrasted with hierarchy and is an important form in contemporary environmental governance. In the debates and in the literature, the market form is often conflated with economic rationality (Thompson et al., 1991), which will be discussed in the subsequent section. The market as a governance form has self-organization as its specific feature. This self-organizing form, although dominated by the idea of the market in practice, can arguably include other self-organizing opportunities in the public sphere, for example, those facilitated by the medium of the internet.

Networks as a governance form are based on resource dependencies between private and public actors and/or individuals (Jordan, 1990; Rhodes, 1990). Resources relevant for interdependency in networks can be economic, political, informational or personal (Kronsell, 1997, pp. 155–84). Trust and cooperation provide the glue establishing links between network participants (Thompson et al., 1991, p. 15). Networks seem to be a preferred governance form in the literature on new modes of governance (Bogason and Musso, 2006; Schout and Jordan, 2005) and are advanced in the normative governance approach as a better alternative to old forms of governance. Networks are interesting from the perspective of deliberative democracy because relations between actors in networks rely on communication, exchange of information, and on trustful and cooperative attitudes, which can provide arenas for deliberation.

Rationalities of Governance

It is useful to investigate governance by combining an analysis of organizational form with an analysis of the 'software' of governance, its underlying logic or rationality. The core of environmental governance is about effecting societal change to lead to stronger environmental performance and effectiveness. Rationality of governance revolves around the optimal forms of steering (governance) and around how the behaviour of different actors can change. The ultimate aim of environmental governance is to transform societies' and individuals' behaviour toward more sustainable and environmentally sound ways. Different rationalities make different assumptions about how to bring about such change.

The three rationalities of environmental governance presented are derived from the debates and experiences with environmental policy since its inception in the 1960s. Inspired by research on governmentality (cf. Miller and Rose, 2008) we critically examine the three rationalities that arguably define environmental governance (cf. Whitehead, 2008, p. 425). The experience of governments and other actors has led to certain insights about the strengths and limitations of governance rationalities. The proliferation of new, mixed or hybrid modes of governance may be seen in this light. They combine the different governance forms and rationalities.

In the 1970s, when environmental problems became politicized in industrialized countries, governments used the traditional domestic regulatory tools available. Many states, such as Sweden, the US, Great Britain and Germany developed and implemented environmental policies (Andersen and Liefferink, 1997; Weale, 1992; Lundqvist, 2004). The problem-solving methods were in line with administrative rationality, which was dominant in governments at the time. In the early 1980s, problems of implementation deficits and weak environmental performance were connected to the failure of governments. The hierarchical governance form, together with administrative rationality, was increasingly recognized as inadequate and ill-equipped to solve environmental problems (Carter, 2007, p. 181). Dryzek (2005, p. 75ff) argues that this is linked to a number of flaws or problems associated with administrative rationality.

Administrative rationality is a governance logic associated with the bureaucratic and expert apparatus of governments. In the classic Weberian sense, problem-solving takes place in a hierarchical organization that tends to separate complex problems and leave them in the hands of experts. Problem-solving capacity is delegated to experts, civil servants and bureaucrats who are believed to have the information, insight and knowledge to transform political will to action (Dryzek, 2005, p. 75). Box 1 in Table 2.1 most resembles the 'state' in the classic Weberian interpretation. It is a hierarchical form whereby administrators and experts carry out governance through rules and principles. Administrative rationality presumes that authoritative institutions and their personnel, which are taken as experts in their field, will make the most informed decisions for the collective good. Consequently, governance is simply about implementing the decisions at the most appropriate level by administrative agencies.

A premise of administrative rationality is that it is the optimal approach to resolve problems and change behavioural patterns as politically appointed administrative staff are the most informed (they have the expertise), legitimate (governments are after all democratically elected) and most effective. Political scientists have pointed out the flaws of administrative rationality and some points of criticism are that administrative rationality cannot deal with long-term problems and that implementation difficulties are abundant due to, for example, street-level bureaucrats, the municipal veto, civil disobedience or illegal behaviour (Dryzek, 2005, pp. 92–6). Administrative rationality has been criticized for being inadequate for solving environmental issues (cf. Carter, 2007, pp. 182–90) and for weakening the legitimacy of polices, which has given impetus to the search for new modes of governance. Despite all these limitations, the tools applied in administrative rationality such as expertise, rule of law and regulation as a way to induce change toward environmental and sustainability goals, remain relevant in environmental governance.

The call for new forms of governance has put much hope in governance forms that rely on economic rationality. Market-liberals are deeply sceptical about interventions and centralized management of environmental problems, apart from establishing the basic rules of markets and property rights (Clapp and Dauvergne, 2005, pp. 4–7). Economic rationality relies on the price mechanism and the making of contracts, where it is assumed that actors respond to costs and benefits by maximizing their self-interest. Depending on the costs or benefits, they will change behaviour accordingly (Dryzek, 2005, pp. 121–42). Many governance modes, for example fees, taxes, charges and subsidies, are based on the assumption that behaviour is guided by economic preferences. Research on various economic policy instruments, such as taxes on sulphur, congestion charges and subsidies for eco-farming, lend support to this as they have been shown to be fairly effective in reducing pollution (Andersen and Sprenger, 2000; Tietenberg, 1990).

The focus on the role of economic costs and benefits in bringing about a change toward environmental sustainability creates certain dilemmas. There are problems related to setting the price right, for example on ecosystem services. Economic rationality only works if the subject of governance is reducible to an economic value. Economic rationality relies on sensitivity to price and thereby raises ethical issues on how groups and individuals are disproportionally affected by price changes. Market principles in environmental governance have become increasingly important as a governance form and are particularly praised by economists (Sterner, 2002). Governments, too, have noted the positive effects of economic incentives for environmental problem-solving and have increasingly employed such means. Governments may also see this as an opportunity to generate revenue (for example congestion charging) used for other purposes than environmental ones. Consequently, it is possible to distinguish between an economic rationality used in the market form (Box 5) and economic rationality that is endorsed in the hierarchical governance form (Box 2) (by states and supranational institutions). Both forms are, nevertheless, guided by the same logic of economic rationality.

A more recent trend in discussions on effective environmental governance is the call for increased participation and democratization of existing governance institutions and forms. This debate takes place within liberal democracies where institutions such as parliaments, political parties and constitutional rights to free speech are already in place. Hagendijk and Irwin (2006) argue that deliberative ideals have taken hold in the governance of most EU countries, and Baber and Bartlett (2001, p. 55) find 'empirical grounding in an inventory of wide-reaching institutionalizations of deliberative environmental democracy'. This deliberative turn, as we call it, has influenced governance in democratic countries in the North, as a deliberative rationality is evident in the governance of environmental and sustainability issues.

A cornerstone of deliberative rationality is that participation, deliberation, accountability, communication and multiple actors' engagement in problem-solving and decision-making, will lead to more effective environmental governance, or what we in this book frame as the promise of new modes of governance. In line with economic rationality, deliberative rationality is seen as a better alternative and a response to the inadequacies of administrative rationality. Accordingly, it is argued that the liberal democratic state and its associated institutions have largely failed in implementing policies and ameliorating environmental problems. As discussed by Lövbrand and Khan (Chapter 3, this volume), environmentalists have posed this critique, but so have other movements embracing democratizing ideals such as feminists, 'anti-globalization' groups and radical democrats. Deliberative ideals articulated in green political theory have been put into practice in contemporary environmental activism and environmental organizations. This is reflected in Box 9 of Table 2.1.

Deliberative rationality is based on the assumption that better decisions are taken if they are done in an inclusive and participatory way. The idea of deliberative rationality has been extended beyond engagement of citizens. 'Stakeholder' participation is expected to render governance legitimate and improve implementation (Bäckstrand, 2006; Dingwerth, 2007). However, deliberative rationality does not only focus on the inclusion of a broad set of actors, it also regards information sharing and communication as important imperatives. Deliberative rationality opens up the governance process to participation, deliberation and arguing among concerned actors (Risse, 2004). The process must be transparent so that it can take in a whole range of perspectives, for example local knowledge, rather than being limited to scientific expertise.

The premise of deliberative rationality is that rational individuals and groups can deliberate around environmental problems and subsequently arrive at the most informed and also the most legitimate decision, consistent with notions of green deliberative democracy as discussed in Chapter 3. The connection between process and environmental outcome is made in green political theory. This Achilles heel of deliberative rationality resonates with the main puzzle of this book, namely whether a deliberative process can also lead to decisions that are environmentally effective. As argued in the introduction, the empirical foundation on whether deliberation leads to more effective governance is weak.

In Table 2.1 forms and rationalities are combined to analyse specific modes of governance. To reiterate, we conceive of new modes of governance as multi-actor governance arrangements that rely on a mix of hierarchical and non-hierarchical steering and collaboration between government, market and civil society actors. New modes appear in a context when political authority is fragmented and there are multiple co-existing governance models centred on states, international organizations, civil society and multi-sectoral public policy networks (Keohane, 2003). The rise of new modes indicates a shift toward more complex and participatory governance arrangements and steering mechanisms that engage non-state actors, the public and citizens (Koening-Archibugi and Zürn, 2006; Treib et al., 2007), combining different rationalities and forms of governance. Although the table contains nine boxes it is not exhaustive of all governance modes. Hybrid modes, which will be examined in several chapters, can fit into several boxes, because they combine different rationalities. Hybrid modes of governance aspire to combine the best aspects of diverse rationalities, which, in turn, raise questions around the possibilities to combine rationalities: do they create synergies, or are rationalities conflicting?

The dark shaded box (Box 1) in the upper left corner represents 'old' modes of governance based on administrative rationality and hierarchical governance forms. The lighter shaded areas (Boxes 2, 3, 4 and 7) are the modes that we explore in this volume. They constitute 'new' modes of governance that are characterized by deliberative and economic rationalities and by market and network forms of governance. The non-shaded areas (Boxes 5, 6, 8 and 9) consist of self-regulation and pure market or civil society governance. As argued in Chapter 1, such modes are usually excluded, as most scholars define new modes of governance as constituting a mix of public–private actors and hierarchical and non-hierarchical steering. In the following, the boxes in the table are briefly discussed.

Boxes 1, 4 and 7 correspond to modes of governance in administrative rationality. Box 1 represents traditional modes of governance but as evident in Hildingsson's contribution in Chapter 8 there are examples of innovation within the context of administrative rationality in hierarchical form. The Swedish Environmental Quality Objectives are such an example. In Box 4 the 'shadow of hierarchy' implies that governments have shadow influence on self-organizing forms like the market by setting, or threatening to set, the rules for the operation of the market. Box 7 is represented by different modes that involve networks of experts, policy makers and administrators.

Boxes 2, 5 and 8 show modes of governance in economic rationality that work with an economic logic and with hierarchical (Box 2), market (Box 5) and network forms (Box 8). Economic rationality relies on economic and business norms for allocating values. In Box 2 modes such as green taxes, regulated carbon markets and certification schemes are found. These are initiated by public authorities, which employ the logic the of price mechanism and economic incentives. Private governance mechanisms, corporate social responsibility (CSR), benchmarking, certification and labelling, are typical examples of economic rationality. Box 5 represents the self-organizing form of the market where economic rationality works in its purest form, represented by green marketing and green consumption and voluntary agreements. Possible modes of governance in Box 8 are networks between actors with a common economic interest or incentive, such as green businesses or climate technology industries and lobbies. Boxes 5 and 8 are beyond the scope of this study.

Finally, Boxes 3, 6 and 9 represent modes of governance in deliberative rationality. Along the vertical axis we can distinguish between modes of governance that employ deliberation in hierarchical (Box 3), market (Box 6) and network forms (Box 9) respectively. Box 3 signifies traditional hierarchical steering by the state, bureaucracy and scientific expertise (Dryzek, 2000) influenced by deliberative ideas. Innovations in deliberative democracy occur within the institutions of representative and electoral democracy (Lafferty, 2004; Meadowcroft, 2004), such as when governments attempt to stage deliberation by engaging citizens and stakeholders through, for example, environmental impact assessment (EIAs), citizen juries and public access to information.

In Box 6 we find such spontaneous self-organizing activities among citizens as individuals making life-style choices, or groups acting together in protests or campaigns. These activities are initiated from the grass-roots level and carried out through the exchange of communication, information and participation. In Box 9 we find modes that are related to the collective organization of deliberative rationality in networks, exemplified by environmental grass-roots organizations and social movements.

If we look at common definitions of new modes of governance (for example PPPs) in the literature they are usually limited to the shaded areas of Table 2.1 (see Chapter 1). For the modes in the remaining boxes there is no public–private interaction and no mix of hierarchical and non-hierarchical steering. While our framework does not make any sharp distinction between different modes of governance, our empirical studies are limited to those modes of governance that are typically labelled as 'new'. This is not a matter of definition but rather because we find it most interesting to study modes that mix hierarchical and non-hierarchical steering. They are likely to have more impact on environmental performance, and there is more at stake with these modes. It is beyond the scope of the book to analyse all the different types of

Table 2.1 *Governance forms and rationalities: a framework*

Rationalities of governance **Forms** of governance	**Administrative rationality** (Delegated by politicians to experts and civil servants) Global/state system delegated via supranational institutions such as the EU	**Economic rationality** Governance is possible through price and contract mechanisms. Economic incentives change behaviour, contracts establish relations.	**Deliberative rationality** Governance is possible through participation, communication, broadened knowledge and deliberation
Hierarchy (principal–agent relations)	1 Administration/experts govern through chains of command via rules, legal norms, etc. Examples: 'Steering by objectives' Traditional regulation, e.g. emission standards, permitting and licensing	2 Hierarchical forms influenced by economic rationality. Examples: Eco-taxes Carbon taxation Labelling schemes	3 Hierarchical forms influenced by deliberative rationality Examples: Advisory boards, Multi-stakeholder panels/consultation Citizen juries/panels

Market (self-organizing)	4 Market exists at the mercy of political will or the will of state/supranational institutions. In the 'shadow of hierarchy'. Examples: 'trade and competition laws' Regulated carbon market such as EU-ETS and CDM Public–Private Partnerships (PPPs)	5 Market works through price and trade mechanisms. Examples: Voluntary carbon markets Self-regulation Certification Green consumption	6 People participate and communicate in self-organized ways. Examples: Campaigns and protests Life-style choices Green consumerism
Networks (interdependent actors)	7 Networks among experts, civil servants, politicians and elites. Examples: Scientific and expert networks City to city networks	8 Networks based on economic ties, interests, contracts. Examples: Green technology lobbies Industrial partnerships	9 Networks of participating citizens. Examples: NGOs Social movements Environmental activists

modes and we do not consider this necessary. The objective is not to test the framework but to explore rationalities and forms in environmental governance and, above all, to assess the legitimacy of new modes of governance.

LEGITIMACY OF NEW MODES OF GOVERNANCE

We have argued that the normative governance approach holds the promise that governance arrangements that encourage broad participation by public and private actors in collective decision-making will bring about more legitimate and effective environmental policies. This section advances a framework for analysing the legitimacy and effectiveness of new modes of governance that will be employed in subsequent chapters on environmental issue areas from the local to the global setting.

Input and Output Legitimacy

Legitimacy is a central and essentially contested concept in social science and political philosophy. Democratic legitimacy has been closely associated with hierarchical forms and administrative rationality that underpin liberal democratic state governance. Democratic legitimacy is only one source of legitimacy and is closely associated with domestic models of electoral democracy (Grant and Keohane, 2005). Democratic state-centred legitimacy is less suitable for evaluating non-electoral, non-territorial governance arrangements and is less applicable to global multi-sectoral networks that consist of governments, business, civil society and multilateral agencies. First, legitimacy has been defined as the acceptance of a particular social order, rule, norm or institution by a set of actors or by a specific community (Hurd, 1999; Risse, 2004) and concerns 'authority granted by the political community to its institutions and structures' (Payne and Samhat, 2004, p. 1). A legitimate political order rests on the approval and consent of the community (Hurd, 1999). Compliance with rules and norms occurs if actors perceive the social and political order as acceptable, and an institution or a rule is legitimate if it is widely believed to be legitimate (Bernstein and Cashore, 2007, p. 2; Buchanan and Keohane, 2006, p. 405).

A second interpretation of legitimacy, normative legitimacy, can be derived from norms, values and principles of liberal democracy, such as accountability, transparency, inclusion, and deliberation and a 'right to rule'. This book starts out from such a normative conception: different modes of governance will be evaluated according to dimensions of procedural legitimacy and problem-solving capacity and effectiveness. An institution, governance system, or political order is legitimate if it is based on values such as transparency, rule of law, accountability, fairness, inclusion, participation, representation and deliberation. In line with a normative notion of legitimacy and in the context of the European Union, Scharpf (1999; 2006) argues that legitimacy has two dimensions: input (or procedural) legitimacy and output legitimacy. Input legitimacy stems from procedural logic and asks: are policies and norms developed in a transparent, fair, inclusive and accountable manner? The participatory quality of the decision-making process is a central element of input legitimacy. Output legitimacy is associated with a consequential logic, collective problem-solving and effectiveness and asks: do norms and institutions result in collective problem-solving and performance? While contested, there are recurrent arguments that a high degree of effectiveness or environmental performance in terms of reducing collective problems such as environmental threats can compensate for low input legitimacy (Scharpf, 1999). Meanwhile, proponents of deliberative democracy claim that deliberation and arguing strengthens input legitimacy and has the potential to increase output legitimacy (Risse, 2004). In sum, the overall legitimacy of governance rests on combining effective environmental problem-solving (reducing negative environmental impacts) with fair, accountable, inclusive and transparent procedures. As discussed in Chapter 1, new modes of governance have been launched as win–win mechanisms that can close the legitimacy and implementation deficits.

The legitimacy of environmental governance has emerged as a central concern among scholars of international relations (Bernstein, 2005; Buchanan and Keohane, 2006; Steffek, 2003), environmental politics (Meadowcroft, 2004) and green political theory (Baber and Bartlett, 2005; Smith, 2003). More recently, attention has also turned to the legitimacy of new modes of public–private environmental governance (Bäckstrand, 2006; Dingwerth, 2007; Schäfferhoff et al., 2007) in issue areas such as GMO governance (Skogstad, 2003), forest certification as a non-state market-driven form of governance (Cashore et al., 2004; Schlyter et al., 2009) and climate politics (Bäckstrand, 2008; Lövbrand et al., 2009).

In the following the concept of legitimacy will be disaggregated to allow for empirical analysis of various modes of governance in the environmental issue areas covered in this book. Table 2.2 summarizes the key dimensions of input and output legitimacy and is the normative standard used to evaluate the overall legitimacy of new modes of governance in this book. We take Dingwerth's (2007) useful categorization of legitimacy as our starting point for the discussion on input legitimacy. He proposes three dimensions of legitimacy; (1) participation and inclusion; (2) democratic control and accountability; and (3) argumentative practice and deliberative quality.

Legitimacy through participation and inclusion
Participation by individuals and societal groups is a core element of democratic theory and practice as well as in environmental governance research and policy practice. The question to be addressed is: to what extent are those subject to a decision represented in the policy-making process? Input legitimacy can be achieved through the inclusion of actors that are affected by collective decision-making. The scope and quality of decision-making are two key aspects (Dingwerth, 2007, p. 28). Scope is about identifying the relevant constituencies and stakeholders affected by the rule-making and asking to what extent key participants are selected and represented in the policy process. In an electoral democracy within the bounds of the sovereign state, individual citizens are key constituencies. Legitimacy through participation also occurs beyond representative democracy in deliberative arrangements such as citizen juries and panels. In new modes of governance, non-electoral, group-based participation with key societal actors is central and exemplified by stakeholder consultations and consensus conferences at local, national, EU and global levels (see Chapters 6 and 7). At the global level where transnational constituencies are affected by decisions, the model of stakeholder democracy has been institutionalized, which entails representation, deliberation and participation of non-state actors, such as NGOs, civil society and business (Chapter 5, this volume; Bäckstrand, 2006; Nanz and Steffek, 2004). Furthermore, the quality of participation is a key concern. These concerns are, for example, whether there are equal opportunities to participate, in what phases of the policy process actors are included (agenda-setting, policy-making, implementation) and if participation is symbolic or real. The agenda-setting and pre-decision phases are often more conducive to deliberation compared to the post-decisional implementation phase.

Legitimacy through control and accountability
A second dimension of legitimacy is when those who govern are subject to control and held accountable, that is those in positions of influence should be responsive to the interests of their constituencies. Accountability is about the relation between an agent and a principal and its dictionary meaning is 'to answer' or 'liable to be called into account'. Accountability 'implies that some actors have the right to hold other actors accountable to a set of standards, to judge whether they have fulfilled their responsibilities in light of these standards, and to impose sanctions if they determine that these responsibilities have note been met' (Grant and Keohane, 2005, p. 29). Accountability can only lead to legitimacy if there are sanctions available when actions or decisions are incompatible with the values and preferences of principals. The ultimate sanction is if an agent is removed from its position because of a failure to comply, deliver promises or implement goals. Transparency and access to

information is a precondition of accountability. We can distinguish between top-down hierarchical accountability on the one hand and horizontal non-hierarchical (market, peer and reputational accountability) on the other. The former, which is aligned with hierarchical governance forms has clear principal–agent relationships: governments are accountable to citizens or international organizations are accountable to member states. They dominate in the governance modes in the top row in Table 2.1 in the context of electoral democracy and intergovernmental organizations. Horizontal accountability implies more complex principal–agent relationships. Private firms are accountable to shareholders and NGOs to their members. Accountability becomes more complex in new modes of governance, because they often include various types of public and private actors, such as public–private partnerships, where there is no coherent principal. Reputational accountability and credibility become crucial. The availability of information, public access and transparency, and monitoring mechanisms are important dimensions of accountability. Publicity, the media and public opinion play a crucial role since hierarchical controls between principal and agents are weak. Market accountability, which is prevalent in modes associated with self-organizational forms such as Box 5 in Table 2.1, relies on market signals to provide the base for reward and punishment for performance by investors, shareholders and consumers. Peer accountability is important in networked governance forms and consists of mutual valuations and rating of organizations by their counterparts. NGOs can, for example, evaluate the performance of other NGO networks.

Legitimacy through deliberative quality

To what extent do new modes of governance capture deliberative democracy ideals? Do new modes of governance use deliberative rationality, such as inclusiveness, unconstrained dialogue, and free and public reason among equal individuals? What is the quality of the deliberation and does it allow for arguing rather than bargaining (Risse, 2004)? Such questions attempt to assess the deliberative quality in new modes of governance that entail a mix of governance rationalities and organizational forms. Dingwerth (2007, p. 31) discusses how to assess deliberative quality. First, barriers that limit participation must be reduced. If the deliberation is limited to negotiations between narrow set of elites it will compromise the deliberative quality. Second, the focus is on how consensus can best be reached. Coercion and power asymmetries between actors are believed to distort communication and rational discourse. Key questions are to what extent the deliberative process is open to competing discourses and arguments from citizens as well as elites, and how the process is conducted. Deliberative theorists suggest that reciprocity assures that arguments of different participants are included and treated in an impartial and respectful manner.

Output legitimacy or effectiveness is the second dimension of legitimacy. There are very few studies of environmental effectiveness in biophysical and ecological terms in the research on the legitimacy of environmental governance, and political scientists have primarily focused on input legitimacy (Dingwerth, 2007; Gulbrandsen, 2008). Legitimate policies do not necessarily make the governance arrangements environmentally effective in terms of reducing the problem of depletion of the stratospheric ozone layer or climate change impacts, to take two examples. The environmental impact of specific modes of governance is a methodologically complex issue, left unanswered by political scientists. The predominant approach in political science and environmental politics is to conceptualize effectiveness in terms of policy, institutional or compliance effectiveness (Gulbrandsen, 2005; Victor et al., 1998; Weiss et al., 2000; Young, 1999). In this literature, environmental effectiveness thus signifies either policy effectiveness (is the right mix of policies/ programmes in place to address the environmental problem?), institutional effectiveness (are the required institutions and resources in place to reduce the problems?) or compliance effectiveness (do states comply with rules, programmes and policies that they adopted?). Implementation studies, also relevant here, focus on the process of implementation rather than its environmental outcomes. Policy, compliance and institutional effectiveness are necessary but far from sufficient preconditions for the environmental effectiveness of policies.

An alternative approach is to study effectiveness in terms of the environmental outcome. To what extent do particular sets of rules, norms or institutions lead to an actual improvement in the state of the environment? It addresses the environmental impact of policies and asks whether objectives are attained and if governance arrangements are effective in addressing the problem it intended to solve. It has been argued that the overall legitimacy of environmental policies largely rests on its environmental effectiveness in terms of biophysical improvements and strengthened ecological protection (Schlyter et al., 2009).

Table 2.2   Dimensions of input and output legitimacy

Input legitimacy (Procedural legitimacy)	• Participation/inclusion • Control/accountability • Deliberative quality
Output legitimacy (Effectiveness)	• Policy effectiveness • Institutional effectiveness • Compliance effectiveness • Environmental effectiveness

CONCLUSIONS

This chapter has proposed a framework for analysing the promise of new modes of environmental governance in terms of legitimacy and effectiveness. The concepts of governance forms and rationalities and input and output legitimacy serve as a basis for discussing the emergence of new modes of governance in the chapters to follow. A range of governance modes explored in this book, such as public–private partnerships, multi-stakeholder dialogues and networks are categorized according to two dimensions. The modes are explored in relation to their organizational form (hierarchy, markets and networks), which relates to the organization or the 'hardware' of governance and governance rationality (administrative, economic and deliberative), which concern the logic underlying governance modes. In evaluating the legitimacy of new modes of governance we distinguish between input and output legitimacy to better understand whether a specific mode investigated can be considered legitimate and if so, on what grounds. In the conclusions in Chapter 12 we will return to environmental governance in terms of forms, rationalities and legitimacy in view of the empirical analysis in Chapters 4 to 11.

REFERENCES

Andersen, Mikael S. and Duncan Liefferink (eds) (1997), *European Environmental Policy: The Pioneers*, Manchester: Manchester University Press.

Andersen, Mikael S. and Rolf-Ulrich Sprenger (eds) (2000), *Market-based Instruments for Environmental Management: Policies and Institutions*, Cheltenham, UK and Northampton, MA, USA: Edward Elgar.

Baber, Walter and Robert Bartlett (2001), 'Toward environmental democracy: rationality, reason, and deliberation', *Kansas Journal of Law & Public Policy*, **11**, 35–64.

Baber, Walter and Robert Bartlett (2005), *Deliberative Environmental Politics: Democracy and Ecological Rationality*, Cambridge, MA: MIT Press.

Bäckstrand, Karin (2006), 'Democratising global governance? Stakeholder democracy after the World Summit on Sustainable Development', *European Journal of International Relations*, **12**(14), 467–98.

Bäckstrand, Karin (2008), 'Accountability of networked climate governance: the rise of transnational climate partnerships', *Global Environmental Politics*, **8**(3), 74–102

Bernstein, Steven (2005), 'Legitimacy in global environmental governance', *Journal of International Law and International Relations*, **1**(1–2), 139–66.

Bernstein, Steven and Benjamin Cashore (2007) 'Can non-state global governance be legitimate? An analytical framework', *Regulation & Governance*, **1**, 1–25.

Bogason, Peter and Juliet A. Musso (2006), 'The democratic prospects of network governance', *The American Review of Public Administration*, **36**(4), 3–18.

Buchanan, Allen and Robert O. Keohane (2006), 'The legitimacy of global governance institutions', *Ethics and International Affairs*, **20**(4), 405–38.

Carter, Neil (2007), *The Politics of the Environment: Ideas, Activism, Policy*, 2nd edn, Cambridge: Cambridge University Press.

Cashore, Benjamin, Graeme Auld and Deanna Newsom (2004), *Governing Through Markets: Forest Certification and the Emergence of Non-State Authority*, New Haven, CT and London: Yale University Press.

Clapp, Jennifer and Peter Dauvergne (2005), *Paths to a Green World: The Political Economy of the Global Environment*, Cambridge, MA: MIT Press.

Dingwerth, Klaus (2007), *The New Transnationalism: Transnational Governance and Democratic Legitimacy*, Basingstoke: Palgrave Macmillan.

Dryzek, John (2000), *Deliberative Democracy and Beyond: Liberals, Critics, Contestations*, Oxford: Oxford University Press.

Dryzek, John (2005), *The Politics of the Earth: Environmental Discourses*, 2nd edn, Oxford: Oxford University Press.

Gill, Stephen (2005), 'New constitutionalism, democratisation and global political economy', in Rorden Wilkinson (ed.), *The Global Governance Reader*, London: Routledge, pp. 174–86, originally published (1998) in *Pacific Review*, **10**(1).

Grant, Ruth and Robert O. Keohane (2005), 'Accountability and abuses of power in world politics', *American Political Science Review*, **99**(1), 29–43.

Gulbrandsen, Lars H. (2005), 'The effectiveness of non-state governance schemes: a comparative study of forest certification in Norway and Sweden', *International Environmental Agreements*, **5**, 125–49.

Gulbrandsen, Lars H. (2008), 'Accountability arrangements in non-state standards organizations: instrumental design and imitation', *Organization*, **15**(4), 563–83.

Hagendijk, Rob and Alan Irwin (2006), 'Public deliberation and governance: Engaging with science and technology in contemporary Europe', *Minerva*, **44**, 167–84.

Hurd, Ian (1999), 'Legitimacy and authority in international politics', *International Organization*, **53**(2), 379–80.

Jordan, Andrew (2008), 'The governance of sustainable development: taking stock and looking forwards', *Environment and Planning C: Government and Policy*, **26**, 17–33.

Jordan, Grant (1990), 'Sub-governments, policy communities and networks', *Journal of Theoretical Politics*, **2**(3), 319–38.

Keohane, Robert O. (2003), 'Global governance and accountability', in David Held and Mathias Koehning-Archibugi (eds), *Taming Globalization: Frontiers of Governance*, Cambridge: Polity Press, pp. 130–59.

Koening-Archibugi, Mathias and Michael M. Zürn (eds) (2006), *New Modes of Governance in the Global System: Exploring Publicness, Delegation and Inclusiveness*, New York: Palgrave Macmillan.

Kronsell, Annica (1997), *Greening the EU: Power Practices, Resistances and Agenda Setting*, Lund, Sweden: Lund University Press.

Lafferty, William M. (ed.) (2004), *Governance for Sustainable Development: The Challenge of Adapting Form to Function*, Cheltenham, UK and Northampton, MA, USA: Edward Elgar.

Lövbrand, Eva, Joakim Nordquist and Teresia Rindefjäll (2009), 'Closing the legitimacy gap in global environmental governance', *Global Environmental Politics*, **9**(2), 74–100.

Lundqvist, Lennart (2004), *Sweden and Ecological Governance: Straddling the Fence*, Manchester: Manchester University Press.

Meadowcroft, James (2004), 'Participation and sustainable development: modes of citizen, community and organisational involvement' in William M. Lafferty (ed.), *Governance for Sustainable Development: The Challenge of Adapting Form to Function*, Cheltenham, UK and Northampton, MA, USA: Edward Elgar, pp. 162–90.

Miller, Peter and Nikolas Rose (2008), *Governing the Present*, Cambridge: Polity Press.

Murphy, Craig (2005), 'Global governance: poorly done and poorly understood' in Rorden Wilkinson (ed.), *The Global Governance Reader*, London and New York: Routledge, pp. 90–104, originally published (2000) in *International Affairs*, **76**(4).

Nanz, Patricia and Jens Steffek (2004), 'Global governance, participation and the public sphere', *Government and Opposition*, **39**(2), 314–34.

Payne, Rodger A. and Nayef Samhat (2004), *Democratizing Global Politics: Discourse, Norms, International Regimes and Political Community*, New York: State University of New York Press.

Petersen, Spike V. (2003), *A Critical Rewriting of Global Political Economy*, London and New York: Routledge.

Rhodes, R.A.W. (1990) 'Policy networks: a British perspective', *Journal of Theoretical Politics*, **2**(3), 293–317.

Risse, Tomas (2004), 'Global governance and communicative action', *Government and Opposition*, **39**(2), 288–13.

Schäfferhoff, Marco, Sabine Campe and Christopher Kaan (2007), 'Transnational public–private partnerships in international relations: making sense of concept, research frameworks and results', DFG Research Center SFB-Governance working paper no. 6, Berlin, August.

Scharpf, Fritz W. (1999), *Governing in Europe. Effective and Democratic?*, Oxford: Oxford University Press.

Scharpf, Fritz W. (2006), *Problem Solving Effectiveness and Democratic Accountability in the European Union*, Political Science series, Vienna: Institute for Advanced Studies.

Schlyter, Peter, Karin Bäckstrand and Ingrid Stjernquist (2009), 'Not seeing the forest for the trees? The environmental effectiveness of forest certification in Sweden', *Forest Policy and Economics*, **11**(5), 375–82.

Schout, Adriaan and Andrew Jordan (2005), 'Coordinated European governance: self-organizing or centrally steered?', *Public Adminstration*, **83**(1), 201–20.

Skogstad, Grace (2003), 'Legitimacy and/or policy effectiveness? Networked governance and GMO regulation in the European Union', *Journal of European Public Policy*, **10**(3), 321–38.

Smith, Graham (2003), *Deliberative Democracy and the Environment*, London and New York: Routledge.

Steffek, Jens (2003), 'The legitimation of international environmental governance', *European Journal of International Relations*, **9**(2), 249–76.

Sterner, Thomas (2002), *Policy Instruments for Environmental and Natural Resource Management*, Washington, DC: World Bank Publications.

Thompson, Grahame, Jennifer Frances, Rosalind Levacic, Jeremy Mitchell (1991), *Markets, Hierarchies and Networks: The Coordination of Social Life*, London: Sage.

Tietenberg, T.H. (1990), 'Economic instruments for environmental regulation', *Oxford Review of Economic Policy*, **6**(1), 17–33.

Treib, Oliver, Holger Bähr and Gerda Falkner (2007), 'Modes of governance: towards a conceptual clarification', *Journal of European Environmental Policy*, **14**(1), 1–20.

Victor, David, Kal Raustilia and Eugene Skolnikoff (1998), *The Implementation and Effectiveness of International Environmental Treaties: Theory and Practice*, Cambridge, MA: MIT Press.

Weale, Albert (1992), *The New Politics of Pollution*, Manchester: Manchester University Press.

Weiss Brown, Edith and Harold Jacobson (2000), *Engaging Countries: Strengthening Compliance with International Environmental Accords*, Cambridge, MA: MIT Press.

Whitehead, Mark (2008), 'Cold monsters and ecological Leviathans: reflections on the relationships between states and the environment', *Geography Compass*, **2**(2), 414–32.

Young, Oran (1999), *The Effectiveness of International Environmental Regimes: Causal Connections and Behavioral Mechanisms*, Cambridge, MA: MIT Press.

3. The deliberative turn in green political theory

Eva Lövbrand and Jamil Khan

INTRODUCTION

As outlined in Chapter 1 in this book, theories of democracy have taken a strong deliberative turn in recent decades (Baber and Bartlett, 2005; Smith, 2003; Dryzek, 2000; Elster, 1998; Bohman and Regh, 1997). In the face of a growing apathy about electoral and representative institutions, democratic theorists have since the early 1990s sought to restore democratic authenticity by revitalizing public debate. In this chapter we trace how this deliberative turn is manifested in green political theory. In parallel to the rise of new modes of environmental governance, green political theorists have in recent years examined the promise of deliberative innovations (cf. Dryzek, 1987; 1990; 2000; Eckersley, 1992; 2004; Torgerson, 1999; Smith, 2003; Baber and Bartlett, 2005; Fischer, 2005; Dobson and Bell, 2000; O'Neill, 2007; Humphrey, 2007). While still diverse, this new school of green political thinkers advances a general belief that deliberative processes will both increase the legitimacy of collective decisions and foster critical self-awareness of the ecological grounds which support our lives (Plumwood, 2001, p. 562). Through free and inclusive reason-giving on questions of common purpose, reflective citizens are expected to bridge the dual goals of strong democracy and demanding environmentalism (Baber and Bartlett, 2005, p. 12).

In this chapter we approach this scholarly commitment to ecological democracy as a normative vantage point for the promise of new modes of environmental governance. Although green political theorizing is often remote from the governance debates found among policy practitioners in the EU and UN, we argue that the deliberative ideals advanced by green theorists have bearing on the deliberative turn in environmental politics and the prospects for more legitimate and effective governance arrangements. More than any other academic field, green political thought has struggled with the challenge to link democratic procedure to sustainable outcomes. Hence, synergies and trade-offs between legitimate and environmentally effective policy-making are at the core of this scholarly debate. After a brief introduction to the deliberative turn in green political theory, this chapter examines three tensions or points of contestation that arise from attempts to reconcile democracy and environmentalism in green political theory. While interesting in their own right, we argue that these tensions are important to this book since they help us to reflect upon potential problems tied to the promise of new modes of environmental governance.

We begin by drawing attention to the tension between means and ends in green deliberative politics. As proposed by Goodin (1992), a green theory of value cannot be equated with a green theory of agency. Whereas the former is concerned with the substantive outcomes of environmental politics (environmental effectiveness, sustainability and so on), the latter tells us about human agency and the procedures required to meet desired ends (for example central government, market liberalism, public deliberations). As we have seen in Chapter 2, this book categorizes such procedures according to forms of governance (hierarchy, market, networks) and rationalities of governance (administrative, economic, deliberative). Although many green political theorists tie high substantive expectations to deliberative procedures, the first section of the chapter highlights potential trade-offs between the procedural ideals of green deliberative politics and its promise to deliver environmentally effective outcomes and performance.

In the second section we address tensions between participation and representation raised by the deliberative conception of legitimacy. As Benhabib (1996, p. 67, emphasis added) puts it, 'legitimacy in complex democratic societies must be thought to result from the free and unconstrained public deliberation of *all* about matters of common concern'. The global and intergenerational reach of many environmental problems stretches the boundaries for the political and moral community involved in such deliberations (Eckersley, 2004; Dryzek, 2000). Since all those potentially affected by environmental degradation (present and future generations, human and non-human subjects) cannot participate in practical discourse at the same time, green deliberative theorists are thus faced with the challenge to develop legitimate and effective means of representation. How and by whom will the concerns of those with no or limited voice be taken into account in environmental deliberations?

Finally, we scrutinize the scope of the deliberative agenda in a time of market environmentalism. As noted by O'Neill (2007), environmental politics has in recent decades been strongly dominated by a market norm that has transformed ecological goods and services into commodities subject to monetary exchange. When recast in the language of capital, environmental governance turns into a marketplace where self-interested consumers seek to satisfy, rather than give reasons for, their preferences. Where, in this expanding marketplace, do green deliberative scholars foresee a political space for deliberative rather than economic rationality? The questions raised in this chapter by no means represent the only challenges facing scholarly attempts to reconcile strong democracy and demanding environmentalism in terms of effective environmental policies. Nor do they result in any easy or final answers. However, they do ask for more empirically informed investigations into the practice of deliberative environmental governance.

While the deliberative turn in green political thought has restored an optimistic belief in the cognitive capacity and the moral potential of the 'ecological citizen' (Dobson and Bell, 2006), our chapter suggests that green deliberative theory is weakly linked to the practical reality in which environmental politics is played out. Although political theorists may approach the deliberative ideal as a critical vantage point from which policy practice can be evaluated (Eckersley, 2004, p. 127), we conclude that serious engagement with the practice of environmental governance is necessary in order to determine the feasibility and desirability of the normative ideal itself. As a consequence, this chapter should be seen as a theoretical starting point for the empirical investigations into the deliberative turn and the promise of new modes of environmental governance offered in the remainder of the book (Chapters 4 to 11, this volume). While green deliberative scholars differ in the emphasis (and hopes) they put on these different deliberative arenas, it is not the aim of this chapter to offer a full account of respective forms of governance, nor to determine which is the most appropriate or promising one. Such an overview is instead offered in Chapter 2 of this book, followed by in-depth empirical case studies in Chapters 4–11. The main focus of this chapter is instead to outline, in more general terms, some crucial points of contestation that arise when the procedural ideal of deliberation meets the substantive promise of environmental politics.

THE PROMISE OF GREEN DELIBERATIVE THEORY

Broadly defined, the deliberative models of democracy forward an ideal of legitimate decision-making that rests upon public reasoning among free, equal and rational individuals (Bohman and Regh, 1997; Elster, 1998). In contrast to aggregate conceptions of democracy, which set out to reflect individual preferences through electoral mechanisms, deliberative democrats ask individuals and their representatives to reason together and to be ready to transform their preferences in light of the better argument (Pellizzoni, 2001, p. 66). When articulating good reasons in public, individuals are expected to think what would count as good reason for all others involved (Benhabib, 1996; Cohen, 1996). At the core of any account of deliberative democracy is a commitment to public reason, that is reasons that transcend individual preferences and are accepted by all those affected by collective decisions (Hicks, 2002, p. 241; Rawls, 1999).

Deliberative democracy can consequently be understood as an expression of the Enlightenment devotion to reason as an arbiter of disagreement (Baber and Bartlett, 2005, p. 231). Largely under the influence of Jürgen Habermas, the theory defends a communicative account of rationality based on free discussion, sound argument and reliable evidence. In contrast to instrumental forms of rationality (for example administrative or economic), which according to Habermas (1971) colonize the life-world and repress individual freedom and creativity, communicative (or deliberative) rationality has been described as a form of social interaction that emancipates the individual from myth, illusion and manipulation (Dryzek, 1990). At the core of the theory are a number of procedural criteria that boil down to two fundamental conditions; inclusiveness and unconstrained dialogue (Smith, 2003, p. 56). Inclusiveness requires that all citizens are allowed to participate in public discourse and have equal rights to advance claims and arguments. The discourse is in turn unconstrained when the only authority is that of a good argument (Dryzek, 1990, p. 15). Hence, communicative rationality requires that social interaction is free from domination, manipulation and strategic behaviour.

While far from all deliberative democrats agree that consensus is a necessary or even desirable condition for successful deliberations (cf. Bohman, 1996; Gutmann and Thompson, 2004; Young, 1996), the deliberative model of democracy rests on a general belief in reasoned argument as the best way of resolving moral conflict. By promoting a public sphere where an informed citizenry can test the validity of their opinions and norms, deliberative democracy aims to foster moral agreement (or reasoned disagreement) on what is good and true (Baber and Bartlett, 2005, p. 87). Considering this procedural emphasis in deliberative democracy, it appears somewhat surprising that the environment has become one of the principal sites for its recent renaissance (O'Neill, 2007, p. 13). As famously put by Goodin (1992, p. 168); 'to advocate democracy is to advocate procedures, to advocate environmentalism is to advocate substantive outcomes'. Since democracy is a political system in which governments respond to the wishes of citizens, many have noted that there is no guarantee that democratic rule is conducive to environmental ends (cf. Saward, 1996). This dilemma led to a turn to centralized and authoritarian solutions to human population growth and natural resource depletion by green thinkers in the 1960s and 1970s (cf. Erlich, 1968; Ophuls, 1977; Heilbroner, 1974).

However, in recent years green political thinkers have instead defended a green version of deliberative democracy as a promising way forward. While the eco-authoritarians of the 1970s did not trust individuals to make altruistic and cooperative choices to manage earth's finite resources, contemporary green thinkers are confident that the citizens in truly democratic societies 'will come to their ecological senses' (Eckersley, 1990, p. 758). At the heart of the deliberative turn in green political theory is a general belief that deliberative processes will help individuals to transcend their self-interested preferences and arrive at morally responsible solutions to collective-action problems. Since deliberative democratic arrangements promote reflexivity, self-correction and the continual public testing of claims (Eckersley, 2004, p. 117), most green deliberative scholars expect that they will lead to an understanding of the irrationality upon which the human domination of nature rests (Torgerson, 1999, p. 123). Hence, by fostering unconstrained and egalitarian deliberation over questions of value and common purpose, green deliberative scholars hope to bring about an age of reflexive ecological modernization when strong democracy and demanding environmentalism go hand in hand (Baber and Bartlett, 2005; Eckersley, 2004; Dryzek et al., 2003; Dobson and Bell, 2006). In other words, in responding to the environmental crisis, how can procedural democratic legitimacy be compatible with strong environmental performance?

In Chapter 2, Kronsell and Bäckstrand outlined a framework for assessing the legitimacy of new governance arrangements by distinguishing between input legitimacy (procedural and democratic qualities) and output legitimacy (problem-solving capacity and performance). In light of the above discussion, green deliberative theory can be seen as an attempt to strengthen both aspects of legitimacy simultaneously. Inclusive and unconstrained public reason-giving holds the promise of rational agreement on the common good, which in turn fosters effective environmental problem-solving. While the deliberative turn in green political theory is characterized by this overall promise, we note that the deliberative ideal is far from homogeneous and promotes different forms governance to reach that end. Meadowcroft (2004, pp. 187–8) makes a useful distinction between deliberative interactions within core political institutions and constitution-making bodies of the state, deliberative innovations at the interface between the state and civil society (for example public–private partnerships, public consultations, consensus conferences), and civic debate and popular will-formation in the public sphere (for example civic networks). The following section discusses the clash between the procedural ideal of deliberation and the substantive promise of environmental politics.

PROCEDURE VS. OUTCOME IN ENVIRONMENTAL DELIBERATIONS

In line with deliberative democratic theory, green deliberative scholars attach high expectations to the cognitive capacity and moral potential of deliberating citizens. When encountering the values, beliefs and arguments of others, the reflective citizen is assumed to extend beyond personal interests and recognize that what is good for the individual is not necessarily good for the social collective (Rosenberg, 2007, p. 8). In the growing literature on environmental or ecological citizenship (Dobson, 2006; Dobson and Bell, 2006), the political-moral space in which citizens operate is often seen as the whole of humanity. Hence, ecological citizenship rests upon a sense of moral responsibility and reciprocity that extends beyond state borders, contemporary generations and, sometimes, also includes the non-human world (Dobson, 2006). However, how to foster such transnational and long-term responsibility remains a central debate. Given the seriousness and urgency of many environmental problems, green political scholars are often faced with the pressing question concerning whether deliberative practices can legitimately be steered towards environmentally sustainable ends.

When following the work of Habermas, deliberative democracy is primarily concerned with creating the right procedural conditions (for example fairness, inclusiveness, open dialogue) for communicative rationality. Green scholars inspired by this procedural ideal (for example Dryzek, 1990; 2000) trust that such reasoned debate will lead to recognition of ecological values since the most rational decision for humanity at large is to minimize the pressure on the planet's life support systems. Hence, the right procedural conditions hold the promise of reflection and morally responsible outcomes. However, not all deliberative scholars agree that deliberative procedures will automatically result in ecologically benign outcomes. Smith (2003), for example, resists any attempt to predetermine green outcomes. In order to avoid the latent authoritarian tendency in green political theory (Smith, 2003, p. 67), he proposes a more modest ambition that faces the risk of disappointing environmentalists:

> The promise of deliberative democracy for greens is that the plurality of environmental values will be voiced and considered in the political process. This is not an argument that there is a necessary connection between environmental values and deliberative democracy. Neither is there any *guarantee* that decisions emerging from deliberative processes will necessarily embody environmental values (Smith, 2003, p. 72, emphasis in original).

Along the same lines Wissenburg (1998, p. 223) argues that deliberative democratic processes indeed may be emancipatory, lead to more informed choices, and increase the legitimacy of policies. However, there is no reason to believe that they will automatically lead to sustainability. Since the interests of the environment are not as close to heart as our more private interests, Wissenburg affirms that more democracy is no guarantee for green decisions. While this observation suggests a potential tension between democratic procedure and green outcomes, many green scholars have been unsatisfied with the vague promise that deliberative processes only *may* lead to the recognition of 'the ecological relations that sustain us all' (Eckersley, 1990, p. 761). Attempts have therefore been made to probe whether environmental rights, which guarantee a certain protection of the environment, can legitimately be included in the constitutional rights of liberal democracies.

Saward (1996) has suggested that such a move is legitimate if it can be shown that environmental rights are part of the internal values of democracy, that is, if they are necessary in order to strengthen democracy. He argues that environmental rights can be viewed as internal values of democracy if connected to health care rights. While adequate health care is essential for citizens to be able to fulfil their democratic rights, Saward concludes that other environmental imperatives are external to the requirements of a democracy. If such imperatives are constitutionally entrenched, democracy will be diluted (Saward, 1996, p. 93). Hayward (2005) has argued more forcefully for the adoption of constitutional environmental rights as fundamental democratic rights. In contrast to Saward, Hayward does not view social rights (for example the right to health care) as necessary preconditions for democracy since the connection between meeting people's needs and their capacity to participate politically is too tenuous. He instead makes a crucial connection between procedural and substantive rights.

Hayward notes that rights to information and participation in environmental decision-making are increasingly common and relatively uncontroversial. Procedural environmental rights are underpinned by a fundamental substantive right to live in an environment adequate for health and well-being (Hayward, 2005, p. 145). Hence, 'if it is rational to affirm procedural environmental rights, then it is rational to affirm all the necessary conditions for achieving the ends for which they were introduced' (ibid., p. 148). Hayward argues that substantive environmental rights are negative rights. Instead of the right to a good environment, environmental rights should protect citizens from environmental harm or degradation. By moving away from the connection between environment and health, environmental rights are here defined in a much broader sense than proposed by Saward. Eckersley takes one step further when including non-human agents in the rights discourse. While Eckersley is critical of the anthropocentric foundation of deliberative democracy (as well as liberal democracy), she notes that procedural ideals such as unconstrained dialogue, inclusiveness and social learning appeal to environmentalists (Eckersley, 2004, pp. 115–17). Her project is thus to reconstruct the Habermasian deliberative ideal so that it accommodates the non-human world.

While Eckersley (2004, p. 122, italics in original) acknowledges that 'we cannot speak for nature in itself; *we can only speak about the nature we humans have constituted*', she maintains that it is sufficient to reach intersubjective understandings of nature. Hence, there is no necessary *moral* objection to including nature as a subject worthy of consideration in its own right in deliberative dialogue (Eckersley, 2004, p. 125). In terms of policy, Eckersley's main suggestion is that the precautionary principle should be constitutionally entrenched in the same way that basic democratic rights are (ibid., p. 135). Such constitutional entrenchment of environmental rights could, indeed, offer a far-reaching regulation towards green outcomes. However, Eckersley also agrees that the environmental values protected by the precautionary principle cannot be predetermined, but instead have to be negotiated in political dialogue. Quoting John Barry, she asserts that 'the concept of sustainability needs to be understood as a discursively created rather than an authoritatively given product' (Eckersley, 2004, p. 119). Does this compromise offer a solution to the intrinsic tension between environmentalism and democracy so elegantly described by Goodin? Not really.

Still, the bottom line is that pure proceduralists will insist that deliberative democracy offers no guarantee of green outcomes, while more radical green thinkers maintain that democracy can (and should) be steered in favour of environmental ends. The extent to which political institutions and decision processes can be shaped to overcome this fundamental tension and dividing line remains to be proven by more real-life examples. In Chapter 8, Hildingsson takes an important step in that direction when assessing recent policy innovations in Swedish sustainability governance. While the study suggests that state-led deliberative procedures indeed can be combined with green outcomes, the causal connection between increased public deliberation and environmental effectiveness remains unclear.

PARTICIPATION VS. REPRESENTATION IN ENVIRONMENTAL DELIBERATIONS

When assessing the democratic legitimacy of environmental governance arrangements, inclusive participation is often brought forward as an important normative principle. Although this principle is only one of several dimensions of the input legitimacy concept advanced by Kronsell and Bäckstrand in Table 2.2 in Chapter 2, it is central to any deliberative account of legitimacy. At the heart of the deliberative ideal is the notion that collective decisions require public justification. Reasons for or against certain courses of action must be given in public so that all those affected have a realistic chance to test and accept them (Dryzek, 2001, p. 651). Hence, Benhabib (1996, p. 68) has defined democratic legitimacy as the result of free and unconstrained public deliberation of all about matters of common concern. This expansive account of inclusion (all affected) is central to the deliberative principle of mutual respect and thus emerges as a non-negotiable condition of legitimacy for deliberative theorists (Hicks, 2002, p. 226). In order to secure legitimate (and effective) outcomes, deliberative processes must give *all* the same chance to initiate speech acts, to question, to interrogate, and to open debate (Benhabib, 1996, p. 70).

However, in practice, this procedural requirement is of course highly problematic. Among many, Michael Walzer (1999) has noted that deliberation is not an activity for the demos '(…) 100 million of them, or even 1 million or 100,000, can't plausibly reason together' (Walzer, 1999, p. 68). Since meaningful participation by more than a fraction of those affected by collective decisions is inconceivable given the practical constraints of time and institutional capacity (Hicks, 2002, p. 227), deliberative practices cannot deliver the legitimate outcomes defined by theory. While this dilemma is by no means exclusive to the environmental domain, it is reinforced by the global and intergenerational challenges of contemporary environmental risks. The environmental harm caused by problems such as forest degradation, water pollution or global climate change (see Chapters 4, 5, 7, 10 and 11, this volume) is not fixed in terms of people or territory. The spatial and temporal community at risk often spans state borders and continents, and may also extend into the future. This extended notion 'all affected' suggests that contemporary environmental decision-making by necessity will fail to involve all relevant communities in collective reason-giving about the common good.

Eckersley (2004, p. 112) has responded to this dilemma by proposing an ecological democracy *for* rather than *by* the affected. Through the concept of political trusteeship, she suggests that persons or groups within the polity could search for meaningful ways of representing the interests and concerns of those who cannot represent themselves (for example non-citizens, future generations, non-human subjects). By thinking and speaking on the behalf of 'excluded others', Eckersley (2004, p. 120) expects that the ecological citizen will fail to justify the displacement of environmental harm. This form of representation resonates with the stakeholder concept as defined in the Anglo-Saxon legal history. According to Whitman (2008, p. 172), the legal discourse of 'the stakeholder' refers to disinterested parties acting to protect the future rights of others. Speaking for those who cannot appear in court on their own behalf, the legal stakeholder seeks to avoid injustice being done (Whitman, 2008). In recent years this stakeholder principle has gained ground in environmental policy practice. Since the 1992 Rio Earth Summit or the World Summit on Sustainable Development in Johannesburg in 2002, we have seen the rise of a range of multi-stakeholder procedures such as consultations, roundtables and partnerships. These participatory mechanisms seek to involve representatives of affected interests in deliberative encounters from the local and national to the global. In Chapter 5 (this volume) Bäckstrand examines in further detail the multi-stakeholder procedures in the Johannesburg partnerships, and in Chapter 6 Bengtsson and Klintman analyse stakeholder deliberations in the European Union's governance of genetically modified food.

However, deliberations mediated by stakeholder representation differ in a significant way from the trusteeship model envisioned by Eckersley. Since the seats at the table are allocated to organized societal groups (for example business, NGOs, academia) rather than individual citizens, Meadowcroft (2004, p. 205) notes that multi-stakeholder processes are more oriented towards representation than transformation of established interests. The stakeholder model does not ask representatives to extend beyond the pursuit of particular group interests and take the perspective of all affected. This deliberative principle is better incorporated into citizen-based governance arrangements (for example citizen juries, consensus conferences, deliberative polling). Individuals participating in such deliberative processes have no formal obligation to represent anyone but themselves. However, through the process of deliberation, they are expected to exercise an enlarged citizenship by thinking beyond what is right and good for the individual in favour of the community at large. While there are strengths and weaknesses in respective models (see Meadowcroft, 2004) critical scholars have questioned the very idea of representation in public deliberations. Following feminist critique of deliberative models of democracy, Phillips (1996, p. 147) has, for instance, claimed that the notion that anyone can 'stand in' for anyone else runs the risk of rendering the multitude of embodied 'subject positions' invisible.

Although most contemporary feminist scholars would reject an essentialist understanding of identity, many have argued that representation in political discourse often privileges the beliefs, experiences and speaking styles of Western, white, well-educated men at the expense of the marginalized 'other' (cf. Young, 1996; 2003; Gould, 1996). By associating the ideal deliberative procedure with virtues such as autonomy, self-determination, rationality and the maintenance of a clear boundary between public and private life, MacGregor (2006, p. 103) argues that theories of deliberative democracy have firmly planted the deliberating citizen on masculinist ground. According to Plumwood (2001), such gender biased interpretations of political life are not only unjust. They will also fail to deliver environmentally effective outcomes. In contrast to Beck's (1995, p. 60) famous claim that '(p)overty is hierarchical, while smog is democratic', Plumwood notes many environmental harms, including smog, are unevenly distributed across boundaries of class, gender and power. While those who have most access to political voice and decision-making power often are those most remote from environmental degradation, those who bear the heaviest environmental burden often have the weakest voice and decision power. Hence, positioned on a high level of remoteness from the ecological consequences of their decisions, Plumwood (2001) sees deliberating elites as poor representatives of the concerns and experiences of those most vulnerable to eco-harm.

While the feminist critique of deliberative democracy seeks to restore its critical edge by bringing the diversity of speaking styles and embodied experiences to the surface, this critical project offers few solutions to the tension between participation and representation discussed here. Approaching political representation as an attempt to silence difference and dissent, feminist scholars have called for a 'politics of presence' (Phillips, 1996, p. 151) that cannot be practically achieved in deliberative forums. While some have seen this dilemma as a reason to reject the deliberative ideal all together (cf. Mouffe, 1999), Dryzek (2000; 2001) identifies a compromise in the public sphere. Rather than asking those affected by environmental harm to reason together in face-to-face deliberations, Dryzek has developed a discursive account of legitimacy. From this vantage point, collective decisions are legitimate when consistent with the prevailing constellation of discourses in the public sphere. In contrast to the trusteeship or stakeholder model, Dryzek (2001, p. 664) sees discursive contestation within civic networks and social movements as a more inclusive form of communication that gives room both for rival discourses and moral constituents beyond the state. Since the reach of the public sphere is not limited by formal boundaries of jurisdiction, it appears more sensitive to the borderless nature of the environmental challenge (Dryzek, 2000, p. 159). Hence, by detaching the concept of legitimacy from the actual 'counting of heads' in formal deliberative settings, Dryzek takes the tension between participation and representation in a different (but far from final) direction.

DELIBERATIVE VS. ECONOMIC RATIONALITY IN A TIME OF MARKET ENVIRONMENTALISM

Efforts to make deliberative democracy more attentive to difference and dissent are often matched by a concern with the large asymmetries of social, economic and institutional power under which public deliberations take place. In contrast to deliberative democrats' belief that sites and processes of deliberation will limit political domination and 'the naked imposition of partisan interests' (Young, 2003, p. 104), many critical scholars are less optimistic and stress the central role of economic imperatives and power structures in political life (cf. Mouffe, 1999). In the following section we approach the marketization of environmental governance as a third dilemma for green deliberative theory that does not arise so much from the theoretical ideal itself, as the political context in which it is applied. According to Newell (2005, p. 189) marketization refers to 'the myriad ways in which the possibilities of environmental politics are being defined according to their ability to serve the broader end of market expansion'. It is a historical juncture when the market is seen as the source of innovation, efficiency and incentives necessary to combat environmental degradation (Newell, 2008, p. 79). It is also a time when tensions between the reflective citizen and the self-interested consumer, deliberative and economic rationalities of governance (see Chapter 2, this volume) are brought to the fore.

In parallel to the renewed interest in deliberative governance arrangements, we have in recent years seen the rise of market schemes such as product labelling and certification, environmental management systems, emission trading and public–private partnerships (see, for instance, Chapters 4 and 5, this volume). Many critical political economists have associated this marketization of environmental governance with an underlying neoliberal agenda of furthering economic growth (Park et al., 2008). Rather than approaching environmental degradation as an opportunity to rethink the capitalist logic of accumulation, market environmentalism has been described as an ideology that relies on market actors to deliver environmental improvements without compromising economic growth (Newell, 2008). As such it emerges as a deregulated (and weak) form of ecological modernization (Christoff, 1996) that promotes private property rights and voluntary standards as more effective environmental governance forms than state-based intervention. According to Eckersley (2004, p. 74), this kind of environmentalism protects global economic processes from policy intervention and deeper questioning and critique. By seeking to decouple, rather than confront, the link between environmental degradation and economic growth, market environmentalism differs substantially from the strong or reflexive version of ecological modernization envisioned by green deliberative scholars.

The attributes attached to the individual represent one of the main dividing lines between these two modernization ideals. According to O'Neill (2007), market environmentalism rests upon a conception of the individual as a self-interested consumer who seeks to maximize rather than give reasons for his/her preferences. In the marketplace ends are treated as wants, and no judgement of their moral rightness is allowed to enter criteria of choice. Following an economic rationality, markets offer decisions without dialogue (O'Neill, 2007, p. 29). For green deliberative theorists, by contrast, environmental decisions are not matters for the market but the forum. Rather than approaching environmental decision-making as an aggregation of individuals' given interests, the deliberative forum builds upon a communicative ideal where preferences are formed and transformed through reasoned dialogue among free and equal citizens. Acting as a responsible citizen rather than a consumer, the individual can no longer express personal or self-regarding wants and interests. By appealing to wider constituencies of interests, the citizen is instead asked to take moral responsibility for the common good. Hence, as argued by Dobson (2006, p. 129), the ecological citizen does the right thing not because of narrow economic or private incentives, but because it is the right thing to do. When speaking and acting on the behalf of humanity as a whole, ecological citizenship emerges as corrective or oppositional work that holds the potential to challenge the underlying causes of unsustainable development (Barry, 2006, p. 32).

Despite these different rationalities and subjectivities, far from all green deliberative scholars reject the consumer as a potential agent of reflection and critique. According to Barry (2006), simplistic distinctions between the citizen and the consumer often overlook the sphere of consumption as a site for the practice of ecological virtue. Consumer activities such as boycotts have a part to play in the struggle for sustainability (Barry, 2006, p. 38). In a similar vein, Boström and Klintman (2008) talk about the politically and ethically motivated 'citizen-consumer' expressing political concerns through active consumer choices. Green consumer movements that seek to alter products and production processes (for example organic food labelling, forest certification schemes) hold democratic potential when fostering civic reflection and debate (Boström and Klintman, 2008). However, in contrast to the ideal deliberative forum, the marketplace is not protected from strategic manipulation or coercion. Underpinned by inequalities of economic and social power, market deliberations often take place in the context of large asymmetries of voice (O'Neill, 2007). As a consequence, caution has been raised against market forms of governance that emphasize cooperation and partnership between public and private actors, business and civil society (for empirical examples see Chapters 4 and 5, this volume). Under the appearance of democratic participation and deliberation, such governance arrangements may in fact defuse the radical potential of green critique and thus function as a legitimizing strategy of global capital (cf. Paterson, 2008; Whitman, 2008). Paterson (2008) talks about 'sustainable consumption' as a mode of regulation that normalizes patterns of accumulation and undermines the radical potential of civic critique. Whitman (2008), in turn, questions stakeholder processes that capture the legitimacy of the participating actors within a management regime that is designed to serve business.

Hence, from the perspective of critical political economy, a tension underpins the relationship between deliberative processes and markets in environmental governance. On the one hand, we have in recent years seen an increased interest and emphasis on democratic participation and deliberation in green political theory, as well as in environmental policy rhetoric and practice. On the other hand the dominance of market environmentalism suggests that the scope for meaningful deliberation is severely restricted. Performed under the umbrella of neoliberal patterns of governance, citizen-based routes to sustainability are increasingly aligned with goals of the capitalist society such as economic growth, private ownership and consumption. Although the critical potential of the deliberative turn remains, market environmentalism appears as an unreliable ally in the theoretical quest to foster strong democracy and demanding environmentalism through inclusive public deliberations. As suggested by Newell (2008, p. 78), decision-making around the economic processes which drive environmental degradation often remains secretive and closed from public participation, driven instead by the commercial interests it seeks to serve.

CONCLUSIONS

We have in this chapter identified and discussed the deliberative turn in green political theory. We have approached the green commitment to deliberation as a normative project that advances public deliberations as a means to link democratic procedure to environmental outcomes. Resting upon an optimistic belief in the cognitive capacity and moral potential of the rational citizen, scholars in this field hope that inclusive and unconstrained reason-giving will help to transform personal preferences in favour of cooperative and collective solutions to environmental problems. Through communicative rationalization, the discursive community is thought to gain recognition of the ecological relations that sustain us all and thus move 'the unfinished project of modernity' (Habermas, 1996) into a reflexive green stage.

Our chapter has addressed three potential tensions built into this theoretical promise. First, we discussed the interplay between means and ends, procedure and substance, in environmental deliberations. We concluded that deliberative politics offers no guarantee that the human life-support capacity of ecosystems, described as '*the* generalizable interest *par excellence*' by Dryzek (1987, p. 204, italics in original), takes priority over the range of private interests that dominate human affairs. If environmental rights are not constitutionally entrenched, all that can be guaranteed is that the plurality of values associated with nature will be articulated and defended (Smith, 2003, p. 67). Hence, green deliberative scholars have to date not offered convincing evidence that their promise holds, even in theory. Thus, whether inclusive and deliberative governance arrangements indeed result in effective environmental problem-solving remains an open question.

Secondly, we analysed the tension between participation and representation generated by the deliberative conception of legitimacy. We discussed the practical challenge of ensuring that all those potentially affected by environmental harm are given equal consideration in environmental deliberations. Since the promise of legitimate and enlightened environmental outcomes rests on this premise, we found that green deliberative scholars are struggling to develop acceptable means of representation. Whether participatory forms of governance (for example public–private partnerships, stakeholder consultations, consensus conferences) can ensure that the diversity of perspectives, concerns and embodied experiences are taken into account in collective decisions, is discussed in further detail in Chapters 5 and 6 in this book. However, considering the cultural differences and range of subject positions involved in environmental deliberations, the quest to give all the same chance to initiate speech acts, to question, to interrogate, and to open debate remains a highly challenging and perhaps even inconceivable ideal.

Finally, we questioned the market as a deliberative site where citizens will be encouraged to 'think from the perspective of everyone else' (O'Neill, 2007, p. 155). We found a widespread concern among green deliberative scholars that the marketplace will encourage individuals to satisfy, rather than give reasons for, their preferences. Underpinned by an economic rationality of governance, market arrangements may indeed counter the deliberative promise of public reflection and moral responsibility for humanity at large. Operating in a context of real asymmetries of power and voice, market deliberations also run the risk of defusing the radical potential of green critique and thus function as a legitimizing strategy of global capital. Hence, in a time of market environmentalism, the potential to realize the ideal deliberative procedure and thus foster legitimate and effective environmental outcomes appears highly constrained. Are these tensions so fundamental that they overthrow the green ambition to reconcile strong democracy and demanding environmentalism all together? And what do they tell us about the promise of new modes of environmental governance?

We conclude that the most ideal forms of deliberative democracy do, indeed, seem highly utopian when translated into environmental politics. Attempts to promote deliberative environmental governance can thus expect to face great challenges. This finding does not, however, mean that public reason-giving on questions of common purpose will automatically fail to contribute to more legitimate and effective environmental decision-making. Since green deliberative theory has emerged as a normative ideal against which environmental policy practice can be critically assessed, we still know too little about the practice of green deliberative politics in order to offer a final answer to this central question. Hence, we conclude that the extent to which the promise of green deliberative theory translates into practice is just as much an empirical as a theoretical question.

Although far from all new governance arrangements in the environmental domain rest upon actual practices of deliberation, we see the remaining chapters in this book as a fruitful step towards a more empirically informed assessment of the green deliberative ideal. Since the promise of new modes of environmental governance shares a similar commitment to democratic procedure *and* environmental outcomes, there is much to gain from linking theoretical insights from this long-standing debate to studies of environmental policy practice.

REFERENCES

Baber, Walter and Robert Bartlett (2005), *Deliberative Environmental Politics*, Cambridge, MA: The MIT Press.
Barry, John (2006), 'Resistance is fertile: from environmental to sustainability citizenship' in Andrew Dobson and Derek Bell (eds), *Environmental Citizenship*, Cambridge, MA and London: The MIT Press, pp. 21–48.
Beck, Ulrich (1995), *Ecological Rationality: On the Politics of the Risk Society*, New Jersey: Humanities Press.
Benhabib, Seyla (1996), 'Toward a deliberative model of democratic legitimacy', in Seyla Benhabib (ed.), *Democracy and Difference: Contesting the Boundaries of the Political*, Princeton, NJ: Princeton University Press, pp. 67–94.
Bohman, James (1996), *Public Deliberation: Pluralism, Complexity and Democracy*, Cambridge, MA: The MIT Press.
Bohman, James and William Regh (eds) (1997), *Deliberative Democracy: Essays on Reason and Politics*, Cambridge, MA and London: The MIT Press.
Boström, Magnus and Mikael Klintman (2008), *Eco-Standards, Production Labelling and Green Consumerism*, New York: Palgrave Macmillan.
Christoff, Peter (1996), 'Ecological modernization, ecological modernities', *Environmental Politics*, **5**(3), 476–500.
Cohen, Joshua (1996), 'Procedure and substance in deliberative democracy', in Seyla Benhabib (ed.), *Democracy and Difference: Contesting the Boundaries of the Political*, Princeton, NJ: Princeton University Press, pp. 95–119.
Dobson, Andrew (2006), *Citizenship and the Environment*, Oxford and New York: Oxford University Press.
Dobson, Andrew and Derek Bell (eds) (2006), *Environmental Citizenship*, Cambridge, MA and London: The MIT Press.
Dryzek, John (1987), *Rational Ecology: Environment and Political Economy*, Oxford: Blackwell.
Dryzek, John (1990), *Discursive Democracy: Politics, Policy and Political Science*, Cambridge: Cambridge University Press.
Dryzek, John (2000), *Deliberative Democracy and Beyond*, Oxford: Oxford University Press.
Dryzek, John (2001), 'Legitimacy and economy in deliberative democracy', *Political Theory*, **29**(5), 651–69.
Dryzek, John, David Downes, Christian Hunold, David Schlosberg and Hans-Kristian Hernes (2003), *Green States and Social Movements: Environmentalism in the United States, United Kingdom, Germany, and Norway*, Oxford: Oxford University Press.
Eckersley, Robyn (1990), 'Habermas and green political thought', *Theory and Society*, **19**, 739–76.
Eckersley, Robyn (1992), *Environmentalism and Political Theory*, London: UCL Press.
Eckersley, Robyn (2004), *The Green State*, Cambridge, MA: The MIT Press.

Elster, John (ed.) (1998), *Deliberative Democracy*, Cambridge: Cambridge University Press.

Erlich, Paul (1968), *The Population Bomb,* New York: Ballantine Books.

Fischer, Frank (2005), *Citizens, Experts and the Environment: The Politics of Local Knowledge*, Durham, NC and London: Duke University Press.

Goodin, Robert (1992), *Green Political Theory*, Cambridge, MA: Polity Press.

Gould, Carol C. (1996), 'Diversity and democracy: representing differences', in Seyla Benhabib (ed.), *Democracy and Difference: Contesting the Boundaries of the Political*, Princeton, NJ: Princeton University Press, pp. 171–86.

Gutmann, Amy and Dennis Thompson (2004), *Why Deliberative Democracy?*, Princeton, NJ and Oxford: Princeton University Press.

Habermas, Jürgen (1971), *Toward a Rational Society: Student Protest, Science and Politics*, London: Heinemann.

Habermas, Jürgen (1996), 'Modernity: an unfinished project' in Maurizio Passerin D'Entrèves and Seyla Benhabib (eds), *Habermas and the Unfinished Project of Modernity*, Cambridge and Oxford: Polity Press, pp. 38–55.

Hayward, Tim (2005), *Constitutional Environmental Rights*, Oxford: Oxford University Press.

Heilbroner, Robert (1974), *An Inquiry into the Human Prospect*, New York: W.W. Norton.

Hicks, Darrin (2002), 'The promise of deliberative democracy', *Rhetoric & Public Affairs*, **5**(2), 223–60.

Humphrey, Matthew (2007), *Ecological Politics and Democratic Theory: The Challenge to the Deliberative Ideal*, London: Routledge.

MacGregor, Sherilyn (2006), 'No sustainability without justice: a feminist critique of environmental citizenship', in Andrew Dobson and Derek Bell (eds), *Environmental Citizenship*, Cambridge, MA and London: The MIT Press, pp. 101–26.

Meadowcroft, James (2004), 'Deliberative democracy', in Robert F. Durant, Daniel J. Fiorino and Rosemary O'Leary (eds), *Environmental Governance Reconsidered: Challenges, Choices and Opportunities*, Cambridge, MA and London: The MIT Press, pp. 183–217.

Mouffe, Chantal (1999), 'Deliberative democracy or agnostic pluralism?', *Social Research*, **66**(3): 745–59.

Newell, Peter (2005), 'Towards a political economy of global environmental governance', in Peter Dauvergne (ed.), *Handbook of International Environmental Politics*, Cheltenham, UK and Northampton, MA, USA: Edward Elgar, pp. 187–201.

Newell, Peter (2008), 'The marketization of environmental governance: manifestations and implications', in Jacob Park, Ken Conca and Mathias Finger (eds), *The Crisis of Global Environmental Governance: Towards a New Political Economy of Sustainability*, London and New York: Routledge, pp. 77–95.

O'Neill, John (2007), *Markets, Deliberation and Environment*, London: Routledge.

Ophuls, William (1977), *Ecology and the Politics of Scarcity*, San Francisco, CA: W.H. Freeman.

Park, Jacob, Ken Conca and Mathias Finger (eds) (2008), *The Crisis of Global Environmental Governance: Towards a New Political Economy of Sustainability*, London and New York: Routledge.

Paterson, Matthew (2008), 'Sustainable consumption? Legitimation, regulation and environmental governance', in Jacob Park, Ken Conca and Mathias Finger (eds), *The Crisis of Global Environmental Governance: Towards a New Political Economy of Sustainability*, London and New York: Routledge, pp. 110–31.

Pellizzoni, Luigi (2001), 'The myth of the best argument: power, deliberation and reason', *British Journal of Sociology*, **52**(1), 59–86.

Phillips, Anne (1996), 'Dealing with difference: a politics of ideas, or a politics of presence?', in Seyla Benhabib (ed.), *Democracy and Difference: Contesting the Boundaries of the Political*, Princeton, NJ: Princeton University Press, pp. 139–52.

Plumwood, Val (2001), 'Inequality, ecojustice, and ecological rationality', in John Dryzek and David Scholsberg (eds), *Debating the Earth: The Environmental Politics Reader*, Oxford: Oxford University Press, pp. 559–83.

Rawls, John (1999), 'The idea of public reason', in James Bohman and William Regh (eds), *Deliberative Democracy: Essays on Reason and Politics*, Cambridge, MA and London: The MIT Press, pp. 93–141.

Rosenberg, Shawn W. (2007), 'An introduction: theoretical perspectives and empirical research on deliberative democracy', in Shawn W. Rosenberg (ed.), *Can the People Govern? Deliberation, Participation and Democracy*, Basingstoke and New York: Palgrave Macmillan, pp. 1–22.

Saward, Michael (1996), 'Must democrats be environmentalists?', in Brian Doherty and Marius de Geus (eds), *Democracy and Green Political Thought*, London: Routledge, pp. 79–96.

Smith, Graham (2003), *Deliberative Democracy and the Environment*, London: Routledge.

Torgerson, Douglas (1999), *The Promise of Green Politics: Environmentalism and the Public Sphere*, Durham, NC: Duke University Press.

Walzer, Michael (1999), 'Deliberation, and what else?', in Stephen Macedo (ed.), *Deliberative Politics: Essays on Democracy and Disagreement*, New York: Oxford University Press, pp. 58–69.

Whitman, Darell (2008), '"Stakeholders" and the politics of environmental policy-making', in Jacob Park, Ken Conca and Mathias Finger (eds), *The Crisis of Global Environmental Governance: Towards a New Political Economy of Sustainability*, London and New York: Routledge, pp. 163–92.

Wissenburg, Marcel (1998), *Green Liberalism. The Free and the Green Society*. London: UCL Press.

Young, Marion Iris (1996), 'Communication and the other: beyond deliberative democracy', in Seyla Benhabib (ed.), *Democracy and Difference: Contesting the Boundaries of the Political*, Princeton, NJ: Princeton University Press, pp. 120–35.

Young, Marion Iris (2003), 'Activist challenges to deliberative democracy', in J.S. Fishkin and Peter Laslett (eds), *Debating Deliberative Democracy*, Malden, MA, Oxford and Melbourne, VIC: Blackwell Publishing, pp. 102–20.

PART II

Global and supranational governance

4. Weberian climate policy: administrative rationality organized as a market

Johannes Stripple

INTRODUCTION[1]

When the Kyoto Protocol[2] to the United Nations Framework Convention on Climate Change (UNFCCC) was agreed upon in 1997, most commentaries revolved around whether the agreed mandatory reductions of greenhouse gases (around 5 per cent in the rich world) should be considered a failure or a success. Very few framed the importance of the Kyoto Protocol as a crucial moment in the marketization of climate governance, as an experiment in a particular mode of governance. The Kyoto Protocol attempts to create markets in emission reductions in various ways. These markets assign a monetary value to emissions and thereby hope to channel clean energy investments around the world. While contemporary environmental policy jargon is littered with notions of certain instruments being 'innovative', or 'new', these labels are actually quite appropriate when its comes to the Clean Development Mechanism (CDM) of the Kyoto Protocol. The CDM can be understood as a response to the trilemma illustrated by Figure 1.1 in Chapter 1. With its broad encouragement of business and civil society, its delegation of authority from public to private actors and its enabling of market forms of governance, the CDM epitomizes the promise of new modes of governance.

This chapter is written at a time when the future state of carbon markets is unclear. The Kyoto Protocol's first commitment period expires in 2012, and the role and relevance of market-based governance in any post-2012 agreement still needs to be decided upon. Since it took four years, from Kyoto (1997) to Marrakesh (2001), to hammer out the details of the CDM, we might expect a similar process to take place after the meeting in Copenhagen in December 2009. The CDM has, as a system of governance, been relatively successful (a fuller account of this judgement follows later on) and many discussions about a future reform of the CDM can be understood as 'tweaks' in the system. But there are also more radical proposals on the table to 'scale-up' the current CDM and to create a mechanism that has greater potential to spur societal transformations into low carbon pathways.

The aim of this chapter is to examine the deliberative turn in the context of the CDM. The present CDM, as well as a future reformed CDM, is conceptualized in terms of forms and rationalities of governance as illustrated in Table 2.1 (see Chapter 2, this volume). Arguably, many of the proposals for a reformed CDM would not imply changes in its forms of governance. But a radically reformed (up-scaled) CDM will imply just that. It seems likely that such a mechanism will be less of a market form and more hierarchical and network-oriented, with a crucial role for governments and technical expertise. I further argue that the CDM can be understood as a market form of governance informed by administrative rationality. By this I mean that governments have constructed a market as well as delegated authority to an international organization (CDM Executive Board) and to private companies (for example large auditing firms). Administrative rationality is not, however, just about relationships among actors but also about the rules and procedures that become established. Whatever happens to the future forms of governance in the CDM, I will argue that its administrative rationality will remain the same.

Has the CDM ensured effective policy performance as well as deliberative and participatory qualities? Deliberation has never been a core concern for the CDM. It remains a market mechanism despite its partnership rhetoric (see Chapter 5, this volume). Although participation can be seen as a success, it is contested whether the CDM is an effective and legitimate way of reducing greenhouse gas emissions. At first glance, CDM represent a prime example of the deliberative turn. Somewhat ironically, while the CDM was not invented in order to democratize global climate governance, its deliberative qualities (participation of non-state actors, state–society communication and broadened knowledge) might be one of its most important legacies.

The chapter is organized as follows. The first two sections outline what the CDM is about and how it is governed. The next two sections conceptualize the present CDM in terms of the deliberative turn and the debate on new modes of environmental governance. I then turn to discuss the future of CDM and ask what a reformed CDM would imply with regard to the promise attached to new modes of governance. The concluding section sums up the changing forms of governance within the CDM and expresses the 'Weberian' perspective on contemporary climate policy adopted; that rationalities of governance ultimately precede forms of governance.

WHAT IS THE CLEAN DEVELOPMENT MECHANISM?

The CDM has a specific political history. Carbon markets have not emerged spontaneously around the world but have been crafted and shaped by political decisions. Carbon markets therefore operate 'in the shadow of hierarchy' and depend on governmental agreements for generating both the supply and the demand for carbon dioxide emission reductions. The CDM entered late in Kyoto negotiations as part of three flexibility mechanisms that were supposed to make the treaty's provisions more acceptable to the US. Ironically, the US did not ratify the Kyoto Protocol but the CDM has nonetheless been established and defended as an important mechanism by the rest of the world. The CDM is intended to lower the cost of complying with the emission targets agreed in the Kyoto Protocol. According to Article 12 of the protocol, the CDM will provide low-cost emissions reductions to Annex 1 countries (developed countries with binding emission targets under the Kyoto Protocol), while at the same time facilitate technology transfer, increase the flow of capital from rich to poor countries, and hereby spur sustainable development in the global South.

The emergence of the CDM should be seen in the context of the long-standing conflict between developed and developing countries in climate change politics. In essence, at the heart of the UNFCCC is an agreement that the respective responsibilities, for causing the problem and doing something about it, are 'common, but differentiated' as Article 3 in the climate convention expresses it.[3] The rich North has a particular responsibility to act first and reduce its carbon footprint because of the past trajectory of emissions and the current level of carbon-generated wealth in this part of the world. But since the cheapest options for reducing emissions do not lie in the North but in the global South, the CDM was supposed to enable reductions to be made where you get most for the money spent (that is in the South).[4] The CDM is a governance mechanism operating at the boundary between the rich and the poor world. It is designed to tap into a variegated political geography and to transcend levels of authority and areas of decision-making. It ultimately enables a connection to be made between a site of responsibility (North), and a site of implementation (South). As Henry Derwant, the President of the International Emission Trading Agency (IETA) (a lobby organization of behalf of carbon market actors) recently put it with regard to the future of the CDM: 'It is very hard indeed to see how the world will not still need a project-based system to identify and incentivize emissions reductions in jurisdictions where economy wide systems have not been, or never will be, introduced' (IETA, 2008, p. 3). Or, in even simpler terms, the CDM works 'by paying developing countries to adopt lower-polluting technologies than they otherwise would' (Wara, 2007, p. 595).

The CDM operates not only on the North–South boundary, but on the boundary between public and private actors (Pattberg and Stripple, 2008). Contemporary climate governance is probably, among all environmental agreements, the one where market-based mechanisms and the role of the private sector is the strongest. In hindsight, the 1997 Kyoto Protocol marks a critical juncture in the making of markets for emission reductions, although it took some years for the markets to start growing. Some markets, like the CDM, are a direct result of the Kyoto Protocol while other markets (like the EU Emission Trading System) are a more indirect result. The carbon economy or carbon markets work on the premise that carbon emission reductions can be turned into tradable commodities (cf. Lövbrand and Stripple, forthcoming). We need to keep in mind that there is not one single international carbon market, but rather a mosaic of markets that can be differentiated in various ways; most commonly between the allowance markets and the project markets. This distinction reflects the method by which the underlying commodity (a carbon credit, which is a tonne of CO_2 equivalents) is created. To simplify, an allowance market, such as the EU Emission Trading System, is created when emitters within a certain jurisdiction receive a cap on their emissions. This enables emitters who reduce their emissions below the cap to trade their unused allowances. In a project market, like the CDM, the carbon credits are the result of a specific offset project.[5] The credit is a measure of the difference that a project makes vis-à-vis a certain baseline of emissions. The CDM therefore works through a counterfactual logic, it credits the difference between doing something, for example by building windmills, and what would have happened anyway, that is burning coal. In CDM governance structure, this difference is referred to as additionality. As specified by Article 12 in the Kyoto Protocol, a CDM project is additional when it leads to reductions in GHG emissions that would not have occurred in the absence of the project.

GOVERNING THE CDM

The CDM is principally interesting since it contains important elements of what in this book is called 'the deliberative turn' and new modes of environmental governance; namely an attempt to engage public and private actors to bring about more effectiveness and legitimacy (see Chapters 1–3). The governance of the CDM can be conceptualized in two major ways. One can either draw attention to actors along a public–private continuum that perform a range of governance functions (Streck, 2007). Or, alternatively, one can draw attention to rules, rationalities and procedures, such as different kinds of measurements and accountant practices, by which carbon markets are made thinkable and operational as administrative domains (Lövbrand and Stripple, forthcoming). To start with the first perspective, it took four years of intergovernmental negotiations (from Kyoto in 1997 to Marrakesh in 2001) to agree on the legal framework of the CDM. The result is an intricate system, in which authority is delegated to a range of non-state actors. Their roles and governance functions diverge in every step of the CDM project cycle; from project identification and design to validation, registration, monitoring and over to verification and certification, and, finally, to the issuance of CERs (see Lövbrand et al., 2009). The supreme authority over the CDM is shared among governments in the CDM Executive Board (EB), and difficult issues are negotiated and resolved under the Kyoto Protocol. The EB is responsible for the approval and registration of the CDM projects, the issuance of CERs, and the accreditation of the so-called Designated Operational Entities (DOE), which are independent third party private actors involved in the validation and verification of CDM projects. The supervision of the CDM is thus delegated from an intergovernmental body (the Kyoto Protocol) to an international organization (the CDM Executive Board) and further to private actors (DOEs). By delegating the on-the-ground supervision of projects to these companies, the EB is supposed to benefit from the companies' existing experience when implementing the CDM (Paulsson, 2009b). The private sector has many roles in the CDM project cycle. Private actors can take on the role as project proponents and thereby identify and design CDM projects. They can also act as consultants and handle project documentation, function as carbon brokers that sell CERs to corporations or individuals seeking to offset their GHG emissions, or, as mentioned previously, verify and validate projects as DOEs. Multilateral organizations (such as the World Bank, the United Nations Development Programme, the United Nations Environment Programme) also take on various roles in the governance of the CDM. Most frequently, they provide technical and scientific advice, capacity assistance and finance to project developers. However, multilateral organizations also set up carbon investment funds and purchase CERs on behalf of governments and corporations.

As indicated above, rather than asking who or which entities are involved in the governance of the CDM, one can also ask how or by which procedures carbon markets emerge as administrative domains in the first place. The success of carbon markets hinges on their ability to make emission reductions the same (cf. MacKenzie, 2008), while generated in different locations and under very different circumstances. Diverse practices such as driving an SUV in Sweden, running a refrigerant plant in China or managing a forest in Kenya are today made equivalent in the carbon accountant's book. Through a range of carbon government technologies (for example standards, baseline methodologies, verification and auditing schemes), combined with certain ways of thinking, derived from climate science and resource economics, one tonne of avoided or sequestered carbon dioxide emissions can today be approached as a standardized good. The implication of this is that the carbon economy can be seen as an imaginary space, a space amenable to policy intervention. This space represents a transformation of politics and statehood, involving a replacement of formal and hierarchical techniques of government with more indirect regimes of calculation (Lövbrand and Stripple, forthcoming). The title of this chapter – Weberian climate policy – is intended to combine these two ways of conceptualizing contemporary climate governance. The CDM is about delegation, about international bureaucracies and private entities becoming involved in day-to-day carbon governance, and about establishing the rules and procedures of carbon markets through administrative rationality.

CDM AS A NEW MODE OF GOVERNANCE

The rest of this chapter will discuss this book's three overarching research questions within the context of the CDM. As mentioned above, the CDM was not invented in order to democratize global climate governance, but rather to provide developed countries with flexibility and cost-effectiveness when meeting their agreed-upon emission reduction targets. The promise of the CDM, as a new mode of governance, is about the engagement of private actors, about making climate governance relevant for business communities usually far from the environmental field. The CDM responds to the implementation deficit (Lövbrand et al., 2009). It is about getting reduction projects off the ground in parts of the world where no incentive for such projects exists. Furthermore, the particular design of the CDM reflects an ambition to make markets in emission reductions more legitimate. When the CDM was proposed in the UN climate negotiations in 1997, creating markets in emissions was considered controversial by both the environmental movement and many industrialized countries. Hence, the bureaucratic and complicated governance system of the CDM is in place to secure the legitimacy of the outcome; in other words, assuring that a tonne of reduced carbon dioxide emissions means the same, regardless of how and where it is produced.

Rationality and Forms of Governance

As a rationality of governance, the CDM is first and foremost administrative. It is about the construction of a market by means of administration. Problem-solving capacity is delegated to civil servants and experts within private companies. Governments delegate decision-making authority to an international organization – the CDM Executive Board – as well as to private companies responsible for validation and verification of emission reductions. According to Paulsson (2009b) this process of delegation has changed from being at the discretion of the DOEs, to being increasingly rule-based through the establishment of the Registration and Issuance Team of the CDM Executive Board. Furthermore, in Chapter 2 the market is defined as a self-organizing governance form. I agree that a market can be understood as a form of governance. Liberal political theory, with its sharp distinction between the state and the market, would contend that only decisions about the market (its constitutive and regulative rules) are governance, while the self-organizing resulting from supply and demand are *not* governance. I argue that the market can be understood as a form of governance *if* it is conceptualized as a possibility to 'structure the possible field of actions of others' (Foucault, 1982, p. 221).

Paterson and Stripple (2010) argue that carbon markets work upon individuals by moulding and mobilizing a specific subjectivity (the individual as carbon emitter), which is able to govern its own emissions in various ways. For example, it has very rapidly become possible to click on a web-link to offset the emissions from an air flight. On the homepage of a carbon offset company it is possible to choose from a series of projects that claim to offset the emissions from the flight. A flight calculator that calculates the emissions from any particular flight is available to guide the purchase.[6] The homepage contains a moral call to manage one's own 'footprint'. Each person's emissions of carbon dioxide in the atmosphere matters, and he or she is made responsible for those emissions. The options are either to reduce the footprint or to offset those emissions. This is not just about a guilty subject seeking absolution for their carbon sins (Smith, 2007); it is also about a charitable subject. The discourse in most offset firms is couched in North–South terms, where the offsetter will not only be absolved for his or her emitting sins but will also be contributing more positively to the development in the South. Such 'conduct of carbon conduct' or 'carbon governmentality' (Paterson and Stripple, 2010) is enabled through calculative practices that simultaneously totalize by aggregating social practices and overall greenhouse gas emissions, and individualize by producing reflexive subjects actively managing their greenhouse gas practices.

Similarly, Lövbrand and Stripple (forthcoming), following the broad field of governmentality studies (see Rose et al., 2006), draw attention to the processes by which carbon markets are made thinkable and operable, which is what Dean (2004, p. 2, emphasis added) calls 'the *how* of governing'. Lövbrand and Stripple (forthcoming) analyse the constituting ways of thinking and acting that make up the carbon economy and render it practicable and amendable to intervention (cf. Miller and Rose, 2008). Such a way of conceptualizing the carbon economy, focusing on procedures, or administrative rationalities in a wide sense, is similar to the way in which the social study of accounting showed how such practices enabled the invention of 'calculative spaces' and 'calculative selves' that enclosed individuals within 'calculative regimes' (Miller, 1992). To sum up, the CDM can be understood as a market that exists at the mercy of states' political will and hence operates in the shadow of hierarchy (see Chapter 2, this volume). But the importance of the CDM is also about its procedures and calculative practices (such as measures about carbon dioxide emissions) that frame the choices open to individuals and influence how we administer the lives of others and ourselves (c.f. Miller and Rose, 2008, p. 11). That is why the CDM can be understood as being Weberian. It is a market form of governance informed by administrative rationality.

The CDM is not heavily influenced by the deliberative ideal, but has some deliberative qualities. Bäckstrand (Chapter 5, this volume) rates deliberation in the CDM as 'weak'. The CDM has, due to its wide engagement of public and private actors, deliberative qualities at the state–society interface. It has some institutionalized mechanisms for public participation and consultation. However, the quality of the deliberative process is adversely affected by barriers to participation. Barriers are power asymmetries between partners, and lack of competing and alternative voices of citizens and marginalized actors. Based on empirical research in China, India and Brazil, by far the three largest CDM host countries, Fuhr and Lederer (2009, p. 22) draw the conclusion that CDM operations have played a fairly important role in raising public awareness of climate change including the need for reducing emissions and to plan for adaptation.

The depiction of the CDM as a market informed by administrative rationality should not be understood as an argument that governments are or should be controlling the development of carbon markets. There is still very little research that is directed towards analysing the various actors, practices and markets of the carbon economy (for an exception, see Lövbrand and Stripple, forthcoming; MacKenzie, 2008). Paterson (2009) has eloquently started to assemble the carbon economy and elaborates on its driving forces. He emphasizes the 'cultural circuit of carbon markets' that concerns the market actors' passion for their work that, in turn, sustains and develops the markets. Paterson refuses to accept the crude distinction between hierarchy, markets and networks as modes of social organization. Market exchanges are constituted not in opposition to networks, but rather, through networks (Paterson, 2009). Clearly, most knowledge about the workings of contemporary carbon markets lies squarely among the market participants themselves. They are the experts, or to frame it alternatively, 'epistemic community' (*sensu* Haas, 1990) and certainly not just on the receiving end of policy-making. But there is not much scholarly research about their actual influence. An overall genealogy of carbon markets that would include loose networks of carbon markets actors, connected in certain sites like London, the carbon finance capital of the world, is still to be written. Through the active and deep involvement of carbon market actors, the CDM has functioned as a site of policy experimentation and innovation. It has brought new actors to climate governance. Examples are large hedge funds, auditing firms, small project developers and companies working with environmental management systems. In the larger scheme of global climate governance, the CDM has also been important as an interface between the developed and the developing world (Streck. 2007, p. 92). We can conceive of the CDM as a kind of 'boundary organization' (*sensu* Guston, 2001, see Chapter 9, this volume) that seeks to bridge the demarcation between countries with emission reduction targets and those without in the UNFCCC. The rhetoric about the CDM as a win–win instrument (Lövbrand et al., 2009) clearly indicates the effort to overcome divergent interests and responsibilities for emission reductions.

Over the years, the modes of governance within the CDM have changed. Benecke et al. (2008) argue persuasively that in the early years, the market was initiated by states and kick-started by public–private partnerships. These were learning experiences in how to create and regulate a market for certified emission reductions. Nowadays, the CDM functions according to its own set of market mechanisms, albeit under the shadow of hierarchy (Benecke et al., 2008, p. 25). Interestingly, the modes of governance have changed as governments have assumed new roles and functions, from establishing the framework conditions, to steering the market through PPPs and the purchase of CERs. Today, governments have outsourced control over compliance with the regulative rules of the CDM project implementation to private certification companies and, as buyers of CERs, governments are complemented by private companies, organizations and individuals (Benecke et al., 2008, p. 26). As a policy innovation, the CDM deserves recognition for its establishment of baseline-and-credit as a method for making value in certified emission reduction units. The voluntary carbon market also rests on this method and even though the CDM, as we know it, might change, commodification by baseline-and-crediting originated and was established in the international scene, through the CDM.

Performance and Participative Qualities

Finally, the verdict is yet to come whether the CDM has ensured effective environmental policy performance. As argued, its deliberate qualities are low by design, so we leave them aside for the moment. In terms of participation, the CDM in its current shape provides a very active role for private actors compared to most other intergovernmental agreements. Not only do private investors finance the majority of CDM projects, they are also entrusted with the development of new methodologies and the monitoring of emission reductions. In this respect, the CDM has been a huge success by mobilizing new investments into emission-reducing activities in developing countries (Sterk, 2008). In May 2009, 500 CDM projects had received CERs and there were another 4733 CDM projects under validation and registration in the pipeline. The projection of the amount of CERs issued until the end of 2012 is now 1343 million (UNEP Risoe, 2009).[7] Climate governance through the CDM is unevenly spread across the globe as four countries; China, India, Brazil and Mexico account for 73 per cent of the projects. Africa is largely bypassed in the CDM investment flows with only 102 projects, most of them in South Africa (UNEP Risoe, 2009).

The institutional and environmental effectiveness of the CDM is debated, which will be further discussed in Chapter 5. Paulsson (2009a) makes an extensive review of the current literature and argues that while many studies acknowledge that the CDM is working quite well in terms of its ability to provide certified emission reductions, the studies also highlight problems such as (1) the unequal geographical distribution of projects; (2) the lack of sustainable development benefits from many projects; and (3) a complex bureaucratic process. A common conclusion is that the market structure of the CDM and the resulting focus on cheap emissions reductions explain these problems (see, for example, Lövbrand et al., 2009).

MODES OF GOVERNANCE IN A REFORMED CDM

In 2012, the commitment period, or the period when states must meet their emission reduction targets according to the Kyoto Protocol, will expire. By all expectations, in order to enter into force on time, a new agreement for the next period will have to be decided upon at the 2009 Conference of the Parties (COP) to the United Nations Framework Convention on Climate Change in Copenhagen. Most authors anticipate that the CDM in some form will be part of the climate regime post-2012 (Streck and Lin, 2008). Contemporary policy practice (discussions at UN meetings and elsewhere in the run-up to Copenhagen) indicates that the current CDM might be subject to major changes (van Asselt and Gupta, 2009). The Ad Hoc Working Group on Further Commitments for Annex 1 Parties under the Kyoto Protocol (AWG-KP) is negotiating possible revisions and extensions of the CDM. The objective of the next two sections of this chapter is to examine the promise of new modes of environmental governance with regard to the debates surrounding a possible reform of the CDM.

Reforming the CDM: Outlining the Policy Options

The most prominent theme in policy and academic circles is the call for scaling-up the CDM. It is argued that CDM's piecemeal project-by-project nature currently limits its potential to engage in a wider transformation of developing countries' pathways to curb greenhouse gas emissions. Currently, the CDM only engages particular companies in specific places and fails to initiate change at the level of a sector or a policy. Many ideas for scaling-up the current project-based CDM are circulating, such as programmatic CDM, sectoral CDM, policy CDM and Sector No-lose Targets (SNLTs) (Michaelowa, 2005; Cosbey et al., 2006; Ellis et al., 2007; Streck and Lin, 2008; Ward, 2008).

Programmatic CDM adds an unlimited number of project activities that follow the same methodology to a larger, overarching project. For example, a project that deals with methane emissions from a particular farm could be scaled-up to include other farms under the same methodology. Such up-scaling reduces the administrative costs and, hopefully, enables larger amounts of emission reductions to be made. Sectoral CDM, in turn, would cover a whole sector like the energy sector of a country. Private entities could claim carbon credits if they emit less than the baseline defined for the sector. Sectoral approaches are viewed as promising since they are assumed to contribute to structural changes and promote necessary long-term mitigation of greenhouse gas emissions in developing countries while they also have the potential to make projects with more sustainable development benefits viable under the CDM (Sterk and Wittneben, 2006).

An evolving and up-scaled CDM will continue to generate concerns regarding additionality, emission reductions, sustainable development, and the transfer of financial and technological resources. Sectoral approaches are popular but would require the development of quite different methodologies for additionality and baseline emissions compared to the current project-based CDM. Another version of sectoral CDM, which credits governments instead of companies, would include the development of a national sector baseline by a developing country government. The government would be responsible for implementing measures to reduce emissions and receive credits that national actors may redistribute based on companies' performance, if emissions are below the baseline (Ward, 2008). Policy CDM would allow any activity that falls under a particular government policy, for example wind power, to claim credits. Implementing Policy CDM would, most likely, run into a difficult measurement challenge. The task of attributing emission reductions to a particular policy is not easy. Emissions are continually and dynamically influenced by a wide range of economic, technical and other factors. Separating the evidence of a particular policy package, let alone of an individual policy, from the many other factors that influence emissions, is an extremely difficult exercise (see Haug et al., 2009).

Callon (2008) has drawn attention to the experimental and laboratory character of emergent carbon markets, where all aspects and components are constantly tested, reflected upon and critically evaluated. One such idea is the

Sectoral no-lose targets, SNLTs (Ward 2008). SNLTs are a form of non-binding emission targets, quite similar to the second version of sectoral CDM outlined above. Developing countries could voluntarily propose (but negotiate internationally) a sector-crediting baseline (for example in terms of emission intensity). Reductions below the baseline would generate credits, but no penalties would be issued if targets were not met. Hence it is a no-lose measure. The main difference between sectoral CDM and SNLTs concerns the institutional requirements for implementing the latter. In sectoral CDM, monitoring and verification, as well as the supervision and approval via the CDM Executive Board, would be maintained (Ward, 2008, p. 27). For SNLT, the national sector baseline would instead be negotiated at the UN level under the climate convention. The baseline would be agreed upon together with the targets for developed countries. The advantage of this approach would be that additionality, so crucial for the legitimacy of the CDM, would no longer be an issue, and the potential for scaling-up would hence be increased (Ward, 2008, p. 28).

There is a range of reforms that would address the geographical inequity of CDMs as well as their lack of contribution to sustainable development (Biermann et al., 2008). Differentiation among project types and among countries is of key importance. Differentiation among projects means favouring projects with clear sustainable development co-benefits and discounting for projects with no or few sustainable development contributions (for example Cosbey et al., 2006). Differentiation among the developing countries could be increased in various ways, for example by further adapting the levies, discounting credits from non-LDCs or even through the use of quota systems (van Asselt and Gupta, 2009, pp. 39–41).

Whither the Market? Administrative Rationality in New Forms

After all, the CDM is a market mechanism, and the basic rationale is the search for the least costly way to reduce emissions. However, cost-effectiveness does not ensure that the other objectives of the CDM are met. Low-cost emission reductions are not enough for the CDM to be considered a legitimate and effective mode of governance. Thus, the suggestions above, for differentiation among project types and countries, are intended to increase the output legitimacy through more sustainability and less geographical inequity of the CDM. No doubt, these suggestions can be quite far-reaching but they are, from the perspective of governance, best understood as tweaks in the system. These are interventions in the form of new rules, intended to govern the market in a more desirable way, at least from the developing countries perspective. The form of governance (market) and its rationality (administrative) would remain the same. If the CDM is understood as a boundary organization, these suggested changes are part of the broader interactions between developed and developing countries in climate politics. As a boundary organization the CDM becomes a site where the developed world can encourage and persuade developing countries to take responsibility for the emissions generated in the global South. Or, to use Foucauldian terminology, it is a site where the possible field of actions of others is structured.

If we look at the advent of a reformed (up-scaled) CDM such development is likely to contain shifts in the forms of governance while the rationality of governance would not change. Probably, governance within an up-scaled CDM will be less about markets and more about hierarchy and networks. The roles of public and private actors will thus have to be reconsidered. Governments in the developing world will have to provide a stronger institutional framework compared to today. In the CDM, the minimum requirement of the host state is to establish a DNA, to assess the sustainability of projects and to approve them. In a reformed CDM, governments will have to play a stronger regulatory role and develop a range of capacities for monitoring and surveillance. Measurements, data collection and modelling have to be coordinated and targeted at the level of a sector or a policy. Surveillance and reporting systems need to be put in place to monitor emissions within a sector or emanating from a certain policy. These are all activities that most likely will enhance and strengthen the role of states. Such development would be in line with a trend long identified in global environmental politics. Environmental agreements lead to sovereignty bargains when states increase their sovereignty vis-à-vis certain dimensions while they suffer losses of sovereignty vis-à-vis other dimensions (Conca, 1994; Litfin, 1997). An up-scaled CDM is not just about data collection and monitoring. Governments in the developing world will also have to play different roles. If the current CDM takes a bottom-up approach, with private actors making project proposals and proposing new methodologies, a reformed CDM can be characterized by more top-down regulation. The concept of 'negotiated baselines' has been introduced in the proposal for SNLTs. Ward (2008, p. 27) writes that

> The main difference between sectoral CDM and SNLTs is that the technicalities referring to baselines, monitoring and verification, as well as the supervision and approval by the CDM Executive Board, would be maintained under a sectoral CDM while the national sector baseline for a sector no-lose target would be negotiated at the COP level.

These negotiated baselines raise several questions about the division between politics and mere technical issues. Sector baselines will be negotiated in conjunction with industrialized countries' targets. The negotiations will hence be political in nature but at the same time require solid technical information. Here networks among experts will certainly play a crucial role for the establishment of the system. One could ask if it is realistic to expect CDM host countries to have the institutional capacity needed for implementing far-reaching policies, setting up or negotiating baselines, or supervising the emissions from large industrial sectors. An independent technical body is needed to provide neutral technical input to the negotiations and raises a whole set of new questions about expert authority in relation to governance (as discussed in Chapter 6, this volume). The ability among developing countries to provide reliable emission statistics is likely to vary substantially, and it might not even be possible to negotiate baselines for all countries. Overall, SNLTs look far less like a market and much more like a target to be achieved through traditional regulation.[8] The possibility for SNLTs to have deliberative qualities, like the original CDM, seems limited, since knowledge and communication is likely to become elitist and confined to closed networks of experts.

CONCLUSIONS

As mentioned above, the CDM was not invented in order to democratize global environmental governance, but to achieve legitimate and effective emission reductions. However, with its delegation of authority beyond the state and non-hierarchical forms of steering, the CDM epitomizes many of the promises attached to new modes of governance. The CDM seems to have delivered with regard to increased participation by public and private actors, but it is contested whether this is converted into environmentally effective and democratic climate governance, issues that will be explored further in Chapter 5. This might change, however, since some of the proposals for a reform of the CDM look promising (such as differentiation and limited up-scaling). Hence, the CDM might enable more fair and effective governance to develop post-2012 by achieving larger volumes of emission reductions (both overall and of higher quality) around the world, not just in a few locations.

How have the forms of governance in the CDM changed over time? In the early days of the CDM, momentum was kept up by organizational forms closely associated with the deliberative turn (like public–private partnerships; see Chapter 5, this volume). As the CDM has matured as a market, the significance of such modes of governance has decreased and public and private actors now engage in normal business activities (Benecke et al., 2008). Looking towards the future, we can anticipate two kinds of development. First, if such suggested changes as increased differentiation among countries and project types are implemented, the mechanism will remain largely the same. Such changes are but tweaks in the system, intended to increase CDM's output legitimacy, but they will not change the way in which the CDM operates as a market form of governance. Second, a thorough up-scaled reform of the CDM would bring fundamental changes. Hierarchical and network forms of governance are then likely to dominate as the CDM becomes more of a governmental and technical affair. As a side effect of this, deliberative qualities of the original CDM of communication and broadened knowledge may be lost along the way.

Contrary to much contemporary thinking, what matters is not whether hierarchies, markets or networks govern, but the kind of rationality that informs the governing. In the CDM, despite changes in the forms of governance, the administrative rationality that informs the CDM seems uncontested. Emission reductions, performed by different people under very different circumstances around the globe, are now transformed into a standardized and tradable commodity. Monitoring, reporting and verification techniques – originally developed for the Kyoto Protocol's project-based mechanisms – are now set to merge into new institutional forms. Climate policy is 'Weberian' in the sense that certain procedures, or carbon government technologies, have been established as legitimate, no matter who happens to supervise or control them. Hence, a general conclusion that emerges from this chapter is that when analysing environmental governance, it is more important to pay attention to rationalities of governance than to forms of governance.

NOTES

1. I would like to express my sincere thanks to the editors for very valuable suggestions on this chapter. I have in general benefited a lot from discussions with my colleagues at Lund University, Karin Bäckstrand and Emma Paulsson, and I would like to extend my thanks to them. I would, in particular, like to thank Eva Lövbrand at Linköping University and Matthew Paterson at University of Ottawa for our inspiring discussions and writings on the overall conceptualization of the carbon economy. I would also like to acknowledge the financial support provided by the ADAM project (EU FP6), the ClimateColl project (Swedish Energy Agency) and the GreenGovern project (The Swedish Research Council, FORMAS).
2. Kyoto Protocol to the United Nations Framework Convention on Climate Change, 11 December 1997, available at http://unfccc.int/resource/docs/convkp/kpeng.pdf. The Protocol entered into force on 16 February 2005.
3. United Nations Framework Convention on Climate Change, UNFCCC, available at http://unfccc.int/resource/docs/convkp/conveng.pdf. The Convention entered into force on 21 March 1994 and is signed by most countries in the world, including all major emitters.
4. Hence, globally, the CDM does not reduce emissions. It allows developed countries to increase emissions to the extent that emissions have been reduced (vis-à-vis a baseline) in developing countries. Nevertheless, it is the only international instrument involving developing countries aimed at reducing emissions in developing countries.
5. Briefly, a carbon offset project entails an investment by those wishing to offset their carbon emissions. Projects can be implemented in a variety of sectors, such as renewable energy, energy efficiency, or forestry. The projects generate credits, which are passed on to the offsetter according to the volume of emissions which would have been emitted if the project had not gone ahead. Carbon offsetting therefore rests upon a complicated system of calculation, monitoring, reporting and verification to both estimate the emissions forgone and to verify that the project realizes these gains. There are also a great variety of companies channelling money from offsetters to the project developers. Most of the latter are entrepreneurs in the developing world.

6. See more at http://www.carbonneutral.com.
7. The CDM/JI Pipeline and Analysis and Database of CDM and JI (Joint Implementation) projects is managed by the UNEP Risoe Centre and contains all CDM/JI projects that have been sent for validation/determination. The Pipeline Overview can be found at http://www.CDMpipeline.org.
8. On the national level, these regulations could of course be about creating a market, such as a national emission trading system, to achieve the given objective.

REFERENCES

Asselt, Harro van and Joyeeta Gupta (2009), 'Stretching too far: developing countries and the role of flexibility mechanisms beyond Kyoto', *Stanford Environmental Law Journal*, **28**(2), 311–78.

Benecke, Gudrun, Lars Friberg, Markus Lederer and Miriam Schröder (2008), 'From public–private partnership to market. The Clean Development Mechanism (CDM) as a new form of governance in climate protection'. Research Center (SFB) 700, SFB-Governance working paper no. 10, April, Berlin.

Biermann, Frank, Harro van Asselt, Ingrid Boas, Philipp Pattberg, Ottmar Edenhofer, Christian Flachsland, Henry Neufeldt, Fariborz Zelli, Johannes Stripple and Monica Alessi (2008), 'Climate governance Post-2012: options for EU policy-making', CEPS policy brief, no. 177, November.

Callon, Michael (2008), 'Civilizing markets: Carbon trading between in vitro and in vivo experiments', *Accounting, Organizations and Society*, **34**(3–4), 535–48.

Conca, Ken (1994), 'Rethinking the ecology–sovereignty debate', *Millennium Journal of International Studies*, **23**(3), 701–11.

Cosbey, Aaron, Deborah Murphy, John Drexhage and John Balint (2006) *Making Development Work in the CDM: Phase II of the Development Dividend Project*, Winnipeg, MB: International Institute for Sustainable Development.

Dean, Mitchell (2004), *Governmentality: Power and Rule in Modern Society*, London and Thousand Oaks, CA: Sage Publications.

Ellis, Jane, Harald Winkler, Jan Corfee-Morlot and Frédéric Gagnon-Lebrun (2007), 'CDM: Taking stock and looking forward', *Energy Policy*, **35**(1), 15–28.

Foucault, Michel (1982), 'The subject and power', in Hubert Dreyfus and Paul Rabinow (eds), *Michel Foucault: Beyond Structuralism and Hermeneutics*, Chicago, IL: University of Chicago Press, pp. 208–26.

Fuhr, Harald and Markus Lederer (2009), 'Varieties of carbon governance in newly industrializing countries', Potsdam University/DGF Research Center 700 paper, under review.

Guston, David H. (2001), 'Boundary organizations in environmental policy and science: an introduction', *Science, Technology & Human Values*, **26**(4), 399–408.

Haas, Peter M. (1990), 'Obtaining international environmental protection through epistemic consensus', *Millennium Journal of International Studies*, **19**(3), 347–63.

Haug, Constanze, Tim Rayner, Andrew Jordan et al. (2009), 'Navigating the dilemmas of climate policy in Europe: evidence from policy evaluation studies', forthcoming in *Climatic Change*, accessed at www.springerlink.com/content/761887rn27n60173/.

International Emissions Trading Association (IETA) (2008), 'State of the CDM 2008: facilitating a smooth transition into a mature environmental financing mechanism', accessed at www.ieta.org/ieta/www/pages/getfile.php?docID=3111.

Litfin, Karen (1997), 'Sovereignty in world ecopolitics', *Mershon International Studies Review*, **41**(2), 167–204.

Lövbrand, Eva, Joakim Nordqvist and Teresia Rindefjäll (2009), 'Closing the legitimacy gap in global environmental governance: examples from the emerging CDM market', *Global Environmental Politics*, **9**(2), 74–100.

Lövbrand, Eva and Johannes Stripple (forthcoming), 'Carbon market governance beyond the public–private divide', in Frank Biermann, Philipp Pattberg and Fariborz Zelli (eds), *Global Climate Governance Post 2012: Architectures, Agency and Adaptation*, Cambridge: Cambridge University Press.

MacKenzie, Donald (2008), 'Making things the same: gases, emission rights and the politics of carbon markets', *Accounting, Organizations and Society*, **34**(3–4), 440–55.

Michaelowa, Axel (2005), 'CDM: current status and possibilities for reform', in *HWWI Research*, Hamburg: Hamburg Institute of International Economics (HWWI).

Miller, Peter (1992), 'Accounting and objectivity: the invention of calculating selves and calculable spaces', *Annals of Scholarship*, **9**(1/2), 61–8.

Miller, Peter and Nicholas Rose (2008), *Governing the Present*, Cambridge: Policy Press.

Paterson, Matthew (2009), 'Assembling carbon markets', paper presented at the International Studies Association Annual Conference, New York, 15–18 February.

Paterson, Matthew and Johannes Stripple (2010), 'My space: governing individuals' carbon emissions', *Environment and Planning D: Society and Space*, **28**(2), 341–62.

Pattberg, Philipp and Johannes Stripple (2008), 'Beyond the public and private divide: remapping transnational climate governance in the 21st century', *International Environmental Agreements: Politics, Law and Economics*, **8**(4), 367–88.

Paulsson, Emma (2009a), 'A review of the CDM literature: from fine-tuning to critical scrutiny?', *International Environmental Agreements: Politics, Law and Economics*, **9**(1), 63–80.

Paulsson, Emma (2009b), 'Dysfunctional delegation: why the design of the clean development mechanism's supervisory system is fundamentally flawed', paper presented at the International Studies Association's 50th Annual Convention, New York, 15–18 February.

Rose, Nicholas, Patrick O'Malley and Marina Valverde (2006), 'Governmentality', *Annual Review of Law and Social Science*, **2**(1), 83–104.

Schneider, Lambert (2007), *Is the CDM Fulfilling its Environmental and Sustainable Development Objectives? An Evaluation of the CDM and Options for Improvement*, Berlin: Öko-Institut.

Schneider, Lambert (2008), A Clean Development Mechanism (CDM) with Atmospheric Benefits for a post-2012 Climate Regime, Berlin: Öko Institut, accessed at www.oeko.de/oekodoc/779/2008-227-en.pdf.

Smith, Kevin (2007), *The Carbon Neutral Myth: Offset Indulgences for Your Climate Sins*, Amsterdam: Carbon Trade Watch.

Sterk, Wolfgang (2008), From Clean Development Mechanism to Sectoral Crediting Approaches – Way Forward or Wrong Turn?, JIKO policy paper 1/2008, Wuppertal: Wuppertal Institute for Climate, Environment and Energy.

Sterk, Wolfgang and Bettina Wittneben (2006), 'Enhancing the clean development mechanism through sectoral approaches: definitions, applications and ways forward', *International Environmental Agreements: Politics, Law and Economics*, **6**(3), 271–87.

Streck, Charlotte (2007), 'The governance of the Clean Development Mechanism', *Environmental Liability Journal*, **15**(2), 91–100.

Streck, Charlotte and Jolene Lin (2008), 'Making markets work: a review of CDM performance and the need for reform', *The European Journal of International Law*, **19**(2), 409–42.

United Nations Environment Programme Risoe (2009), CDM/JI Pipeline Analysis and Database, accessed at www.CDMpipeline.org. 1 May 2009.

Wara, Michael (2007), 'Is the global carbon market working?', *Nature (London)*, **445**(7128), 595–6.

Wara, Michael and David G. Victor (2008), 'A realistic policy on international carbon offsets', Stanford University Program on Energy and Sustainable Development, working paper no. 74, Stanford, CA.

Ward, Murray (2008), 'The role of sector no-lose targets in scaling up finance for climate change mitigation activities in developing countries', report prepared for the International Climate Division, Department for Environment, Food and Rural Affairs, United Kingdom.

5. The legitimacy of global public–private partnerships on climate and sustainable development

Karin Bäckstrand

INTRODUCTION

Global public–private partnerships (PPPs) for sustainable development have been framed as new modes of governance that can potentially reduce the three deficits of global governance, namely the implementation, governance and legitimacy deficits. '"Partnerships" as a term is rapidly becoming the new mantra shaping the UN discourse on global politics' (Martens, 2007, p. 4). Partnerships are underpinned by discourses of participatory democracy, private governance and sustainable development (Mert, 2009). Multi-stakeholder partnerships are presented as win–win solutions that can increase the democratic credentials of global governance and simultaneously strengthen environmental performance and effectiveness. Accordingly, global public–private partnerships are key tests of the promise of new modes of governance and the deliberative turn, which represent the core themes of the book. Three questions are addressed in this chapter. First, what are global environmental public–private partnerships and how can they be seen as examples of new modes of governance? Second, what is their legitimacy record: do they promote environmental effectiveness and procedural legitimacy? Third, are these partnerships examples of deliberative multilateralism or do they reflect a turn to market environmentalism?

Two types of multi-stakeholder partnerships for climate and sustainable development are examined: the Johannesburg partnerships adopted at the World Summit on Sustainable Development (WSSD)[1] and projects under the Kyoto Protocol's Clean Development Mechanism (CDM), which are also analysed in Chapter 4 (this volume).[2] These are examples of global public–private partnerships and networked governance. Partnerships are frequently highlighted as innovative and new forms of public–private collaboration that hold the promise of more effective and legitimate governance (Benner et al., 2003, 2005; Streck, 2004). In the debate it has been argued that the Johannesburg and CDM partnerships represent new modes of deliberative and multi-stakeholder multi-lateralism. These debates have taken place between governments, civil society and business actors at the sessions of the UN Commission on Sustainable Development (CSD) and the Conference of the Parties (COP) to the United Nations Framework Convention on Climate Change (UNFCCC) (Bäckstrand, 2006). Both types of partnerships have rule implementation in terms of the Kyoto Protocol and the Johannesburg Plan of Implementation (JPOI) as their primary function.

This chapter reviews scholarly work on global partnerships on environment and sustainable development and draws upon the UN partnerships database and the CDM project registry.[3] The chapter does not evaluate individual partnerships. Rather it is a meta-assessment of existing studies of partnerships in the context of multilateral environmental diplomacy and summitry. The first section conceptualizes PPPs as new modes of governance representing a mix of organizational forms and governance rationalities. The normative and critical governance perspectives, on whether PPPs represent tools for effective and legitimate governance, are contrasted. The second section argues that the Johannesburg and CDM partnerships can be conceived as public–private partnerships. Starting out from the two-fold concept of legitimacy developed in Chapter 2, the third section compares the input and output legitimacy of the Johannesburg and CDM partnerships. The concluding section summarizes the legitimacy record of these partnerships and revisits the question of whether partnerships are deliberative innovations or instruments for market environmentalism.

GLOBAL ENVIRONMENTAL PUBLIC–PRIVATE PARTNERSHIPS AND THE DELIBERATIVE TURN

Since the 1990s, public–private partnerships have been promoted as tools for good governance that can increase legitimacy, effectiveness and efficiency of multilateral environmental politics. Partnerships in areas of global health, environmental protection and sustainable development, have even been seen as instruments to promote global deliberative democracy (Börzel and Risse, 2005). How can PPPs be conceptualized in theoretical terms? They have been interpreted as governance arrangements that lead to the reconfiguration of authority towards non-state actors. Partnerships are hybrid modes combining different rationalities and forms of governance. PPPs are here defined as 'institutionalized transboundary interactions between public and private actors, with the goal to provide public goods' (Schäferhoff et al., 2007, p. 8). The functions of partnerships are varied and include agenda-setting, rule-making, advocacy, implementation, and service provision (Bull and McNeill, 2007;

Martens, 2007). Partnerships appear in different sectors such as health, human rights development, security and finance and vary in degree of institutionalization and permanence. Some partnerships are established institutions in themselves while others are looser networks for collaboration for a limited time. Finally, partnerships have different geographical scope from the local, national, regional to global level.

The concept of partnerships is used in the literature as an all-inclusive term that seems to encompass everything from informal cooperation between two actors to multilateral organizations. Martens (2007, p. 4) has argued that a partnership 'now covers virtually every interaction between state and non-state actors, particularly between UN and the business sector'. There is a positive connotation in the partnership discourse both in academic and policy circles, where multilateral organizations, companies and non-profit actors are engaged in mutual and symmetric cooperation in the pursuit of global common goods (Benner et al., 2003). It is therefore problematic to identify partnerships based on the actors' own definition of their activities as a 'partnership'. Instead it is argued that public–private partnerships should be conceived as network governance combining different government rationalities and organizational forms, as illustrated in Table 2.1 in Chapter 2. The Johannesburg and CDM partnerships are networks in their primary organizational form as they bring together governments, business and civil society. While this chapter focuses exclusively on public–private partnerships, there are other examples of global networked governance such as private partnerships, intergovernmental networks and international city networks (see Chapter 11, this volume), which represent organizational forms other than hierarchy and market (Bäckstrand, 2008).

Non-hierarchical steering and a mix of public and private actors are two characteristics of transnational public–private partnerships. PPPs are often contrasted with old modes of governance associated with administrative rationality and based on hierarchical steering, such as top-down regulation, enforcement and threat of sanctions (Börzel and Risse, 2005). They entail a mix of government rationalities. The reason for adopting the Johannesburg partnerships, also referred to as Type II agreements, was that they were seen as complements to Type I agreements or intergovernmental treaties. As will be argued, PPPs also rest on market rationality. The CDM partnerships, which in 2010 amounted to 2140 projects, are networks of public actors like governments and private actors such as investors and NGOs, which are part and parcel of the global carbon market. Public–private partnerships also rest on a deliberative rationality. Both the Johannesburg and CDM partnerships have institutionalized mechanisms for stakeholder participation and consultation.

In the International Relations literature, two competing accounts explain the emergence of PPPs. In the win–win story of functional liberal-institution-alism, which is a mix of normative and empirical governance perspectives (see Chapter 1, this volume), PPPs are seen as a response to market and state failure, shaped by a functional need to supply better governance (Buchanan and Keohane, 2006). Partnerships can decrease the implementation, governance and legitimacy deficits, as well as promote the democratization of global governance institutions. The emergence of PPPs is conceived of as a response to state failure, governance gaps and inadequacies of inter-state bargaining. Governance functions such as agenda-setting, monitoring, verification, enforcement and service provision can be outsourced to PPPs by governments and multilateral agencies. In the literature on principal–agent and delegation, a core argument is that states or multilateral institutions (the principal) delegate functions to subsidiary bodies, private actors or partnerships for gains in effectiveness, specialization and implementation (Green, 2008).

The critical perspective views PPPs as neoliberal instruments that shift power from multilateral institutions to the corporate sector and thereby reinforce market environmentalism (Levy and Newell, 2002; see Chapter 3, this volume). The turn to partnerships reinforces marketization, privatization and commodification of global governance, leading to market multilateralism (Maartens, 2007, p. 4). The neo-Gramscian critique targets the neoliberal environmental order, manifested as the global carbon market and the rise of corporate driven public–private partnerships (Matthews and Paterson, 2005). Partnerships reflect trends of new public management, a hollowing out of the state, the rise of the corporate sector, the fragmentation of global governance and the retreat of state responsibility in environmental affairs. These contrasting perspectives view PPPs a priori as either effective/legitimate or ineffective/illegitimate. Between these competing accounts, the empirical evidence for the win–win and lose–lose argument of PPP is at best mixed or weak.

CONCEPTUALIZING THE CDM AND JOHANNESBURG PARTNERSHIPS AS PPPS

In what ways can Johannesburg and CDM partnerships be understood as public–private partnerships? The Johannesburg partnerships have been advanced as innovations in global sustainability governance and generally hailed as a success (United Nations, 2008). Similarly, the CDM has also been framed as a mechanism that can deliver better governance in terms of both cost- and environmental effectiveness (Streck, 2004; Streck and Chagas, 2007, p. 62). After briefly analysing each of the partnerships, we move on to a comparison.

Since the late 1990s and under General Secretary Annan's leadership, the UN has promoted multi-stakeholder partnerships from the Johannesburg partnerships to the UN Global Compact, as a way to restore legitimacy for the UN as a result of the weakened multilateral system (Bull and McNeill, 2007; Martens, 2007). The voluntary multi-stakeholder partnerships adopted at the 2002 Johannesburg summit, also known as Type II agreements, were said to serve as an important complement to Type I agreements, which represent negotiated agreements between governments (United Nations, 2008). A more pessimistic interpretation is that it was the failure of the 2002 summit to deliver binding international Type I agreements that paved the way for voluntary partnerships (Mert, 2009). There are currently (April 2010) 348 Johannesburg partnerships registered at the United Nations Commission on Sustainable Development (CSD) secretariat, and they are seen as central to the implementation of Agenda 21 and Johannesburg Plan of Implementation. These partnerships involve participation from the UN's nine major groups: business, NGOs, youth, farmers, scientific communities, women, indigenous people, local governments and trade unions. More than half of the partnerships have a thematic focus, mainly on natural resource protection and management (United Nations, 2008, p. 6).

As analysed in Chapter 4 (this volume), the overall function of the CDM is to implement Article 12 in the Kyoto Protocol with the twin objectives of assisting developed countries in achieving cost-effective GHG emission reductions and promoting sustainable development in host countries (Streck, 2004). In Chapter 4 it is argued that the CDM had more characteristics of public–private partnership in its early phase, while subsequently being developed into a market-based mechanism, an argument that is derived from Benecke *et al.* (2008). However, this chapter analyses private–public interaction not only in the projects but in the whole CDM project cycle, where tensions between hierarchical, market and network governance forms play out. Public–private interaction thus occurs both in the CDM project cycle and in the individual projects. The CDM project cycle, from project design to validation, involves various actors such as private investors, carbon buyers and brokers, host governments, multilateral organizations, accredited independent verifiers and NGOs. Many of the approximate 2140 registered CDM projects can be described as multi-sectoral networks involving project investors (governments or private actors), multilateral institutions, non-profit organizations, carbon brokers and developing countries. The CDM is advanced as an instance of delegation to private actors to perform governance functions. The CDM Executive Board (EB) can be seen as a collective principal who delegates tasks of validating and verifying CDM projects to Designated Operational Entities (DOEs), which currently represent around 18 private auditing firms accredited by the EB (Green, 2008; Paulsson, 2009b).

What are the similarities between the partnerships? One commonality is that they are multilaterally sanctioned, under the auspices of the UN. They exist under the shadow of hierarchy, under the supervision of UN agencies. The operation of the CDM market is ultimately dependent on intergovernmental climate negotiations in the Kyoto process (see Chapter 4, this volume). The Johannesburg partnerships are registered under the CSD and reviewed at its annual sessions. The CDM projects are registered after screening in a seven-step project cycle, where the Executive Board has final power to issue credits. Secondly, the Johannesburg and CDM partnerships are multi-stakeholder instruments, which involve a diverse set of actors, such as intergovernmental organizations, governments, NGOs and business. Thirdly, their primary function is rule implementation of multilateral targets and provisions in the Kyoto Protocol and the JPOI. Fourthly, they have an overlapping sectoral focus on climate and sustainable development. The Johannesburg partnerships cover sustainable development but 25 per cent have climate and energy as a primary focus. In turn, the dual goal of the CDM partnerships is to reduce greenhouse gas emissions and promote sustainable development in developing countries.

However, there are also significant differences between these two partnerships. The CDM is the most important instrument in the emerging carbon markets and is expected to generate almost 3 million carbon credits or certified emission reductions (CERs) by the end of 2012. The Kyoto Protocol has enabled a tradable commodity, carbon credits or certified emission reductions, which has developed into a global carbon market. In contrast, the Johannesburg partnerships have no linkage to global markets or trading arrangements such as the carbon market. The Johannesburg partnerships can be seen as an instance of a soft law arrangement to implement a voluntary action plan, such as Agenda 21, while the CDM partnerships constitute hard law in terms of the legally binding Kyoto Protocol. CDM partnerships are linked to scientific assessment processes through the Intergovernmental Panel on Climate Change (IPCC) and the various methodology panels in the CDM project cycle, while the Johannesburg partnerships lack a scientific assessment body or process. Finally, the CDM partnerships have strong mechanisms in place for monitoring, supervision and implementation review through the CDM project cycle. The Johannesburg partnerships, on the other hand, rely on voluntary reporting and lack enforcement power, an issue that will be discussed more in the subsequent sections (Green, 2008).

THE LEGITIMACY AND EFFECTIVENESS OF THE CDM AND JOHANNESBURG PARTNERSHIPS

Starting out from the two-fold conception of input and output legitimacy in

Chapter 2, this section evaluates the legitimacy of Johannesburg and CDM partnerships. To reiterate, input legitimacy refers to procedures, which indicates the participatory and deliberative qualities of the decision-making process as well as issues of accountability and transparency. Output legitimacy, which is used interchangeably with effectiveness, refers to institutional effectiveness, environmental performance and problem-solving capacity (see Table 2.2, Chapter 2, this volume). To measure environmental effectiveness in terms of environmental impacts, such as reduced greenhouse gas emissions and sustainable development benefits, is methodologically problematic and challenging. As will be demonstrated below, the environmental effectiveness of Johannesburg partnerships cannot be assessed because quantitative goals and monitoring are lacking.

The empirical evidence of the ability of public–private partnerships to generate win–win solutions in terms of increased capacity for problem-solving as well as democratization of global governance is generally weak. There are some studies of the legitimacy or effectiveness of Johannesburg partnerships for sustainable development (Andonova and Levy, 2003; Biermann et al., 2007; Bäckstrand, 2006; Hale and Mauzerall, 2004). However, the research on the performance and legitimacy of partnerships for environment and sustainable development in general is fragmented and lacks systematic comparative studies between various types of partnerships (Martens, 2007; Meadowcroft, 2007; Schäferhoffer, et al., 2007). Most studies of partnerships are single case studies with an exception of one quantitative study (Biermann et al., 2007, p. 240). Moreover, there is a methodological problem of selection bias towards successful public–private partnerships.

The legitimacy and effectiveness of the CDM has been analysed by employing the input–output legitimacy distinction with the recurrent conclusion that there is a trade-off between low-cost projects that generate the maximum amount of carbon credit and participatory small-scale projects that provide sustainable development benefits (Lövbrand et al., 2008; Olsen, 2007). The transparency and accountability of the CDM have increasingly been brought into focus following the frequent critiques of the procedural legitimacy and bottlenecks in the CDM project cycle (Streck and Lin, 2008). The CDM partnerships have been criticized on various grounds, such as limited contribution to sustainable development, poor environmental integrity, imbalance in geographical distribution of CDM projects, inadequate governance structures, high transaction costs and a limited ability to reduce GHG emission. In the following sections the different dimensions of input and output legitimacy of the Johannesburg and CDM partnerships are analysed and summarized (see Table 5.1).

Inclusion and Participation

What are the patterns of representation, inclusion and exclusion of different types of public and private actors in the CDM and Johannesburg partnerships? What type of actor predominates and what is the geographical representation? Turning to the Johannesburg partnerships, three dimensions of participation are highlighted: 1) geographical representation of Northern and Southern partners; 2) participation of non-state actors; and 3) representation of marginalized stakeholders. The Johannesburg partnerships demonstrate a geographical imbalance as Northern actors predominate. Sixty per cent of the registered partnerships have industrialized country partners, while only 17 per cent are led by a developing country (Hale and Mauzerall, 2004, p. 30, Biermann et al., 2007). In 70 per cent of the partnerships led by an industrialized country, another OECD country is the country of implementation. Hence, relatively few partnerships are directed to neglected regions with high poverty and environmental pressures. Large developing countries, such as South Africa and Indonesia that hosted the preparatory meetings of the 2002 Johannesburg summit, are more frequent as partners. In this respect, the Johannesburg partnerships represent a 'coalition of the willing' between industrialized countries and a few large developing countries, as Andonova and Levy (2003) argue.

Public actors dominate the Johannesburg partnerships while NGOs and business actors have a more marginal presence. A general pattern for the Johannesburg partnerships is that governments or international agencies are often the lead partners: 83 per cent of partnerships involve governments, 62 per cent UN organizations and 61 per cent other intergovernmental organizations. Only 8 per cent of the approximate 400 partnerships are led by NGOs, while business actors lead only 3 per cent. Furthermore, there has been a 30 per cent decline of NGO-led partnerships between 2003 and 2007 (Biermann, 2007). Private sector involvement is lower than expected, since business actors choose their own partnerships with less formalized reporting mechanisms, and the financing of partnerships by private sectors has been minimal (Mert, 2009, p. 7).

Concerning actors from the nine major groups defined by the UN, participation is low and particularly so when it comes to marginalized groups. Only 1 per cent of the partnerships involved women's groups, youth, trade unions, indigenous people and farmers. The more institutionalized major groups were better represented. 30 per cent of the partnerships involved NGOs, 38 per cent business, 18 per cent science and technology communities and 8 per cent local authorities (United Nations, 2008, p. 10). This pattern reveals that partnerships are geared towards well-established non-state actors such as large NGOs, the scientific community and business primarily from the Northern hemisphere. Local actors, least developed countries and Southern grassroots movements are represented to a lesser degree.

Due to the differences in the legal and governance structure of the CDM and Johannesburg partnerships, participation and inclusion in CDM partnerships has to be operationalized differently. Participation can be seen on two levels: 1) participation of affected local stakeholders, international stakeholders and developing countries in the projects; and 2) geographical distribution of CDM projects.

The CDM has formalized procedures for local and international stakeholder participation in the project cycle. However, the procedural ideal of stakeholder participation clashes with the realities of the CDM regulatory process, which is highly expert-driven, opaque and unpredictable (Lövbrand et al., 2008). CDM stakeholders are defined as 'the public, including individuals, groups and communities affected or likely to be affected, by the proposed clean development project activity' (Green, 2008, p. 32). There are several provisions in the CDM that allow public participation of stakeholders (Green, 2008, p. 4). At meetings of the UN annual climate summits, interested stakeholders can engage in dialogue with the EB at public events. In addition, the project-planning phase allows for public consultation with affected stakeholders from the local community. Public participation is also made possible through a notice and comment period when methodologies under consideration are available on the website. It is mandatory that the Project Design Document (PDD) is available to the public for a 30-day period for comments by stakeholders. Local stakeholders in CDM projects and NGOs with UNFCCC accreditation are also given opportunity to participate by registering complaints with the EB concerning activities of DOEs. Despite these procedural mechanisms for civic participation there is recurrent and widespread criticism of the quality of stakeholder participation in the CDM. Lövbrand et al. (2009, p. 85) argue that in order for participation to be meaningful, it is not sufficient to make information available to the public, it must also be accessible to local stakeholders. For example, translation of documents into local languages is limited.

The geographical distribution of CDM projects shows patterns of inclusion and exclusion. The answer to the question concerning whether CDM partnerships allow for the poorest regions and countries in the world to participate in the CDM market, is discouraging. Three countries (China, Brazil and India) account for the majority of volume traded. The poorest countries in the world with the lowest flow of foreign direct investments also attract the smallest share of CDM projects. Only 4 per cent of the total number of CDM projects can be found in Africa. Apart from a few registered projects in South Africa and the Maghreb region, the African continent is void of CDM projects (Lecocq and Ambrosi, 2007). There are several reasons for this. First, CDM investments require good governance conditions with a stable political regime as well as institutional and legal capacities. Secondly, sub-Saharan Africa has a small supply of industrial non-CO_2 projects that generate cheap carbon credits on the CDM market. Thirdly, land-use and forestry activities, which are a potentially important supply of projects in Southern Africa, are not allowed under the EU-ETS (Lecocq and Ambrosi, 2007, p. 146).

To sum up, both the Johannesburg and CDM partnerships have skewed representation. They are dominated by Northern actors or large developing countries with the most advanced capacity, who reap the benefits of partnerships rather than those with the largest needs. Partnerships mirror rather than transform existing patterns of power, inclusion and exclusion between North and South, public and private authority and professional NGOs and local grass-roots movements. The demand for CDM projects from the poorest countries is not matched by supply.

Accountability and Transparency

Transparency and accountability are closely linked, as accountability depends on access to information about the performance of partnerships and the monitoring of goal achievement. In terms of the availability of accountability mechanisms there is a substantial difference between the Johannesburg and CDM partnerships. The CDM partnerships rest on hierarchical and legal accountability through the CDM project cycle while the Johannesburg partnerships lack formal mechanisms for accountability. The absence of a single principal and agent in the Johannesburg partnerships raises the question: to whom should partnerships be accountable?

The Johannesburg partnerships have no centralized agency overseeing goal attainment in partnerships. There is no formalized supervision, monitoring and implementation review of partnerships, and they completely lack coercive elements. The Bali guidelines, which were an outcome of preparatory meetings a few months before the 2002 Johannesburg summit, did not grant the CSD secretariat, which is the responsible body, the power to enforce reviewing and reporting of partnership activities (Mert, 2009, p. 6). Instead a Partnership team of 2–3 people was set up at the CSD, and this team can only screen partnerships that apply for registration. Due to this lack of formal accountability, transparency has been emphasized in the partnership initiative. There are three indicators of transparency of the Johannesburg partnership initiative: a website, a reporting system and a monitoring mechanism (Hale and Mauzerall, 2004, p. 227). What is the transparency record for the Johannesburg partnerships? A website of all partnerships was set up in 2004 under the CSD and has been updated and amended in 2006 and 2007 (United Nations, 2008). Only a third of the partnerships fulfil all three indicators of transparency, and around half lack mechanisms for monitoring effectiveness and progress of partnerships (Hale and Mauzerall, 2004, p. 228). Systematic monitoring of the progress of partnerships remains a challenge because monitoring is based on voluntary reports compiled by the partnerships themselves

(United Nations, 2008, p. 23). Of the registered partnerships, only 20 per cent have submitted updates on progress concerning organizational activities, coordination activities and implementation activities. Only 1 per cent of the partnerships reported that they had met their stated goal (Andanova and Levy, 2003, p. 22). The weak accountability mechanisms of Johannesburg partnerships stem from the unclear and vague guidelines as well as lack of mandatory reporting requirements. No Johannesburg partnership has been removed from the registry because of insufficient performance. 'Partnerships fairs' with showcases of Johannesburg partnerships have instead become a new practice at the annual CSD sessions as a way of information sharing.

The CDM partnerships display a higher degree of accountability compared to the Johannesburg partnerships. The delegation and accountability chains and scope of authority were hammered out in the Marrakesh Accords, which spell out details of the CDM. The legal and supervisory accountability comes in two forms: 1) States at the COP/MOP hold EB accountable; 2) EB through its supervisory functions holds private auditing companies (DOEs) accountable. First, the COP/MOP, which is the ultimate authority of the CDM, has delegated daily supervision and oversight to the EB. The CDM is often highlighted as a far-reaching example of delegation to private actors (Green, 2008; Paulsson, 2009b). Secondly, the EB (the principal) has delegated screening of CDM projects to 18 accredited auditing companies (the agent), which validate and verify CDM projects to ensure the credibility of the issued CERs. The EB exercises supervisory authority through screening the accreditation process of DOEs, which is quite a lengthy and complex process. Once DOEs are accredited, the EB can review if DOEs act in accordance with the Kyoto Protocol through the Regulation and Issuance Teams. Availability of sanctions is a key dimension of accountability. The EB has the power to penalize DOEs that do not perform their validation and verification properly by revoking their accreditation. This occurred for the first time in November 2008 when the EB suspended one of the largest DOEs on the market, DNV, for six months (UNFCCC, 2008). On transparency, the CDM project cycle allows for 19 types of information on the CDM to be made 'publicly available' (Streck and Lin, 2008, p. 424). Documentation and meeting notes are available on the website and stakeholders can follow webcast meetings of the EB via the UNFCCC website. However, while there is transparency and access to the CDM project cycle, open EB meetings are limited (Streck and Lin, 2008, p. 425).

Despite the existence of rather advanced hierarchical accountability and transparency mechanisms in the CDM, there is a recurrent critique of the institutional performance of the CDM coupled with calls to reform administrative procedures. Decisions by the EB are not always predictable and there is no independent tribunal within the CDM regulatory framework for review of EB decisions. Consequently, there have been proposals for due process, that is administrative law-like processes for private actor participants who are adversely affected by the decisions of the EB (Green, 2008; Streck and Lin, 2008).

Deliberation

To what extent do the CDM and Johannesburg partnerships live up to the deliberative democracy ideals, such as communicative rationality, unconstrained dialogue and free and public reason as discussed in Chapter 3? Whether public–private partnerships actually promote a venue for deliberation largely depends on the partnership function. In partnerships whose primary function is rule implementation, such as the Johannesburg and CDM partnerships, the room for deliberation and problem-solving is more limited compared to partnerships for rule-making, agenda-setting or service provision. Deliberative processes tend to be cosmetic and symbolic and are often added on or serve to legitimize decisions already made.

Deliberative quality also depends on the context of deliberation. This chapter has analysed mega-summitry deliberation *about* partnerships by various public and private actors at the CSD and COP/MOP annual sessions rather than deliberation *within* public–private partnerships. The Johannesburg partnerships clearly have a more institutionalized model for deliberation about partnerships through partnership fairs and multi-stakeholder deliberations between the nine major groups (Bäckstrand, 2006). This can be compared with the CDM where stakeholder input is limited to open sessions of the EB. The CDM partnerships fare better in the CDM project cycle, due to institutionalized mechanisms for public participation and consultation. However, deliberation tends to take place in the later phase of the policy process as in the CDM projects where stakeholder consultations often occur after the project has been designed (Lövbrand et al., 2009, p. 86). The hope associated with increased deliberation is an ideal and '[i]t may indeed be utopian to expect a market mechanism such as the CDM to function as a deliberative site where all those affected by the growing trade in CERs have an equal and meaningful opportunity to influence the making and implementation of rules' (Lövbrand et al., 2009, p. 96).

Finally, the quality of deliberation is adversely affected by barriers to participation, such as power asymmetries between partners and the lack of competing and alternative voices from citizens and marginalized actors. The bias of representation and participation in both the CDM and Johannesburg partnerships toward Northern states, large developing countries, professional NGOs, climate change capitalists, and multilateral bureaucracies at the expense of least developed countries, local grass-roots movements, women and indigenous people limits free and authentic discursive contest between equals. Yet in the case of the CDM partnerships in particular, the scientized and expert-driven discourse on the complexities and intricacies of the relationship between CDM governance and the carbon market requires detailed and specialized knowledge and readership in economics, climate science and policy. This may be beyond the scope for the ordinary educated citizens to comprehend.

Table 5.1 summarizes the input legitimacy record for the Johannesburg and CDM partnerships. Overall, the CDM partnerships score slightly higher due to more advanced and formalized mechanisms of accountability and transparency.

Institutional Effectiveness

The UNEP Executive Director described the 2002 Johannesburg conference as a summit for 'implementation, accountability and partnership' (Bäckstrand, 2006, p. 297). The overall rationale was that the implementation gap in sustainable development could be reduced by results-based and outcome-oriented partnerships. However, several studies have demonstrated a low implementation record of Johannesburg partnerships. 'Partnerships are most frequent in those areas that are already heavily institutionalized and regulated. They are predominantly not concerned with implementation, but rather with further institution building' (Biermann et al., 2007, p. 259). Partnerships lack capacity as a majority of them are unfunded and seek funding. The WSSD summit did not garner new and additional resources in terms of official development assistance. Due to the bias of Northern countries as lead and implementing states, partnerships are fewer in least developed regions in the world. Less than a third of Johannesburg partnerships focus on direct environmental impacts. Instead they are process-oriented, by building capacity, increasing awareness and strengthening means of implementation. In sum, the Johannesburg partnerships have no clear quantitative goals that can be used as a yardstick for measuring their performance. The weak implementation review and institutional machinery for reporting, monitoring and control as discussed above, precludes an analysis of the environmental effectiveness of the Johannesburg partnerships. On the other hand, the hard law character of the CDM governance structure, results in greater institutional effectiveness in terms of compliance, implementation and review. We now turn to analyse the environmental effectiveness of the CDM partnerships.

Environmental Effectiveness

As discussed in Chapter 2, environmental effectiveness relates to the direct environmental impact of governance arrangements. Does the CDM lead to real and substantial reductions in GHG emissions? Article 12 in the Kyoto Protocol states that CDM projects should lead to '[r]eal, measurable and long-term benefits related to the mitigation of climate change' and 'additional to any that would occur in the absence of certified project activity'. The credibility of the CDM ultimately rests on the above notion of environmental additionality. The projected reduction of greenhouse gases in the CDM scheme amounts to 1.75 billion tonnes of CO_2 equivalent emissions (Wara, 2007, p. 59), which represents an annual reduction of 278 million tonnes. This is a small share of total global CO_2 emissions, which add up to 26 billion tonnes per year. In response to the critics of the environmental ineffectiveness of the CDM, it can be argued that as an offsetting mechanism, the CDM was not designed to contribute in itself to any net reduction of total emissions (Paulsson, 2009a). It was set up as an instrument to channel low carbon investments into developing countries, promote sustainable development and enable cost-effective emission reductions in industrialized countries. Accordingly, at best and ideally the CDM is a zero-sum game to the atmosphere given that emission reductions from projects are real, measurable and verifiable (Schneider, 2008). Environmental additionality refers to whether the CDM projects generate real emission reductions, and that is critical to the environmental integrity of the mechanism. If the CDM remains as an offsetting mechanism, it will have limited potential to bring about the large emission reductions stipulated in the IPCC assessment and the Stern report. Critics argue that if the goal of the CDM was to create a market that enabled a low carbon energy transition in developing countries, the mechanism has failed (Wara, 2007). Instead of investments to promote low-carbon energy infrastructure in developing countries, almost a third of all CERs stem from brown-field low-cost projects for capture of non-CO_2 industrial gases, such as HFC-23, nitrous oxide and methane.

Turning to the second goal of the CDM, which is to promote sustainable development in developing countries, there are no mechanisms available for screening, monitoring and evaluating sustainable development outcomes of projects. Host countries define the criteria for sustainable development and there is no price tag on sustainable development benefits on the CDM market. In this vein, the CDM is designed with an economic rationality creating incentives for low-cost carbon mitigation options. Sustainable development values that are not priced are not incorporated in the CDM's incentive structure. The trade-off between cheap emission reductions and sustainable development benefits to host countries has been a recurrent critique in numerous studies (Ellis et al., 2007; Lövbrand et al., 2009; Olsen, 2007). The CDM functions as a market and identifies the cheapest alternatives for emission reductions, that is, cheap credits from industrial gas projects described above, which are profitable compared to small-scale community projects that can generate sustainable development.

Table 5.1 Input legitimacy and output legitimacy of the Johannesburg and CDM partnerships

| | INPUT LEGITIMACY | | | OUTPUT LEGITIMACY | |
	Deliberation	Inclusiveness	Accountability	Institutional Effectiveness	Environmental Effectiveness
Johannesburg partnerships	**Weak** Summitry deliberation between nine major groups at CSD annual sessions partnerships fairs	**Medium** Imbalance between nine major groups *Geographical imbalance*: Northern states dominate *Public-private actor imbalance*; IOs and governments dominate *Marginalized actors*: very low participation	**Low** No accountability mechanism, weak transparency	**Low** CSD lacks power to approve, review, monitor and sanction partnerships for non-compliance	**Not available** Partnerships lack standards and benchmarks for goal attainment and environmental performance
CDM partnerships	**Weak** Mechanisms for stakeholder consultation for individual projects, Summitry deliberation at the EB COP/MOP sessions	**Medium** *Stakeholder participation* in project planning: Mandatory but weak in practice *Geographical imbalance*; Host countries China, India and Mexico dominates project portfolio, few investor countries	**Medium/High** Formalised accountability and transparency through the CDM project cycle, EB exercise supervision, monitoring and reporting	**High/medium** A system for monitoring, verification and control by third parties and EB Compliance and implementation review	**Low** Off-set mechanism Environmental additionality questioned No measurable sustainable development benefits

Small projects usually have higher transaction costs. The CDM is contested precisely due to the conflict between large-scale carbon credit generating projects and locally owned stakeholder projects with a high development dividend (Lohman, 2006).

In Table 5.1 the effectiveness of the CDM and Johannesburg partnerships is compared. The CDM fare better both on institutional and environmental effectiveness compared to Johannesburg partnerships.

CONCLUSIONS

Do the CDM and Johannesburg partnerships pave the way for more effective and legitimate governance? This chapter has argued that the Johannesburg and CDM partnerships can be seen as prime examples of PPPs at the intersection of different government rationalities and involving a mix of organizational forms such as hierarchy, market and networks. Moreover, they operate in the shadow of hierarchy and, which particularly applies to the CDM, are situated between two different logics, that is multilateral bargaining between sovereign states and a global carbon market with business actors. The debate on the promises and pitfalls of partnerships is also polarized between the liberal-functionalist perspective claiming that partnerships are win–win instruments that can decrease the three deficits, and the critical governance perspective arguing that partnerships reinforce market environmentalism and privatization. Beyond this contested debate there is a need for a comparative empirical research agenda to assess the performance of public–private partnerships across different sectors and in different multilateral settings. As the partnership term is very broad and inclusive, this chapter started off with conceptualizing and differentiating between different categories of public–private partnerships, which are preconditions for judging if PPPs constitute legitimate and effective tools.

The legitimacy and effectiveness record of the Johannesburg and CDM partnerships show a mixed picture. The Johannesburg partnerships generally score higher on deliberative quality and inclusion than the CDM partnerships. The CSD has institutionalized stakeholder participation and dialogue between the major UN groups during its annual sessions. However, the deliberative quality on the ground within individual partnerships is difficult to evaluate. Furthermore, the Johannesburg partnerships have virtually no mechanisms for accountability and a weak transparency record compared to the CDM, where there are formalized mechanisms for transparency and accountability. Moreover, the CDM's EB can hold private companies accountable while governments in turn can hold the EB accountable through the COP/MOP. Compared to the Johannesburg partnerships, the CDM partnerships display a higher degree of accountability and transparency through institutionalized mechanisms of monitoring, validation and verification, and through mandatory stakeholder consultations in the whole project cycle.

The output legitimacy or effectiveness record of the Johannesburg and CDM partnerships is difficult to ascertain. Due to the methodological challenges there are few studies taking stock of the environmental effectiveness of these partnerships. A core argument is that governance structures are crucial for institutional effectiveness. Functioning mechanisms for compliance, monitoring and implementation are decisive for environmental performance. The Johannesburg partnerships score low on both institutional effectiveness and environmental effectiveness, which it is not even possible to evaluate given the absence of quantitative goals and monitoring. A reason is that these partnerships rely on voluntary action, and the CSD has no mandate to review, monitor, supervise or enforce implementation. There are no benchmarks or yardsticks for goal attainment and environmental performance. In contrast, the CDM partnerships have a governance structure for project screening, verification and certification by the EB. While there is a recurrent critique of the CDM for inadequacies in accountability, predictability and transparency and proposals for reform of the mechanism to increase procedural legitimacy, there are at least instruments for accountability and sanctions in place.

Do these partnerships reflect deliberative multilateralism or market environmentalism, consistent with the fears and hopes of liberal-functionalism and critical theorists? To some extent, the CDM consolidates the rise of market environmentalism in line with neoliberal climate politics which is legitimatized through economic rationality and the market. The boom of the CDM and the carbon market involving a plethora of business actors such as investors, carbon brokers and verification companies lends some support to the neo-Gramscian critique. However, the CDM is also a prime example of the delegation of authority and in this respect reflects the significance of the shadow of hierarchy. The EB's supervision, control and regulatory power as well as its mandate to punish individual companies for not performing adequate governance tasks reflect the continuity of hierarchy and the logic of intergovernmental bargaining. The Johannesburg partnerships do not reflect trends of privatization and free market environmentalism but signify the continued power of intergovernmental organizations that have found new tasks in being facilitators and administrators of voluntary multi-partnerships. The separation between 'new' modes of public–private partnership governance and 'old' modes of regulation, command and control is an analytical distinction that does not hold in political reality. PPPs operate in the shadow of the hierarchy with background conditions of state authority, intervention, steering and control.

NOTES

1. The partnerships adopted at the World Summit on Sustainable Development (WSSD) are referred to as the 'Johannesburg partnerships'.
2. In this chapter the 'CDM partnerships' refer to the projects under the Kyoto Protocol's Clean Development Mechanism (CDM).
3. The CDM projects are available at http://cdm.unfccc.int and the Johannesburg partnerships database can be accessed at http://webapps01.un.org/dsd/partnerships/public/welcome.do

REFERENCES

Andonova, Liliana and Marc Levy (2003), 'Franchising global governance: making sense of the Johannesburg Type II Partnerships', in Olav Schram Stocke and Øystein B. Thomessen (eds), *Yearbook of International Cooperation on Environment and Development 2003/04*, London: Earthscan, pp. 19–31.

Bäckstrand, Karin (2006), 'Multi-stakeholder partnerships for sustainable development: rethinking legitimacy, accountability and effectiveness', *European Environment*, **16**, 290–306.

Bäckstrand, Karin (2008), 'Accountability of networked climate governance: the rise of transnational climate partnerships', *Global Environmental Politics*, **8**(3), 74–104.

Benecke, Gudrun, Lars Friberg, Markus Lederer and Miriam Schröder (2008), 'From public–private partnership to market. The Clean Development Mechanism (CDM) as a new form of governance in climate protection', Research Center (SFB) 700, SFB-Governance working paper no. 10, April, Berlin.

Benner, Thorsten, Wolfgang H. Reinicke and Jan Martin Witte (2005), 'Multisectoral networks in global governance: towards a pluralistic system of accountability', in David Held and Mathias Koenig-Archibugi (eds), *Global Governance and Public Accountability*, Oxford: Blackwell Publishing, pp. 67–86.

Benner, Thorsten, Charlotte Streck and Jan Martin Witte (eds) (2003), *Progress or Peril? Networks and Partnerships in Global Environmental Governance: The Post-Johannesburg Agenda*, Berlin and Washington DC: Global Public Policy Institute.

Biermann, Frank, Man-san Chan, Aysem Mert and Philipp Pattberg (2007), 'Multi-stakeholder partnerships for sustainable development: does the promise hold?', in Pieter Glasbergen, Frank Biermann and Arthur P.J. Mol (eds), *Partnerships, Governance and Sustainable Development: Reflections on Theory and Practice*, Cheltenham, UK and Northampton, MA, USA: Edward Elgar Publishing, pp. 239–60.

Börzel, Tanja A. and Thomas Risse (2005), 'Public–private partnerships: effective and legitimate tools of transnational governance?', in Edgar Grande and Louis W. Pauly (eds), *Complex Sovereignty: Reconstituting Political Authority in the Twenty-first Century*, Toronto: University of Toronto Press, pp. 195–216.

Buchanan, Allen and Robert O. Keohane (2006), 'The legitimacy of global governance institutions', *Ethics and International Affairs*, **20**(4), 405–37.

Bull, Benedicte and Desmond McNeill (2007), *Development Issues in Global Governance: Public–Private Partnerships and Market Multilateralism*, New York: Routledge.

Dingwerth, Klaus (2007), *The New Transnationalism: Transnational Governance and Democratic Legitimacy*, Houndmills: Palgrave Macmillan.

Ellis, Jay, Harald Winkler, Jan Corfee-Morlot and Frederic Gagnon-Lebrun (2007), 'CDM: taking stock and looking forward', *Energy Policy*, **35**(1), 15–28.

Green, Jessica (2008), 'Delegation and accountability in the clean development mechanism: the new authority of non-state actors', *Journal of International Law and International Relations*, **4**, 21–55.

Hale, Thomas N. and Denise L. Mauzerall (2004), 'Thinking globally and acting locally: can the Johannesburg partnerships coordinate action on sustainable development?', *Journal of Environment and Development*, **13**(3), 220–39.

Lecocq, Franck and Philippe Ambrosi (2007), 'The Clean Development Mechanism: history, status, and prospects', *Review of Environmental Economics and Policy*, **1**, 134–51.

Levy, David and Peter Newell (2002), *The Business of Global Environmental Governance*, Cambridge, MA: MIT Press.

Lohmann, Larry (2006), 'Carbon trading: a critical conversation on climate change, privatisation and power', *Development Dialogue*, 48.

Lövbrand, Eva, Joakim Nordquist and Teresia Rindefjäll (2009), 'Closing the legitimacy gap in global environmental governance. lessons from the emerging CDM market', *Global Environmental Politics*, **9**(2), 74–100.

Martens, Jens (2007), 'Multistakeholder partnerships: future models of multilateralism?', Friedrich-Ebert Stiftung occasional paper no. 29, January, Berlin.

Matthews, Karina and Matthew Paterson (2005), 'Boom or bust? The economic engine behind the drive for climate change policy', *Global Change, Peace & Security*, **17**(1), 59–75.

Meadowcroft, James (2007), 'Democracy and accountability: the challenge for cross-sectoral partnerships', in Pieter Glasbergen, Frank Biermann and Arthur P.J. Mol (eds), *Partnerships, Governance and Sustainable Development: Reflections on Theory and Practice*, Cheltenham, UK and Northampton, MA, USA: Edward Elgar Publishing, pp. 194–213.

Mert, Aysem (2009), 'Partnerships for sustainable development as discursive practice: shifts in discourses on environment and democracy', *Forest Policy and Economics*, **11**(2), 109–22.

Olsen, Karen Holm (2007), 'The Clean Development Mechanism's contribution to sustainable development: a review of the literature', *Climatic Change*, **84**, 59–73.

Paulsson, Emma (2009a), 'A review of the CDM literature: from fine-tuning to critical scrutiny?', *International Environmental Agreements: Politics, Law and Economics*', **9**(1), 63–80.

Paulsson, Emma (2009b), 'Dysfunctional delegation: why the design of the clean development mechanism's supervisory system is fundamentally flawed', paper presented at the International Studies Association 50th Annual Convention New York City, 15–18 February.

Schäferhoff, Marco, Sabine Campe and Christopher Kaan (2007), 'Transnational public–private partnerships in international relations: making sense of concepts, research frameworks and results', DFG Research Center (SFB) 700, SFB-Governance working paper no. 6, August, Berlin.

Schneider, Lambert (2007), *Is the CDM Fulfilling its Environmental and Sustainable Development Objectives? An Evaluation of the CDM and Options for Improvement*, Berlin: Öko-Institut.

Schneider, Lambert (2008), 'A Clean Development Mechanism (CDM) with atmospheric benefits for a post-2012 climate regime', Öko-Institut discussion paper, 25 September, Berlin.

Streck, Charlotte (2004), 'New partnerships in global environmental policy: the clean development mechanism', *The Journal of Environment Development*, **13**, 295–322.

Streck, Charlotte and Jolene Lin (2008), 'Making markets work: a review of CDM performance and the need for reform', *The European Journal of International Law*, **19**, 409–42.

Streck, Charlotte and Thiago B. Chagas (2007), 'The future of CDM in a post-Kyoto World', *Carbon and Climate Law Review*, **1**, 53–63.

United Nations Framework Convention on Climate Change (UNFCCC) (2001), 'Report to the conference of the parties on its seventh session. Part two: action taken by the conference of the parties', FCCC/CP/2001/13/Add2, Marrakesh.

UNFCCC (2008), 'Meeting report of the forty-fourth meeting of the executive board of the Clean Development Mechanism', 28 November 2008, CDM-EB-44.

United Nations (2008), *Partnerships for Sustainable Development: Report of the Secretary General*, E/CN.17/2008/1, Commission on Sustainable Development, 16th session, 5–16 May, New York: Department of Economic and Social Affairs.

Wara, Michael (2007), 'Is the global carbon market working?', *Nature*, **445**, 595–6.

Wara, Michael and David G. Victor (2008), 'A realistic policy on international carbon offsets', Stanford University Program on Energy and Sustainable Development, working paper no. 74, Stanford, CA.

6. Stakeholder participation in the EU governance of GMO in the food chain*

Beatrice Bengtsson and Mikael Klintman

INTRODUCTION

In this chapter we analyse the role of new modes of governance and deliberation in the context of the European Union (EU) policies on food safety and genetically modified organisms (GMOs). European food safety governance is an interesting case, since it appears as a deliberative rationality has influenced policy-making in a multi-level context between governments, supranational institutions and a range of public and private actors. Yet there is a strong shadow of hierarchy in food safety and GMO governance. These issues represent high stakes policy areas where governance functions are delegated to a less degree to networks of private–public actors in co-regulation and self-regulation arrangements. The chapter traces the deliberative turn in the food safety domain by examining stakeholder consultations as a new mode of governance. By employing the framework of input and output legitimacy (see Chapter 2, this volume), we investigate and evaluate what types of stakeholder-consultative processes can be found in the food safety domain, and how they have addressed GMO-related issues. The first section provides an overview of the regulatory activities within food safety and GMOs. The second section analyses governance of GMOs in the European food safety domain. In the third section problems of legitimacy in the authorization procedures of GMOs is examined. Sections 4, 5 and 6 assess whether stakeholder consultations in the food safety domain promote input and output legitimacy. Stakeholder consultations with regard to both risk assessment and risk management are analysed. Specific attention is drawn to the Advisory Group on the Food Chain and Animal Health at DG SANCO, the Commission Directorate on Health and Consumer Protection. The analysis is based on extensive research of documents and a series of interviews with central stakeholders and policy-makers.[1]

FOOD SAFETY REGULATION IN THE EU

In the context of the EU, food safety is a new policy field. Traditionally, the food policy domain was addressed in separate sectors: farming, fisheries, development, health, environment, transport, consumer affairs, and so forth (Lang, 2003). Since 2000, the EU has employed an integrated and comprehensive approach on food safety. It is officially termed 'From the Farm to the Fork'. The guiding principle is that food safety policy must ensure a high level of food safety through the entire food chain as well as a high level of human health and consumer protection (European Commission, 2000). The latter two objectives are new, because free trade and market harmonization have previously been the only concern of EU food regulation. In fact, it was not until the mid-1990s that consumer affairs were interpreted as important in their own right: from that time, it was no longer considered sufficient to address new challenges through only the economic lens of the internal European Market (Alemanno, 2006; Bergeaud-Blackler and Ferretti, 2006; Knowles et al., 2007). The shift from a market focus to a 'market- *and* consumer-driven' policy domain is typically explained by the multiple and high-profile food scares that hit the European market during the mid- and late 1990s. Examples include 'mad cow disease' or Bovine Spongiform Encephalopathy (BSE) (Great Britain in the 1990s), dioxin in animal feed (Belgium in 1999), E-Coli and salmonella (Knowles et al., 2007). Consequently, food entered the debate as a complex and abstract system of governance. Naturally, the food scares and surrounding turmoil were an economic catastrophe for many groups of farmers and other agricultural actors. Yet there is wide agreement among observers that the BSE crisis was, above all, a political crisis. The failure of the control system during this period was considered to be just one instance of the malfunctioning of European food regulation. Moreover, a popular view was that the existing decision-making processes regarding risk were inadequate, lacked transparency and were biased towards industrial interests. Politicians, public officials and scientific advisers had downplayed the risks and safety issues and could not be trusted (Bartlett, 1999; Vos, 2000; Borrás, 2006). In 1998, the Eurostat survey revealed that most consumers in Europe trusted NGOs more than national governments or EU institutions with respect to information on food safety risks (Ansell et al., 2006). This, among other things, precipitated a re-conceptualization and re-organization of the policy-making context of food in Europe (Ugland and Veggeland, 2006). Based on the principles expressed in the White Paper on Food Safety, as well as in the General Food Law, a number of institutional reforms were initiated, among them the establishment of a more integrated food policy under the Commission Directorate on Health and Consumer Protection (DG SANCO), and a new agency – the

European Food Safety Authority (EFSA). The following section analyses governance of GMOs in the EU food safety landscape.

THE REGULATORY LANDSCAPE OF GMO GOVERNANCE

The regulatory framework on GMO is based on a diffusion of institutional authority, and is an example of network governance within a supranational–intergovernmental organization. Network governance is here understood as 'regular and non-hierarchical interaction among relevant and resourceful state and societal actors in policy formulation' (Skogstad, 2003, p. 330; cf. Caduff and Bernauer, 2006). The Commission has the exclusive right to propose legislation, but the European Parliament (EP) and the Council of Ministers are co-legislators on all GMO issues. The Commission thus needs an absolute majority in the EP and a qualified majority in the Council in order to pass new legislation (Skogstad, 2003). While the regulatory system is based on hierarchical forms of governance, where national governments have the main authority (albeit share some competence with supranational institutions), it also exemplifies a move away from administrative rationality. DG SANCO, as well as Members of the European Parliament, rely on information, knowledge and feedback from non-state actors. As an example, DG SANCO consults stakeholders and gives them access to policy formulation. The purpose, according to the Commission, is to ensure that proposals are technically viable, practically applicable and acceptable by all the players involved (European Commission, 2004).

Since 2004 there have been two different sets of rules governing the authorization of GM products in the EU: one concerning the use of genetically modified plants (Directive 2001/18/EC) and the other concerning food and feed made from such plants (Regulation 1829/2003). The first legislation was adopted in 2001 by a co-decision between the Council and the European Parliament. The central objective of the directive was to protect the environment and human health when GMOs are released into the environment and placed on the market 'as or in products', in accordance with the precautionary principle (Shaffer and Pollack, 2009, p. 279). Due to complaints from certain member states, new regulations for labelling and traceability were adopted in 2003 (Regulation 1829/2003). As with the former legislation, there was a lengthy bargaining process among the Commission, the Council and the European Parliament.[2] As a supplement to the protection of the environment, human life and health, the legislation from 2003 includes the rather vague criterion of 'consumer interest in relation to genetically modified food or feed' (Shaffer and Pollack, 2009, p. 281).

The governance of GMO needs to be understood in the light of the General Food Law. According to this law, risk analysis is the basis for European food policy. In line with the general definition as determined by the WHO and Codex Alimentarius (an international programme promoting coordination of food standards and consumer protection), risk analysis consists of (1) risk assessment; (2) risk management; and (3) risk communication. Risk assessment is a scientifically based process carried out by an independent scientific body: the European Food Safety Authority (EFSA). Risk management, on the other hand, is the process of weighing policy alternatives in consultation with interested parties. It takes into account the result of risk assessment, the precautionary principle and other relevant factors, and is done by policy-makers. Risk communication refers to the interactive exchange of information and opinions throughout the risk analysis process among all the involved actors (Vos, 2009). According to Caduff and Bernauer (2006), the establishment of EFSA has particularly strengthened the risk-assessment phase of the decision-making process. Skogstad (2006) refers to the EU regulatory framework on GMO as a consensual, meditative regulatory policy style. The framework combines the authority of scientific expertise (risk assessment) with the authority of democratic values, such as transparency, deliberation and public accountability and other dimensions of input legitimacy as elaborated in Table 2.2 (Chapter 2, this volume). It is often stated that the EU's GMO legislation is the most stringent in the world, and that politicians who are directly accountable (risk managers) have the final authority to approve GMOs (Skogstad, 2006). Nevertheless, the regulatory framework has, and still is, fiercely debated and contested (cf Vos, 2009; Kupier, 2009).

LEGITIMACY CHALLENGES OUTSIDE THE REALM OF STAKEHOLDER CONSULTATIONS

The regulatory power in the area of food safety and GMO exemplifies multi-level governance as it has become increasingly centralized at the EU level while, at the same time, the European Commission's authority has constantly been challenged by member states and other actors (Shaffer and Pollack, 2009). In this section we focus on several problems of legitimacy in the EU governance of GMO. Why do certain actors perceive the authorization procedure as unacceptable, and what reforms have been made to enhance input or procedural legitimacy as well as output legitimacy (policy and compliance effectiveness)? One important conclusion from this analysis is that stakeholder consultation has little or no role to play here. Instead, deliberation on high-stake issues (such as GMO authorization) has taken place in other informal and formal public spheres and between the Commission, state and non-state actors.

The first problem concerns the authorization procedure and what is typically referred to as the 'Deadlock in the Council'. In short, this criticism refers to an alleged dysfunction within the institutional system. For a decade, the Standing Committee on the Food Chain and Animal Health (SCFCAH) as well as the Council of Ministers have been unable to either approve or reject GMOs. Therefore, the European Commission is free to authorize them based on a special regulatory procedure.[3] Since neither the SCFCAH nor the Council can make a decision, proposed decisions are returned to the Commission. In that sense, the exception has become the main principle and this undermines the procedural and input legitimacy of the authorization procedure. In addition, the entire procedure is seen as biased towards the EFSA, and ultimately towards industrial interest. A second procedural problem relates to the framework for risk analysis and the division between risk assessment and risk management. The worries are that the opinions of the EFSA create excessive spillovers to risk management, in the sense that the Commission too frequently treats the opinions of the EFSA as a result of both risk assessment *and* risk management, and not just risk assessment. Certain EU member states, NGOs and EU-parliamentarians have repeatedly criticized the EFSA for representing pro-GMO bias, and argue that the Commission's responsibility to act as risk manager is de-politicized: the Commission simply relies on EFSA's assessments, overlooking the expertise of the member states and independent scientists (cf. EurActiv, 2006). Critics argue that the European Commission is not responsive to public concerns and does not fulfil its responsibility as risk manager. To a certain extent, this is also a problem of accountability. This problem emerges as member states argue that risk managers do not fulfil their responsibilities. As a result, member states react by imposing sanctions and national protectionism, something that we will explore in the following section.

A third problem concerns disputes over the methods of risk assessment. National governments, environmental ministers and research groups have repeatedly challenged the scientific authority of the EFSA (cf. Séralini et al., 2007; EFSA, 2007). A fourth and closely related problem is the member-state 'revolt'. This has implications for policy and institutional effectiveness of GMO governance as illustrated in Table 2.2 (see Chapter 2, this volume). Several member states have repeatedly invoked a EU safeguard clause enabling them to suspend the marketing or cultivation of GM crops within their borders even though they have EU-wide authorization. But the EU executive has never substantiated their applications and has always ordered them to lift the national bans. In that sense, institutional and compliance-related effectiveness is not just undermined, but obstructed when member states simply ignore the Commission's recommendations backed by scientific assessments from the EFSA. During the Austrian (2006) and French (2008) presidencies, important steps were taken to review the procedures for authorization and risk assessment of GMOs.[4] In December 2008 the EU Environment Ministers adopted a conclusion on GMOs (Council Conclusion, 2008). Separately, the EFSA has initiated a review to update its guidelines on environmental risk assessments of GMOs, at the request of the European Commission. However, the calls for introducing socioeconomic criteria into the GM crops registration process, and to give member states greater freedom to establish GMO-free areas, have not been supported by the other ministers.

One important conclusion from this analysis is that measures to improve the legitimacy of the authorization procedure of GMO have mainly taken part outside the realm of stakeholder consultation. It has not, as the respondents point out, been a topic for stakeholder consultation. Stakeholders have certainly exercised influence on this matter, yet mainly through channels other than the open and transparent mode of governance that stakeholder consultation represents. Hence, the formal inclusion of actors in the policy-making process regarding the authorization procedure on GMO has been narrow and mainly driven by government actors. Furthermore, we argue that the reforms aimed at improving the authorization process are based on an administrative and a deliberative rationality. First, the new reform proposals are based on administrative governance logic since the discussion has taken place on a high ministerial level, between agencies, scientific experts and regulators. In addition, the tools applied are 'hard law' or traditional regulation as the EFSA's new guidelines for risk assessment are supposed to be regulated. According to a respondent from the EFSA's GMO-panel, the regulatory approach of the Commission to science and risk assessment has caused criticism among scientists in the EFSA GMO-panel. Scientists are not pleased with politicians controlling the realm of science and deciding on best approaches to risk assessment. Secondly, the governance logic is deliberative in the sense that the debate and criticism from civil society and environmental organizations has taken hold in the governance institutions. Through the organizational form of networks (between EU public institutions, the EFSA and member states) and stakeholder consultation (at DG SANCO and by the Barroso Commission), multiple actors have been engaged in problem-solving activities. In addition to the expanded guidelines for environmental risk assessment (on long-term environmental effects of growing GM crops and the potential effects on non-target organisms), the deliberative rationale has prompted a pluralized conception of, and an interdisciplinary approach to, risk (cf. Council Conclusion, 2008, section 7).

So far, we have focused on deliberative interactions within the core political institutions (EU Member States and EU institutions). In the following sections we turn the attention to stakeholder consultations, that is, deliberative innovations at the interface between EU institutions, NGOs and the industry.

STAKEHOLDER CONSULTATIONS: GOVERNANCE FOR OR BY THE AFFECTED?

Scholars regularly conceptualize stakeholders as representatives of affected interests or as societal actors who have an interest (a stake) in a specific policy issue (cf. Renn et al., 1993; Von Winterfeldt, 1992) and include companies, NGOs, EU member states and individual citizens. In contrast, the EFSA defines stakeholders more specifically as organizations that (a) have specific expertise; (b) are representatives in their respective field of competence; (c) are permanently established at the EU level; and (d) are well known at the Community level for their activities in the area of food safety (EFSA, 2007). This stricter definition of stakeholders by the EFSA should not be confused with the more general discussion about public or institutional stakeholders. According to an ideal of broader stakeholder participation, such a restricted definition threatens to reduce the input legitimacy of decision-making within the EFSA, particularly if suspicions emerge that experts from the NGOs, the governments and the business community become an exclusive group of too intimate friends.

The research on modes of governance within the GMO field typically concerns national experiences with consensus conferences and public consultations. It focuses on the general public rather than on stakeholders, and on nation-states rather than the EU (Klüver, 1995; Nielsen et al., 2007; Blok, 2007; Irwin, 2001; 2006). GMO food is already a frequent topic for public consultations on a national level and remains an important and publicly recognized food safety issue in the EU. For that reason we expected to find several European policy processes open to the public. However, we did not find empirical support for our expectations. The governance of GMOs at the EU level (so far) takes place within the core political institutions and constitution-making bodies. In fact, we could not find any examples of formalized deliberative innovations at the interface between the state and civil society that has a specific focus on GMOs and the public at the EU level. Neither could we find examples of a EU-wide consensus conference, nor citizen juries or the like. Such stakeholder conferences have instead taken place in member states. It can therefore be argued that GMOs are, at the EU-level, governed *for* rather than *by* the affected (cf. Eckersley, 2004, p. 112). Previous analysis indicates that the input legitimacy of GMO governance at the EU-level has been limited to informal and ad hoc interest representation and parliamentary representation (Borrás, 2006), as well as non-formalized stakeholder dialogue with the EFSA (Ferretti, 2008).

However, important initiatives have been taken more recently in the food safety domain in general. New arenas have been established that are based on formal and direct participatory mechanisms for stakeholders. Stakeholder consultation, involvement, engagement, participation and dialogue have become familiar key words in the EU food safety domain, and the terminology applies to an array of activities. There are clear indications that the EU food safety domain is an experimental arena for deliberative mechanisms, and that DG SANCO makes its own participatory and policy-innovative reflections. These reflections are manifested in at least two comprehensive and deliberative reviews: 'The Healthy Democracy Process' (DG SANCO, 2007) and the 'Future Challenges exercise' (DG SANCO, 2009a). In addition, the EFSA also practises stakeholder dialogue in its Stakeholder Dialogue Platform. For these reasons, we argue that European policy-makers in this particular policy area experiment with stakeholder-related policy innovations based on participation and deliberation.

STAKEHOLDER CONSULTATION IN RISK ASSESSMENT AND POLICY-MAKING: EMPTY PROCEDURALISM OR DELIBERATIVE QUALITY?

Oels (2006) classifies stakeholder dialogues according to three main purposes. Stakeholder dialogues for science have the aim to clarify and improve knowledge. Stakeholder dialogue for policy-making aims to garner political acceptance after deliberations. Finally, the aim of stakeholder dialogue in management is to strengthen implementation. The following overview of stakeholder consultations in the European food safety domain rests on this classification. However, we add a fourth purpose, which is stakeholder consultation as development of procedures for decision-making and participation. In Table 6.1, the four types of stakeholder consultations are listed along with examples from the EU food safety domain. With respect to the governance of GMOs the examples that are most relevant for this chapter are EFSA's Consultative Stakeholder Platform and the Advisory Group on the Food Chain and Animal Health at DG SANCO. Nevertheless, Table 6.1 includes all inclusive and transparent arenas for stakeholder participation in the food safety domain (EFSA, 2007; DG SANCO, 2007; 2009a). Since the EU Platform on Diet, Physical Activity and Health concerns health rather than food safety, we have chosen to focus our analysis on the other three examples of stakeholder consultation.

The first type of stakeholder consultation concerns the risk assessment process. The creation of the EFSA Stakeholder Consultative Platform was agreed upon in 2005. It consists of EU-wide stakeholder organizations working in areas related to the food chain. The purpose of this platform is to meet and assist the EFSA in the development of its overall relations and policy with stakeholders. The meetings provide a 'platform for honest exchange of opin-

Table 6.1   Typology of stakeholder consultation

Purpose	Example	Institutional position
Stakeholder consultation as contribution to risk assessment and/or risk communication	EFSA's Consultative Stakeholder Platform	EFSA
Stakeholder consultation as policy advice	The Advisory Group on the Food Chain and Animal Health	DG SANCO/ Food safety
Stakeholder consultation as management	EU Platform on Diet, Physical Activity and Health	DG SANCO / Health
Stakeholder consultation as development of procedures for decision-making and participation	DG SANCO Stakeholder Dialogue Group	DG SANCO / General

ions and ideas' (EFSA, 2009). Since 2005, ten meetings have taken place. No particular platform meeting has had an exclusive focus on GMO. As an alternative, the EFSA chose to have a 'Technical meeting with non-governmental organizations on GMO' in 2006. This meeting was followed up in 2008. These two meetings have been highly criticized on both input and output legitimacy grounds. For example, Greenpeace has raised concerns about holding separate meetings with NGOs and about including too few stakeholders, and have questioned the meaning and outcome of interactions with the EFSA. However, this platform is where stakeholders come closest to the realm of science/risk assessment and it might be assumed that this science-based stakeholder dialogue is set up as a structured communicative process linking scientists with selected actors who are relevant for the research problem at hand (cf. Stoll-Kleemann and Welp, 2006). However, the platform does not seem to live up to this aim and has been criticized for lacking in-depth discussions, for having an unclear rationale and for giving results that are perceived as insufficient (Paeps, 2008). In addition, stakeholders are clearly ambivalent about their participation and contribution in this arena. Instead of 'up-stream involvement in risk assessment' (Wynne, 2008) or deliberation, stakeholders agree that this arena comes down to risk communication and monitoring. While it is possible to get up-to-date information, meetings are perceived as tedious and costly. As a consequence some of the stakeholders who attend the meetings send a secretary or assistant instead of a policy adviser. Several stakeholders see the EFSA as overly instrumental. These stakeholders claim that the EFSA exercises 'empty proceduralism' (Chalmers, 2003, p. 552). If this practice is addressed in terms of input legitimacy, the principle of inclusion seems most satisfied. Moreover, transparency has also been improved. Agendas and minutes are available online. In addition, observers are allowed to participate in the meetings. However, some actors claim that the objective of transparency may also hamper the quality of the debate: one respondent, for instance, mentioned that observers sitting at the back at EFSA stakeholder meetings have the effect of hindering the dialogue. Therefore, the respondent's organization will not speak about issues that it does not want to see in the press. In spite of not having any visible output legitimacy, some stakeholders are content with the established procedure and input legitimacy in terms of inclusiveness and transparency.

Stakeholder consultations can also contribute to the policy process in the development of procedures for decision-making and participation (as summarized in the fourth row in Table 6.1). The DG SANCO Stakeholder Dialogue Group (SDG) was created as a direct result of the DG SANCO 2006 Peer Review Group on Stakeholder involvement, in September 2007. The objective of the group is to advise the Director General and the European Commission on different procedural issues that will facilitate stakeholder involvement in the work of DG SANCO. The group is currently chaired by Mr Robert Madelin, Director-General of DG SANCO, and consists of 19 members of various stakeholder groups (DG SANCO, 2009b). The SDG's tasks are a more transparent comitology, improved consultation, 'engaging the unengaged' and to reduce stakeholder asymmetry. Since this group focuses on procedures rather than on food safety topics, the SDG has not had any impact on the regulations of GMO. Nevertheless, this type of consultation may have an impact on future regulations. In comparison with the other arenas of stakeholder participation, this is one where the transformation of preferences and exchange of arguments seems to take place, which relates to deliberative quality as a key dimension of input legitimacy (see Table 2.2, Chapter 2, this volume). Several respondents draw specific attention to the positive feedback from SANCO, and emphasize Robert Madelin (Director General of the European Commission's DG SANCO) as a driving force behind the overall deliberative approach towards stakeholders. An important outcome of the SDG is the Comitology Planner, published yearly to allow stakeholders to anticipate consultations in the forthcoming year so that they know in advance when they will be consulted and on what particular topic. There are also more visionary plans to develop deliberative innovations at the interface between SANCO, civil society and the public. However, citizen juries as a deliberative innovation are perceived by stakeholders as practically unworkable and more of a theoretical idea.

So far, we have examined the approach of policy-makers to stakeholders and stakeholder consultation as a contribution to risk assessment and risk communication (the first row in Table 6.1) and as a development of procedures (the fourth row in Table 6.1). Two important conclusions can be made so far. First, there are clear indications that policy-makers in the food safety domain have an increased interest in stakeholder consultation. Various forms of stakeholder consultation have indeed been implemented as a complement to network governance and traditional regulation (cf. the earlier sections in this chapter). Secondly, there are great differences between the EFSA's Consultative Stakeholder Platform and DG SANCO's Stakeholder Dialogue Group. The deliberative quality seems to be higher in the latter (SDG), which focuses on procedures. The former consultative process (at the EFSA) is an example of risk communication and one-way communication rather than deliberation. However, input legitimacy in terms of transparency and inclusion is strong in both stakeholder consultations.

STAKEHOLDER PARTICIPATION IN RISK MANAGEMENT

In the food safety domain (the food unit of DG Sanco), there is mainly one opportunity for stakeholders to participate in risk management and to discuss technical issues and legislative proposals, namely the Advisory Group on the Food Chain and Animal and Plant Health (hereafter called 'The Advisory Group'; see the second row of Table 6.1). Although incorporated in a public authority, the Advisory Group is distinctive in the sense that it is based on stakeholder participation and consultation that is transparent, inclusive and formalized. The Advisory Group was formed in 2004 (DG SANCO, 2009c) and replaced old committees such as the Advisory Committee on Foodstuffs and the Advisory Committee on Agricultural Product Health and Safety, as well as certain standing groups attached to it. Its purpose is to establish a dialogue between the Commission's departments and the socio-professional circles involved in the fields covered by food legislation. The dialogue is said to make sure there is an opportunity to 'anticipate and pinpoint the nature of the difficulties and uncertainties which the Union may have to address, with an eye to taking decisions and ensuring that the risks can be clearly explained to the public' (Commission Decision, 2004a, p. 1). Another promise of this group is to ensure that the Commission's proposals are 'technically viable, practically applicable and acceptable by all the players involved' (Commission Decision, 2004a, p. 2).

The Advisory Group on the Food Chain and Animal Health brings together key stakeholders including farmers, the food industry, retailers, consumer organizations and others to advise the European Commission on food safety policy. It meets in principle twice a year in plenary sessions to discuss general policy issues that have an interest for all the 36 member organizations, or in Working Groups when more technical issues are examined. The representative bodies must meet the following criteria: (1) that the general nature of the interests are protected; (2) that they represent all or most member states; and (3) that they have a permanent presence at Community level to allow direct access to members' expertise and to permit swift and coordinated reactions (Commission Decision, 2004b). If necessary, the Commission may invite additional experts or observers, including representative bodies from non-member states, to participate in the work of the Advisory Group or its working groups. The purpose of the working groups is both to collect more technical contributions from the different fields involved and to provide information on the implementation of the existing law and rules of procedure. The possibility to expand in terms of scale, scope and participants is an example of the inclusive nature of the process. Nevertheless, critics such as Greenpeace are not satisfied with representativeness because of structural inequalities. Despite improvements, consumer interests remain a minority and there are great disparities between participants in terms of access to resources. Stakeholders as well as civil servants are open about these problems. As an example, stakeholder representativeness and stakeholder asymmetries have been discussed in the DG SANCO Stakeholder Dialogue Group (SDG) (DG SANCO Stakeholder Dialogue Group, 2009b). In particular, the asymmetry in access and production of information is a key issue that may lead to stakeholder inequality. Stakeholder consultation in the Advisory Group is based on an integrated approach to the food chain. Representatives from the different components of the food chain are included in this forum. This is a clear difference compared to the earlier Advisory Committee in which, for instance, food and feed were treated individually. There are two important differences between these groups that are related to procedural aspects of deliberation. First, the regulation 178/2002 states that consultation shall be open and transparent, which means, for example, that the minutes of the Advisory Group are now published on the webpage. This differs from the former secrecy of the meetings. Secondly, this forum represents an established procedure for stakeholder participation and is an institutionalized forum for stakeholders to deliberate. There are some limitations to the process because while the consultation may be ongoing, the Commission is not obliged to use input from the consultation or the Advisory Group. Therefore, the potential output legitimacy of this forum, in terms of reduced risks to health or the environment (as perceived by the public), may be questioned. Since the implementation phase of GMO regulations has already taken place, DG SANCO's new experimental and participatory approach towards stakeholders has not had any major effect on the governance of GMO.

It may appear as though stakeholders can be consulted on every occasion and on every topic in the EU food safety domain. This is definitely not the case. There are strict limitations on stakeholder participation. They are never authorized to participate directly in risk assessment or risk management. As an example, the EFSA keeps the Stakeholder Consultative Platform at arm's length, and the GMO panel meetings are held behind closed doors. On the risk management side, stakeholders operate (as professional stakeholders and as lobbyists) outside the comitology system. Another important remark is that consensus is not the purpose of any stakeholder consultative process examined in this chapter. The EFSA's and DG SANCO's approach to consultation does not follow the conventional view of deliberative decision-making. In contrast, the emphasis is on constructive discussion and elaboration of difference: the reason why DG SANCO consults stakeholders is to gather different opinions and to get different types of feedback on a proposal (cf. Sabel and Zeitlin, 2008). However, decision-making is never in the hands of stakeholders. Consultation can never replace the procedures and decisions of legislative bodies. Another important conclusion is that stakeholder consultation always takes place in the initial phase of the policy-making process. A consultation concerns 'hard-law', and occurs in the shadow of hierarchy. In a similar way, GMO governance is based on hard law or traditional regulatory approaches, rather than soft forms of governance. Neither policy-makers nor the biotech-industry favours self-regulatory measures on GMO. As discussed in the case of forestry governance (Chapter 10, this volume), the strong shadow of hier-archy may be explained by the fact that food policy is an issue area that repre-sents high stakes for the population in terms of public safety.

CONCLUSIONS

This chapter has argued that there has been a deliberative turn in the EU food safety domain and in the governance of GMOs. Stakeholder consultations on food safety governance have been employed as means to strengthen input legitimacy. Yet in this domain the deliberative elements are not manifested in ways that one could expect them to be. Despite the multi-level governance context and a move to a deliberative rationality, the question of food safety and GMOs is highly influenced by the interest of member states and supranational institutions. We have claimed that deliberative interaction takes place within or close to core political institutions and legislative bodies. Thus deliberation is mainly exercised within a hierarchical governance form. In the governance of GMO, as well as in the food safety domain in general, policy-makers use a deliberative logic in relation to certain stakeholders, whereas the public is, per definition, excluded from the concept of 'stakeholders'. Consequently, we have not been able to find many policy innovations at the interface between the Commission/DG SANCO and the public.

What is the legitimacy and effectiveness record of the GMO authorization process? In our view, there are specific problems here, which can be conceived as problems relating to input as well as output legitimacy. Criticism of the 'Deadlock in the Council', the EFSA's pro-GMO bias and a de-politicized Commission, among other issues, have in some cases entailed a breakdown of normal EU decision-making processes. Since several actors (among them EU member states) do not approve of the authorization process, institutional, policy and compliance effectiveness are hampered (cf. Chapter 2, this volume). To be sure, important reforms have been made such as new guidelines for risk assessment and a more pluralized conception of risk. Yet this has taken place at a high ministerial level and outside of the realm of stakeholder consultation.

Looking more specifically at the prevalence of deliberative as well as participatory processes of stakeholder consultations, it is clear that civil servants at the EFSA and at DG SANCO are eager to experiment with, and to implement, participatory processes for stakeholders. As mentioned earlier, stakeholder consultations are used in the initial phase of the policy-making process surrounding food safety. Yet, the form is clearly hierarchical. Or put the other way round, DG SANCO and the EFSA represent an 'old mode of governance', although their hierarchical forms are influenced by a deliberative rationality (Klintman and Kronsell, 2009). Yet the Habermasian position on deliberative democracy (see Chapter 3) has little relevance in this particular policy domain. When stakeholders are consulted, the purpose is rarely to transform their preferences in the light of the better argument (Pellizzoni, 2001, p. 66). Instead, the purpose is typically to bring together diverse voices, so that civil servants can make informed choices when drafting a piece of legislation.

As we have indicated, stakeholder consultations in the food safety domain are typically strong with respect to transparency and inclusion. It is interesting to note that respondents are satisfied with the organizational set-up, even though the effectiveness and problem-solving capacity of these processes are unclear. The stakeholders have problems explaining the output of consultation, yet they appreciate the opportunity to meet and exchange information. Not all respondents, but most of them, perceive the stakeholder consultations as acceptable and legitimate. Another important conclusion is that the deliberative quality differs among the various stakeholder consultations examined in this chapter. Our analysis suggests that the closer stakeholders come to the scientific core, the less there is of stakeholder deliberation in the Habermasian sense. In the DG SANCO Stakeholder Dialogue Group (SDG), for instance, stakeholders deliberate on procedural issues with little of particular relevance to substantive knowledge sharing on food safety or GMO. At the Advisory

Group on the Food Chain and Animal Health, stakeholders may (depending on the topic) deliberate, not only with other stakeholders and civil servants, but also with experts and invited guests. At the EFSA's Consultative Stakeholder Platform, on the other hand, the communication comes down to risk communication, not deliberation. Altogether, our analysis suggests a deliberative turn in the EU food safety domain and in GMO governance. However, the deliberative quality seems to be higher in low-stake issues. In addition, there are signs that stakeholder consultations are stronger in terms of input legitimacy (inclusion and transparency) than in output legitimacy (effectiveness). As to the actual impact that stakeholders have on policy proposals, this remains to be examined in future research.

NOTES

* This article is based on research projects financed by the Swedish Research Council for Environment, Agricultural Sciences and Spatial Planning (2005-1014, project leader Karin Bäckstrand) and Swedish Research Council (2005-1720, project leader Mikael Klintman). We thank both research foundations.
1. The data used in this chapter corresponds to document analysis and interviews conducted between January and May 2009. The documentary sources are derived from a wide range of sources: (1) scientific books and articles; (2) DG SANCO/EFSA; (3) stakeholders; and (4) news media. Sixteen interviews were conducted in Sweden and Brussels. The respondents correspond to six different categories: national authorities, environmental organizations, scientific experts, consumer organizations, policy-makers and business federations (representing farmers, commerce, biotech and food).
2. One of the most controversial elements of the new regulation was the establishment of a set of thresholds for permitted traces of genetically modified ingredients. Environmental and consumer groups, as well as the European Parliament, thought that the initial suggestion (of 1 per cent GM material) was too high, while biotech companies and the United States Government criticized it as too low. The final regulation was set to vary from 0.5 per cent to 0.9 per cent (Shaffer and Pollack, 2009, p. 291).
3. Both the special regulatory procedure and the role of the EFSA have been the subject of criticism (see EurActiv 05/12/05 and 10/03/06).
4. In spring 2008, the EU executive mandated the agency to update its guidelines as regards the long-term environmental risk assessment of GM plants. In summer 2008, the French EU Presidency created a series of proposals to consider ways of solving the current deadlock and make product approval or rejection easier.

REFERENCES

Alemanno, Alberto (2006), 'Food safety and the single European market', in Christopher Ansell and David Vogel (eds), *What's the Beef? The Contested Governance of European Food Safety*, Cambridge, MA: MIT Press, pp. 237–58.
Ansell, Christopher and David Vogel (eds) (2006), *What's the Beef? The Contested Governance of European Food Safety*, Cambridge, MA: MIT Press.
Ansell, Christopher, Rahsaan Maxwell and Daniela Sicurelli (2006), 'Protesting food: NGOs and political mobilization in Europe', in Christopher Ansell and David Vogel

(eds), *What's the Beef? The Contested Governance of European Food Safety*, Cambridge, MA: MIT Press, pp. 97–122.

Bartlett, David (1999), 'Mad cows and democratic governance: BSE and the construction of a "free market" in the UK', *Crime, Law & Social Change*, **30**(2), 237–57.

Bergeaud-Blackler, Florence and Maria Paola Ferretti (2006), 'More politics, stronger consumers? A new division of responsibility for food in the European Union', *Appetite*, **47**(2), 134–42.

Blok, Anders (2007), 'Experts on public trial: on democratizing expertise through a Danish consensus conference', *Public Understanding of Science*, **16**(2), 163–82.

Borrás, Susana (2006), 'Legitimate governance of risk at the EU level? The case of genetically modified organisms', *Technological Forecasting & Social Change*, **73**(1), 61–75.

Buonanno, Laurie (2006), 'The creation of the European Food Safety Authority', in Christopher Ansell and David Vogel (eds), *What's the Beef? The Contested Governance of European Food Safety*, Cambridge: the MIT Press, pp. 259–78.

Caduff, Ladina and Thomas Bernauer (2006), 'Managing risk and regulation in European food safety governance', *Review of Policy Research*, **32**(1), 153–68.

Chalmers, D. (2003), '"Food for thought": reconciling European risks and traditional ways of life', *Modern Law Review*, **66**(4), 533–62.

Commission Decision (CD) (2004a), 'Concerning the creation of an advisory group on the food chain and animal and plant health' (2004/613/EC).

Commission Decision (CD) (2004b), 'The Advisory Group on the Food Chain and Animal and Plant Health, rules of procedure', accessed 12 August 2009 at http://ec.europa.eu/food/committees/advisory/rules_procedure_en.pdf.

Council Conclusion on Genetically Modified Organisms (GMOs) (2008), 2912th Environment Council meeting, Brussels, 4 December 2008, accessed 12 August 2009 at www.consilium.europa.eu/ueDocs/cms_Data/docs/pressData/en/envir/104509.pdf.

DG SANCO (2007), 'Healthy Democracy', Conclusions and Actions following the DG SANCO 2006 Peer Review Group on Stakeholder Involvement, accessed 10 March 2009 at http://ec.europa.eu/health/ph_overview/health_forum/docs/ev_20070601_rd08_en.pdf.

DG SANCO (2009a), 'Future Challenges paper: 2009–2014', accessed 5 June at http://ec.europa.eu/dgs/health_consumer/events/future_challenges_paper.pdf.

DG SANCO (2009b) 'Stakeholder Dialogue Group', accessed 17 February at http://ec.europa.eu/dgs/health_consumer/sdg/index_en.htm.

DG SANCO (2009c), 'Advisory Group on the Food Chain and Animal and Plant Health', accessed March at http://ec.europa.eu/food/committees/advisory/index_ en.htm.

Directive (2001), 2001/18 of the European Parliament and of the Council of 12 March 2001 on the deliberate release into the environment of genetically modified organisms and repealing Council Directive 90/220/ECC.

Eckersley, Robyn (2004), *The Green State*, Cambridge, MA: MIT Press.

European Food Safety Authority (EFSA) (2007), 'EFSA reaffirms its risk assessment of genetically modified maize MON 863', press release 28 June 2007, accessed 12 August 2009 at www.efsa.europa.eu/EFSA/efsa_locale-1178620753812_1178621165358.htm.

EFSA (2009), 'Consultative platform', accessed 12 August at www.efsa.europa.eu/EFSA/PartnersNetworks/StakeholderInitiatives/efsa_locale-1178620753812_EFSAConsultativePlatformAndArchive.htm.

EurActiv (2006), 'Austria criticises EFSA on GMO bias', accessed November 2008 at http://www.euractiv.com/en/food/austria-criticises-efsa-gmo-bias/article-153305, March.

European Commission (2000), White Paper on Food safety, COM (99) 719 final, 12 January, Brussels.

European Commission (2001), European Governance: A White Paper, COM (2001) 428 final, 25 July, Brussels.

European Commission (2004), 'Communication from the Commission concerning the creation of an advisory group on the food chain and animal and plant health and the establishment of a consultation procedure on the food chain and animal and plant health through representative European bodies', COM (2004), 6 August, Brussels, accessed 12 August 2009 at http://ec.europa.eu/food/animal/welfare/tasks/index_en.htm.

European Parliament (2003), Regulation 1829/2003 of the European Parliament and of the Council of 22 September 2003 on genetically modified food and feed, OJ L268/1.

Ferretti, Maria Paola (2008), 'Participatory strategies in the regulation of GMO products in the EU', in Jens Steffek, Claudia Kissling and Patrizia Nanz (eds), *Civil Society Participation in International and European Governance: A Cure for its Democratic Deficit?*, Basingstoke: Palgrave Macmillan, pp.166–84.

Gutmann, Amy and Dennis Thompson (2004), *Why Deliberative Democracy?*, Princeton, NJ and Oxford: Princeton University Press.

Irwin, Alan (2001), 'Constructing the scientific citizen: science and democracy in the biosciences', *Public Understanding of Science*, **10**(1), 1–18.

Irwin, Alan (2006), 'The politics of talk: coming to terms with the "new" scientific governance', *Social Studies of Science*, **36**(2), 299–320.

Klintman, Mikael and Annica Kronsell (2009), 'Challenges to legitimacy in food safety governance: the case of the European Food Safety Authority (EFSA)', *Journal of European Integration*, **32**(3), 309–27.

Klüver, Lars (1995), 'Consensus conferences at the Danish Board of Technology', in Simon Joss and John Duran (eds), *Public Participation in Science: The Role of Consensus Conferences in Europe*, London: Science Museum, pp. 41–52.

Knowles, Tim, Richard Moody and Morven G. McEachern (2007), 'European food scares and their impact on EU food policy', *British Food Journal*, **109**(1), 43–67.

Kupier, A. Harry (2009), 'The role of scientific experts in risk regulation of foods', in Michele Everson and Ellen Vos (eds), *Uncertain Risk Regulated*, Abingdon: Routledge-Cavendish, pp. 389–98.

Lang, Tim (2003), 'Food industrialization and food power: implications for food governance development', *Policy Review*, **21**(5–6), 555–68.

Nielsen Porsberg, Annika, Jesper Lassen and Peter Sandøe (2007), 'Democracy at its best? The consensus conference in a cross-national perspective', *Journal of Agricultural and Environmental Ethics*, **20**(1), 13–35.

Oels, Angela (2006), 'Evaluating stakeholder dialogues', in Susanne Stoll-Kleemann and Martin Welp (eds), *Stakeholder Dialogues in Natural Resources Management: Theory and Practice*, Berlin: Springer, pp.118–50.

Paeps, Frederic (FPA) (2008), 'Stakeholder activities evaluation', accessed at http://www.efsa.europe.eu/EFSA/DocumentSet/sh_presentation_fpa_7thmeet_en, 0.pdf?ssbinary=true.

Pellizzoni, Luigi (2001), 'The myth of the best argument: power, deliberation and reason', *British Journal of Sociology*, **52**(1), 59–86.

Renn, Ortwin, Thomas Webler, Horst Rakel, Peter Dienel and Branden Johnson (1993),

'Public participation in decision-making: a three-step procedure', *Policy Sciences*, **26**, 189–214.

Roosen, Jutta, Jayson L. Lusk and John A. Fox (2003), 'Consumer demand for and attitudes toward alternative beef labelling strategies in France, Germany and the UK', *Agribusiness*, **19**(1), 77–90.

Sabel, Charles F. and Jonathan Zeitlin (2008), 'Learning from difference: the new architecture of experimentalist governance in the EU', *European Law Journal*, **14**(3), 271–327.

Séralini, Gilles-Eric, Dominique Cellier and Joël Spiroux de Vendomois (2007), 'New analysis of a rat feeding study with a genetically modified maize reveals signs of hepatorenal toxicity', *Archives of Environmental Contamination and Toxicology*, **52**, 596–602.

Shaffer, C. Gregory and A. Mark Pollack (2009), 'The EU regulatory system for GMO', in Michelle Everson and Ellen Vos (eds), *Uncertain Risk Regulated*, Abingdon: Routledge-Cavendish, pp. 269–94.

Skogstad, Grace (2003), 'Legitimacy and/or policy effectiveness? Networked governance and GMO regulation in the European Union', *Journal of European Public Policy*, **10**(3), 321–38.

Skogstad, Grace (2006), 'Regulating food safety risks in the European Union: a comparative perspective', in Christopher Ansell and David Vogel (eds), *What's the Beef? The Contested Governance of European Food Safety*, Cambridge, MA: MIT Press, pp. 213–36.

Stoll-Kleemann, Susanne and Martin Welp (2006), 'Linking case studies to the integrative theory of reflexive dialogues', in Susanne Stoll-Kleemann and Martin Welp (eds), *Stakeholder Dialogues in Natural Resources Management: Theory and Practice*, Berlin-Heidelberg: Springer, pp. 348–71.

Ugland, Trygve and Frode Veggeland (2006), 'Experiments in food safety policy integration in the European Union', *Journal of Common Market Studies*, **44**(3), 607–24.

van Dijk Ingénieurs Conseils with Arcadia International EEIG (2005), Brussels, 5 December 2005, 'Evaluation of EFSA final report', accessed at www.efsa. europa.eu/cs/BlobServer/Non_Scientific_Document/final_report_evaluation1.pdf? ssbinary=true.

Von Winterfeldt, Detlof (1992), 'Expert knowledge and public values in risk management: the role of decision analysis', in Sheldon Krimsky and Dominic Golding (eds), *Social Theories of Risk*, London: Praeger Publishers, pp. 321–42.

Vos, Ellen (2000), 'EU food safety regulation in the aftermath of the BSE crisis', *Journal of Consumer Policy*, **23**(3), 227–55.

Vos, Ellen (2004), 'Overcoming the crisis of confidence: risk regulation in an enlarged European Union', Universitet Maastricht: Unigraphic.

Vos, Ellen (2009), 'The EU regulatory system on food safety: between trust and safety', in Michelle Everson and Ellen Vos (eds), *Uncertain Risk Regulated*, Abingdon: Routledge-Cavendish, pp. 249–68.

Wynne, Brian (2008), 'Does genetics have any democratic public(s)? Normative imaginations and risk discourses in modern genetics and genomics', presentation at the seminar Genetics, Normality and Democracy, 10 December, Lund University.

7. Participation under administrative rationality: implementing the EU Water Framework Directive in forestry

Lovisa Hagberg

INTRODUCTION

Few environmental issues illustrate the dilemmas and specificities of environmental governance as well as water (cf. Carter, 2007, pp. 174–80). Water moves across boundaries, in spatial units that rarely match administrative space. Water also cycles in ways that seldom correspond to the time-dimensions of policy and water management. Ground water, surface waters and coastal waters are sensitive in different ways, but are also related to each other through the water cycle. The quality of water is extremely dependent on the area of land it drains from. The effects of water use on a small scale, at the very local level, accumulate downstream. This is why what happens to small streams high up in the stream order is often more important than measures close to the coast or a big river. Furthermore, water use is sectorized and there is often a mismatch between those that use water and those who bear the consequences of the use. Water can both be a common and private resource. Because of its vital importance, the right to water is a controversial normative issue.

Water was one of the first environmental issues to be regulated in the European Union (EU) due to the need for similar criteria for different kinds of water use within the common market. As a commodity, water was open to community regulation before the environment was added to EU competencies through the Single European Act. At the same time other water issues remained under the jurisdiction of member states (MS), such as the regulation of drainage and floods (McCormick, 2001). The early EU water directives, for example the drinking water directive (Directive 73/404/EC), represented a traditional, highly sectorized approach to water governance. By the end of the 1980s, there was growing concern that European water governance suffered from a triple failure in terms of deficits regarding governance, implementation and legitimacy (see Figure 1.1, Chapter 1, this volume; cf. Lundqvist, 2004).

In recent years, the sectorized approach has been challenged by integrated water resources management (IWRM) and sustainable river basin management. In the negotiation processes for the Water Framework Directive (WFD) (Directive 2000/60/EC), participation was introduced as one of the requirements for the legitimate formulation and effective implementation of European water policy.

This book analyses the promise implied in 'new modes' of environmental governance, which assumes that public participation and deliberation will improve the legitimacy of environmental policies while contributing towards increased environmental effectiveness. The WFD is an exemplary case of this promise, since it is perceived to have the potential to reduce the legitimacy, governance and implementation deficits in water management. Even though it represents a hierarchical form of governance (see Table 2.1, Chapter 2, this volume) by establishing the water district as the administrative basis for water management, the WFD has raised high expectations of increased environmental effectiveness through its emphasis on public participation throughout the whole policy process. Studies of EU environmental policy often refer to the WFD as a good example of novel approaches to environmental regulation (cf. Gouldson et al., 2008; Hedelin, 2008; Kastens and Newig, 2008). Policy practitioners have also highlighted the promise of the WFD's participatory approach. For instance, the European Environmental Bureau (EEB) stated that

> (p)ublic participation will make the measures adopted to achieve the WFD's objectives much more effective. It will also help to create legitimacy and foster public acceptance of EU water policies. And finally it will be a major tool for a better and more efficient implementation of EU water policies than in the past' (EEB, 2001, p. 4).

In this chapter, the promise implied in the WFD is analysed in the context of EU multi-level governance.

As discussed in Chapter 2, one can distinguish between two major sources of legitimacy, input legitimacy (or procedural legitimacy) and output legitimacy (or effectiveness). The trend that procedural sources of legitimacy grow in importance can be observed in the context of European nature conservation policy in general. Decision-makers increasingly find that they rely on procedural sources of legitimacy rather than substantive ones, such as science and expertise. One reason for the growing importance of procedural legitimacy is the increasing complexity of the policy problems addressed, as well as the growing recognition that different sources of knowledge are needed in order to manage natural resources (Engelen et al., 2008).

A reading of the WFD indicates that the directive, which is the result of a long and cumbersome negotiation process, is constructed around several of the rationalities of governance presented in Chapter 2. Moreover, the legitimacy of the measures established in the directive seems to draw on both substantive and procedural sources. Scientific standards for what constitutes good water status are to be implemented through a water management cycle in which stakeholders as well as the general public are expected to participate. This chapter analyses how the mix of governance rationalities employed in the WDF affects the legitimacy and effectiveness of European multi-level water governance. Can synergies be expected from combining different sources of legitimacy, or are there potential tensions and contradictions?

In order to answer these questions, a content analysis of the WFD is first used to identify what governance rationalities it represents. Second, the logic behind participatory implementation measures is explored through an analysis of key texts in the burgeoning literature on implementation advice produced at the European level (CIS, 2003; ADVISOR, 2004). This literature, though eloquent on the need to adapt participatory measures to different contexts, is less concerned with potential conflicts and trade-offs between participatory and other approaches to water governance. Third, since potential clashes are more easily examined at the local level where practical implementation takes place, the empirical analysis proceeds by studying the results from Life Forests for Water (FFW), one of numerous projects initiated with the aim of facilitating the implementation of the WFD. Reports and recommendations from the project, complemented by information collected through participant observation provide the empirical base for the analysis.[1]

GOVERNANCE RATIONALITIES IN THE WATER FRAMEWORK DIRECTIVE

By the end of the 1980s, the governance, implementation and legitimacy deficits in EU water policy grew glaringly obvious (see Figure 1.1, Chapter 1, this volume; cf. Richardson, 1994). In Northern member states the importance of diffuse source pollution was brought into focus while Southern member states criticized the EU for pursuing problems of water quality at the cost of water quantity. Furthermore, the effectiveness of water policy was hampered by the fragmentation of water use policies. Issues of water quantity and quality were separated, policies relied on input from highly specialized and separate groups of professional expertise, detailed regulation of water usage was combined with badly designed subsidies, and the implementation of agreed measures was unsatisfactory.

The aim of the Water Framework Directive (WFD) (Directive 2000/60/EC) was to address these problems by creating a common framework for all uses of water, and by basing the assessment of water on ecological criteria in addition to physical or chemical ones. Water should be governed in river basin districts that match the flow of water through the landscape. Whereas the directive arguably is a traditional piece of legislation, the fresh approach is that a water management cycle is set up which provides the opportunity for adapting and improving goals and measures in predetermined steps. The first step is characterization, or mapping and classifying the status of water bodies.[2] The second step is to establish environmental quality standards for different kinds of water so that goals can be set for each water body. Third, river basin management plans and programmes of measures should be developed for each river basin district in order to reach the goals. The resulting plans should be revised every six years in order to ensure progress in relation to water quality. Thus, the fourth step is to set up monitoring programmes of water status in each river basin district. These programmes serve both as a basis for developing environmental quality standards and programmes of measures, and for detecting change in water status within the river basin district. As the fifth step, each member state should regularly report back to the European Commission (EC) and other concerned member states, on the progress in the river basin districts (Directive 2000/60/EC, Article 8, 11, 13, 15).

The water management cycle includes components that are both highly technical (such as establishing classification of waters comparable across the various ecological conditions in Europe) and process dependent (developing programmes of measures with the participation of stakeholders). It works across multiple levels (from local implementation to reporting to the EC) and had, from the beginning, a very tight schedule of implementation, which is why timing of activities becomes crucial for fulfilling different steps of the cycle. For member states like Sweden, this means that the first cycle is tentative. It was necessary to forgo some degree of detail and to work at a larger scale than was originally foreseen in order to be able to report back to the EC on time. The implications of this are that water bodies tend to be designated on a larger scale than may seem relevant from a local perspective, where the variation in environmental quality, and thus the potential need for different measures, do not appear unless the resolution is high enough (Jägrud, 2007, p. 3).

The dynamics between the time and spatial scales of implementation points to some of the potential difficulties in achieving the participatory ambitions of the WFD. Article 14 of the directive on public information and consultation states that member states should encourage 'the active involvement of all interested parties in the implementation of this Directive, in particular in the production, review and updating of river basin management plans' (Directive 2000/60/EC, Article 14). 'To encourage' is arguably not a very strong requirement; nevertheless, Article 14 has generally been interpreted as having to do with active public participation that goes beyond consultation and information sharing (CIS, 2003, pp. 10–12). Many observers do note, however, that the provisions in the directive are rather weak, and that there is a gap between how integrated the deliberative governance rationality is in the directive text, and the extent to which 'the spirit of the law' has been interpreted in deliberative terms by affected actors (Hedelin, 2008; Ker Rault and Jeffrey, 2008).

Despite the focus on achieving working processes revealed in the water management cycle, administrative rationality is strongly embedded in the WFD (the different forms and rationalities of governance expressed in the directive are summarized in Table 7.1). The comprehensive provisions for how water status should be classified, monitored and reported exemplify this. Since these provisions are binding, member states can be taken to the European Court of Justice (ECJ) if they do not fulfil their obligations. Consequently, there is a strong incentive to prioritize administrative implementation before more process-oriented measures towards environmental effectiveness. For instance, there is an incentive to report large water bodies since the 'risk' of falling below the level that requires potentially costly measures is less than for smaller watersheds, which would be more relevant from an environmental or participatory perspective (Jägrud, 2007, p. 4). The setting of environmental quality standards is also a highly technical process. Participatory and deliberative activities, such as consultation on the standards, often occur late in the process.

One of the problems identified in the preamble of the directive is the existence of inappropriate subsidies for water use in many European states. Thus, proper pricing of water is one of its objectives. Also, the economic use of water is to be described in the characterization of each water district. At the same time, water is designated as a common heritage in the preamble, which implies that it cannot be a concern of the market exclusively. The tension between water as a common heritage and as a market resource is built into the directive. Thus, while economic rationality is present in the directive, it does not foresee a pure market governance form for water (cf. Table 7.1).

The governance rationalities expressed in the WFD are also reflected in how actors have interpreted the reasons for working in river basins rather than conventional administrative units. Actors at different policy levels expressed different views on what the river basin represents in spatial terms (Hagberg, 2003). For some, the river basin is perceived as more or less a redrafting of existing administrative boundaries. While they recognize that the fit between ecosystems and institutions is improved, an administrative rationality is still expected to reign, implying, for example, that environmental standards should apply equally to all actors within the river basin regardless of their location. Others tend to view the river basin as a functional space, which means that effectiveness rather than fairness legitimizes policy measures. In this view, it is legitimate to differentiate between actors; for example, depending on how close they live to the river. Especially in the process leading up to implementation,

Table 7.1   Governance rationalities in the Water Framework Directive (WFD)

Governance rationalities:	Administrative	Economic	Deliberative
Forms of governance:			
Hierarchy	Article 3: Coordination of administrative arrangements within river basin districts. Article 4: Environmental objectives Article 5: Characteristics of the river basin district, review of the environmental impact of human activity and economic analysis of water use Article 6: Register of protected areas Article 7: Water use for the abstraction of drinking water Article 8: Monitoring Article 10: The combined approach for point and diffuse sources Article 11: Programme of measures Article 13: River basin management plans	Article 5: Characteristics of the river basin district, review of the environmental impact of human activity and economic analysis of water use	Article 14: Public information and consultation
Market		Article 9: Full recovery of costs for water services	
Networks			

many actors viewed river basin management as a way of working with place rather than space. This would imply a stronger emphasis on caring for and identifying with the water you interact with daily, be it a river, a lake or coastal water. In this view deliberation becomes important because it allows participants from a river basin to learn more about relations in place and to articulate shared problems. By identifying problems in place, one also learns which contacts are needed in order to address them; for example, with the community downstream that has built a dam that hinders fish from migrating. Such deliberative rationality would most likely amount to networked forms of governance. However, the technical demands of the directive seem to have prevented developments in that direction (Hagberg, 2003, pp. 221–3).

PARTICIPATION IN WFD IMPLEMENTATION AT THE EUROPEAN LEVEL

Central ideas of the WFD have been adapted from the IWRM and sustainable river basin management traditions. These management traditions hold the promise of more successful water management by paying more attention to scale, involving stakeholders and the public and by addressing sectorization in ways that traditional water management has not (Jöborn et al., 2005). Hedelin (2008) concludes that the directive does not pose any formal barriers to democratic participation but provides weak legal support for such practices. Yet the professional and academic debate on participation has intensified during the first round of the water management cycle. One may ask what degree of participation the directive intended. Arnstein's (1969) ladder of participation as employed by Hansen and Mäenpää (2007) helps us to analyse this question. Arnstein's ladder can be divided into three major levels of public participation. The lowest level, non-participation, represents manipulative or therapeutic uses of participation, where those who participate do not have any real influence on decisions. The intermediate level is tokenism, where participants may receive information, be consulted on recommended solutions, or asked to contribute to the definition of interest, actors and agenda without being able to make final decisions. The highest level is citizen power, where citizens control decisions either through partnerships, for instance in risk assessment, through delegated power, or through total control over decisions (see Table 7.2).

Examples of deliberation and participation in environmental governance are often taken from early stages of the policy cycle. It should be noted that for the WFD public participation should take place at all stages and at all levels of water governance. This means that public actors are involved as much in decision-making as in the implementation of overarching policy principles.

Table 7.2   Participatory methods in the FFW sorted according to Arnstein's (1969) ladder of public participation

Level of participation		Participatory method
Citizen power	Citizen control (PP in final decisions)	
	Delegated power (PP in final decisions)	Participatory groups
	Partnership (PP in risk assessment and recommendation of solutions)	Participatory groups
Tokenism	Placation (PP in defining interests, actors and setting the agenda)	Participatory groups
	Consultation (PP in risk assessment and discussion of recommended solutions)	Participatory groups, study groups, excursions
	Informing (one-way information)	Leaflets, pedagogic footpaths, demonstration areas of good practice, public information evenings, excursions, study material produced for study groups, on-site computerized forest training models 'martelodrôme'
Non-participation	Therapy	
	Manipulation	

What were the arguments for giving a prominent role to public participation in the directive and its implementation? The factors that help finalize the negotiations of a directive are not necessarily the same as those that facilitate implementation. As one national official explained, once the directive was finally agreed upon, the member states and the EC '[...] realised what a monster of a directive we had created and the vast practical, technical, legal and political difficulties and problems its implementation entailed. Then we drew the only possible conclusion and that was that we were obliged to co-operate and help each other in developing guidance' (Hagberg, 2003, p. 198). The Water Directors of the member states were responsible for this novel form of cooperation, known as the Common Implementation Strategy (CIS). The process resulted in a number of guidance documents based on experience gained in the member states and accession countries. However, since institutional and administrative arrangements belong exclusively to national competence, they were not to be discussed within the informal framework of the CIS (CIS, 2003). Somewhat problematically, this suggests that it is possible to separate institutional matters from technical and methodological issues. The guidance document on public participation, about 200 pages long, initially warns that its advice cannot be used as a blueprint for participation in all member states, since political, organizational and cultural conditions vary between countries (CIS, 2003, p. 2). Participation is viewed as necessary in order to deal with the complexities of water management, not as an end in itself (CIS, 2003, p. 14).

Parallel to the CIS process, other organizations also launched initiatives to strengthen the implementation of the WFD as well as the participatory components of river basin management. The European Commission and the World Wide Fund for Nature (WWF) hosted a water seminar series with some 300 European water stakeholders that resulted in a report on good practice in integrated river basin management (WWF/EC 2001). The European Environmental Bureau (EEB), representing approximately 140 environmental NGOs, had launched a water campaign to closely follow the development of the WFD on its way between the EC, the European Parliament and the Council. Because the final text was so complex, they published a handbook directed at NGOs and the wider public. In the handbook the EEB notes that '[f]rom the early beginnings of the legislative process, the Water Framework Directive developed into a compromise of numerous particular interests and most demanding technical expertise. As a result, the current legal text is unusually complex and virtually incomprehensible for a wider public' (Lanz and Scheuer, 2001, p. 1).

What motives for public participation can be found in these texts? First, it is observed that there is a need to distinguish between the components of 'information', 'consultation' and 'participation' in the WFD's Article 14. Participation is 'a *dynamic, interactive process* [that] relies on building trust and confidence that public/stakeholder views will be accommodated and *have a real influence* on developments of RBMPs' (WWF/EC, 2001, p. 24, emphasis in the original).

The motives for public participation include: (1) that key water management issues will be correctly identified and agreed upon at the river basin level; (2) that the knowledge, experience, aspirations and concerns of local communities will be included in river basin management plans and action programmes; (3) that programmes of measures will be more realistic but also more acceptable culturally and politically; (4) that conflicts can be minimized or avoided; (5) that costs will be lowered by avoiding errors in implementation; and (6) that regulatory and voluntary approaches are more likely to be enforceable if they have been developed in cooperation with stakeholders (WWF/EC, 2001, p. 23).

Participation is seen simultaneously as adding to the effectiveness of programmes of measures under the WFD and bolstering their legitimacy or 'acceptance'. It is emphasized that stakeholder views have to be seriously considered for this to happen but it still seems as if participation is essentially about securing harmony in the river basin. An instrumental take on participation is advanced through frequent calls for tailoring participatory models to the needs at different scales and of different stakeholder groups (CIS, 2003; WWF/EC, 2001, p. 24). Subsequent projects reflect this in their guidance on deliberative tools in sustainable river basin management, for instance ADVISOR (2004). These documents occasionally recognize that participatory approaches may clash with other approaches to water management. However, they do not discuss if different approaches may be inherently contradictory or what risks such contradictions may pose to policy legitimacy.

PARTICIPATION IN THE IMPLEMENTATION PHASE

The WFD was partly constructed in order to overcome the sectorization of water policy. To administer waters in river basins entails a landscape perspective that integrates other land uses and sectors in water management (Lundqvist, 2004). Forestry is such a land use that has potentially large impacts on the health of water ecosystems by affecting nutrient cycling, erosion, morphology, local climate as well as food chains (Life Forests for Water, 2007b).

Unlike agriculture, forest policy does not fall under EU competency, which means that forest stakeholders do not have the same basis for working with the WFD as, for example, farmers. Nevertheless, informal EU cooperation on forests has grown substantially in the last decades, for example through the forest strategy and action programme (Andersson, 2007, p. 1). New forest policy issues are often debated in pan-European contexts. The relationship between forests, forestry and water ecosystems has been addressed by the UN Economic Commission for Europe and the Ministerial Conference on the

Protection of Forests in Europe. An example is the need for preserving ecosystem services provided by forests, such as water purification. The conclusions from the pan-European meetings support the development of informal forest cooperation within the EU, like the forest strategy.

One of the many projects launched to support the implementation of the WFD was Life Forests for Water (2003–2007) (FFW). It concerned how European forests and forestry could contribute to the implementation of the WFD, by drawing on practical experience from river basins in Sweden, France and the UK and with additional expertise from Italy, Austria and Estonia. Project members were forest and water public authorities, research institutes, NGOs, sector organizations and local communities. The project addressed social, environmental and economic aspects of forests and water. Apart from having a cross-sectoral perspective, the project took into account the multi-level character of WFD water governance by establishing participatory groups at local, regional and national levels (Life Forests for Water, 2007b).

The main participatory measure employed by the FFW was to establish these participatory groups. Since forestry is but one of several land uses affecting water, sometimes project members joined existing participatory structures. Demonstration areas of best practice were established in cooperation with participatory groups. Information and education on forests and water were provided as well. It was directed toward stakeholders as well as the general public through leaflets, special editions of journals, courses, information evenings, excursions and pedagogic footpaths (see Table 7.2).

The project's ambition was to establish partnerships that could contribute to the characterization of water bodies as well as recommend and implement measures in order to improve water quality. This level of participation was only reached in groups at the local level in France. The participatory groups also contributed by identifying partners, interests and by setting the agenda. That this level of participation was easier to achieve in France and the UK was because institutions were already in place that could channel the groups' contributions into the decision-making process. At the local level in Sweden, forest owners met in study circles in which they identified common problems and discussed potential solutions. The provision of information and education formed an important basis for further participation in all MS who participated in the project (Life Forests for Water, 2007a; 2007b, pp. 14–16).

Participation under Administrative Rationality

The WFD is a complex piece of regulation, and this complexity is a challenge to participation. In Sweden, forestry is an important economic sector and, naturally, there has been widespread concern about the consequences of the directive for forestry practices. The concern was aggravated by the delay of environmental standards that would decide which waters need particular consideration. In May 2009, the editor of one of the major farming journals wrote: 'Who can explain the water directive? The more you try to grasp the water directive, the less you understand. Its introduction into Swedish legislation, the classification of water and the programmes of measures – all are extremely difficult to understand' (Vernersson, 2009, author's translation). However, on his way to a local water walk, Vernersson concludes that every new occasion to discuss the directive adds to his understanding, even though he has long given up expectations to suddenly understand it all (Vernersson, 2009). Vernersson's experience highlights the importance that participatory processes have continuity. This is particularly relevant for forestry where there is often a gap of decades between forestry operations. However, it may be difficult to motivate active participation when concrete results will only occur in a distant future (Life Forests for Water, 2007a).

The complexity of the directive combined with the immense time pressure has entailed processes where it has been difficult for officials from other sectors than water or the general public to give input. The technical aspects of the directive have been managed by experts and professionals. A general observation is that implementation at local and regional levels in many cases had to begin before standards and regulations were completed, or before the relevant CIS documents became available. This means that there was uncertainty not only about the directive per se, but also about how its content would be interpreted. The prolonged absence of established standards, for example on whether a water body should be regarded as having good ecological status or not, has entailed uncertainty as to which measures would actually be required and thus also about the scope for decisions by participatory groups (Life Forests for Water, 2008). For those initiating participatory processes at the local level, two alternative strategies were available: either you extrapolate the likely outcomes of national processes establishing environmental criteria, and risk increased scepticism among stakeholders should you be wrong, or you avoid talking much about the project's connection to the directive, and instead motivate activities by the problems at hand in the local context. In the long run, downplaying the importance of the directive may negatively affect its legitimacy, which would be paradoxical given that increased legitimacy would be the reason for adopting a participatory approach in implementation in the first place.

An example of when the technical setting of standards with limited transparency risked the legitimacy of the directive can be seen in the set of biological criteria for good water status in Northern Sweden. The criteria were based on the presence of a set of indicator species and initially worked on a 'one missing, all out' principle. As there are natural variations in the presence of species, water streams that seemed to be of very good quality, but missing species, could drop one class. From a scientific perspective this seemed perfectly legitimate.

However, this did not make sense to those who experienced the stream in reality, and this made the whole system seem questionable. Fortunately, it was possible to modify some of these counter-intuitive effects at later stages in the process (Jägrud, 2007 p. 16, Life Forests for Water, 2007b, p. 38).

Participation under Economic Rationality

Van Ast and Boot (2003, pp. 558–9) have argued that public participation would be useful for managing the economic dimensions of the WFD. Interested stakeholders could contribute to the definition of the scales at which economic analyses should be performed and the design and implementation of economic policy instruments. In general, economic rationality is absent in the participatory context of the directive, especially in cases where water is perceived to be a plentiful resource, as in Sweden. Indeed, in the negotiations of the directive, Swedish forestry and hydropower sectors were exempted from the principle of full cost recovery for water use. In Sweden, water fees are only paid to municipal waterworks. The pricing of water has remained a controversial issue and the implementation of the WFD's pricing policy is subject to a government investigatory committee (Dir. 2008:157). This means that the fees or recovery schemes expected in the directive to fund programmes of measures are not yet in place in Sweden. In France, a system of water fees is used to finance water-related projects. This facilitated the timely implementation of ideas for measures developed in the participatory groups, and thus increased the sense that the process contributed to something concrete (Life Forests for Water, 2008).

Participation under Deliberative Rationality

The deliberative rationality includes the notion that participants in a policy process can transform their ideas, preferences and perceived interests through interaction with others, which in turn promotes social learning (see discussion in Chapter 2). A major practical obstacle is the time available for different groups of actors to deliberate (Jonsson, 2005). Although groups might be highly interested in the issue, the increased use of participatory approaches puts certain groups under pressure, forcing them to prioritize. Sectorization aggravates this situation, for example when public authorities establish participatory processes on issues where actors' engagement overlap (for example on water issues in agriculture and forestry respectively), or when different authorities set up deliberative processes in the same sector (Life Forests for Water, 2007a). When the ambition is to work at different levels, as is the case in river basin management, the capacity of stakeholder groups to take part varies, which can skew the discussion. For example, in Germany, Kastens and Newig

(2008) found that environmental NGOs have employed representatives only at higher levels, while there may not be enough volunteers to engage in all sub-basin groups at the local level. Similar problems are found in Sweden. Even professionals representing large forest companies were concerned that they could not participate in all groups, since there are so many at the local level (Johansson, 2007).

Another important question concerns to what extent those invited to take part in a participatory process perceive a common problem. In the case of forests and water in the Mediterranean river basins, problems such as floods were perceived as very serious and also caused conflicts between upstream and downstream communities. Here, participatory methods worked quite well, and it was not difficult to motivate the presence of forest representatives in established water management structures. In Southern Sweden, there was great interest in taking care of one's own water, and a number of groups were established locally within the project. In Northern Sweden, the sparse population and the water-rich landscapes made it less obvious to actors why they should initiate activities in order to restore damaged waters. Here, public officers and experts played the role of public informers. Public officers active in the project began with the ambition that groups be self-governing and responsible for ideas and activities, but found that they had to contribute with suggestions (Life Forests for Water, 2007a; Johansson, 2007). The challenge was not so much about giving the public access to the process (even though that problem also existed), but to motivate actors to get involved when they were not even convinced that there was a problem in the local water ecosystems (Life Forests for Water, 2008, p. 30). In this respect, information and educational activities can be important, even though they belong on the lower rungs of the participatory ladder.

In some groups, forest actors expressed concern that they, by participating, would be held accountable for views or decisions that they did not support. This risk is perceived to be more pronounced in informal structures that have weak connections to the political system. Participation takes place in contexts that are politicized to different degrees. In Sweden, stakeholder representatives, experts from research organizations and public agencies generally dominated the participatory groups. Local politicians were interested in the benefits of collaboration between forestry and water managers (for example wilderness tourism), but they were not involved in the practical discussions or in any conflicts about water management because they regarded such issues as technical rather than political. In France, by contrast, the institutional framework, as well as the importance of the local mayor, made local politics a crucial aspect of promoting water–forest collaboration. Tangible conflicts around river management contributed to this situation and concerned, for example, the relation between forest management and downstream floods (Life Forests for Water, 2008).

Knowledge Transfer and Sense of Place

Experts on forests and water from research organizations, NGOs and public agencies came to play an important role in the FFW project. These experts were often invited to participatory groups at different levels. In some river basins they were responsible for guiding the process to implement measures together with stakeholders. The experts, mainly researchers but also employees of NGOs or sector organizations, were also important because they interpreted the WFD in relation to various contexts when national policies were not yet in place. Whereas public officers and stakeholders often worked at the same policy level as the stakeholders in a group, the experts who participated did so at various policy levels. Thus, experts came to have access to information that was not readily available at one single level. Even though scientific knowledge per se may only to a lesser extent result in substantive legitimacy in European environmental policy, the experts' access to information and their role as trusted translators of that information contributed to procedural legitimacy (cf. Engelen et al., 2008). The experts also contributed to the networked character of water governance in forestry by functioning as nodes between sector representatives and public officers.

In the discussions on how to implement the WFD in Sweden, the potential importance of a sense of place was often alluded to (Hagberg, 2003). By working in watersheds or river basins, people would recognize their particular relations to water, and through increased familiarity with local circumstances come to care more for water and how it is managed. The sense of place could blunt the edge of conflicting interests in the watershed, and contribute to the legitimacy of different policy measures. Observations from the FFW project indicate that communities can easily relate to water when building a sense of place. For example, the restoration of cultural remnants in the riverbed creates a sense of historic continuity to a community while promoting the social value of the place, for instance for tourism. However, rather than an existing tie to place leading to spontaneous activities, the participatory activities initiated by public officers contributed to the construction of a sense of place and care for the watershed (Life Forests for Water, 2007b, pp. 27–8).

LEGITIMACY AND EFFECTIVENESS IN THE CONTEXT OF MULTIPLE GOVERNANCE RATIONALITIES

The simultaneous presence of multiple governance rationalities offers both synergies and clashes. In the case of the WFD in forestry, one of the greatest challenges was the delay in the development of standards and environmental quality norms under administrative rationality. Consequently, participatory approaches had to be implemented in the shadow of hierarchy, in the shape of a regulation the practical consequences of which were difficult to predict. There were also synergies between rationalities. One example was the system of water fees in France, which made it possible to realize some of the recommendations from the participatory groups. It is, however, striking that no conscious efforts were made to analyse the potential effects of employing different governance rationalities during the negotiation of the directive. Participation in the WFD was meant to contribute to the legitimacy and effectiveness of water policy. Yet there was little discussion on how, for example, the technical standards of the directive may risk legitimacy.

The sense that the rules of the game shift over time renders the agreements reached in participatory processes fragile, especially in the context of multi-level governance. Here, experts who move between administrative levels can alleviate some of the uncertainty through first-hand information on likely outcomes of technical processes taking place at the European or national levels. Still, there is a very tangible dilemma of accountability, which is aggravated by the mix of formal and informal networks for participation. Who should be held accountable for agreements reached through deliberation? The existence of a coherent institutional context for deliberation, like in France, improves the chances for accountability. At the same time, formalization may be less attractive to actors adverse to administrative procedures. Public officers, who are often responsible for initiating participatory processes, can contribute to long-term legitimacy of participation by taking into account the discrepancy between the sectorized public sector and the everyday conditions of local actors at the level of management.

Participation is encouraged if affected actors can unite around a common problem. A common awareness of, for example, flooding problems existed in the UK and France but not in Sweden. For deliberative rationality to be successful it is crucial that those who can actually affect the problem are involved. This was illustrated in a small watershed in Northern Sweden where the members of the participatory group maintained that it was not forestry that caused the most severe problems, but farming practices by land owners who did not participate (Life Forests for Water, 2007a). Such situations undermine the legitimacy of the process as well as hinder environmental effectiveness.

Generalizing from the experience of FFW it seems that input legitimacy of the WFD in forestry can be strengthened through participatory processes that involve stakeholders as well as the public. It should, however, be recognized that not all relevant actors either want or have the opportunity or capacity to participate. Accountability in relation to participation is endangered when the regulative dimensions of the directive are not yet in place, which causes large degrees of uncertainty about 'the rules of the game'. It should be stressed that education and information, low on the rungs of Arnstein's ladder of public participation, can contribute significantly to long-term deliberative quality. When participants gather to learn about a problem it provides an opportunity for equal exchange on the issue. Also the presence of a voice from 'outside' the group may open up discussions that would otherwise risk getting stuck in interest-based arguments.

Does participation render EU water policy more effective? This question on policy effectiveness is difficult to answer based on the material of the present study. The first water management cycle is not yet complete. Nevertheless, it is clear that some measures contributing to improved ecological status of water could not be implemented without the participation of forest owners and professionals. This is especially true for measures addressing diffuse source pollution and the health of small streams. In terms of effectiveness related to compliance, the EC has already brought complaints to the ECJ concerning member states that have not managed to implement institutional reform in time. The experience from the FFW shows that participation is hampered by the absence of institutions adapted to the water management cycle. In other words, institutional effectiveness is crucial for qualitative participation, rather than the other way around.

NOTES

1. Participant observation was conducted by the author in her function as project manager of the FFW 2004–2006.
2. Each river basin is divided into water bodies, or elements of surface or ground water that are monitored and evaluated according to environmental quality norms, for example a lake, a river or a stretch of coastal water (2000/60/EC, Article 2).

REFERENCES

ADVISOR (2004), 'Integrated deliberative decision processes for water resources planning and evaluation', guidance document, accessed 10 April 2008 at http://ecoman.dcea.fct.unl.pt/projects/advisor.

Andersson, Therese (2007), 'En gemensam europeisk skogspolitik? En integrationste-oretisk studie av ett politikområde på tillväxt', ['A common European forest policy? An integration theoretical study of a growing political field'], PhD dissertation, Department of Political Science, Umeå University, Sweden.

Arnstein, S. (1969) 'A ladder of participation', *Journal of the American Institute of Planners*, **35**(4), 216–24.

Carter, Neil (2007), *The Politics of the Environment: Ideas, Activism, Policy*, 2nd edn, Cambridge: Cambridge University Press.

CIS (2003), *Common Implementation Strategy for the Water Framework Directive (2000/60/EC)*, Guidance document No. 8 on public participation in relation to the Water Framework Directive, Luxembourg: Office for Official Publications of the European Communities.

Directive 2000/60/EC of the European Parliament and of the Council of 23 October 2000 establishing a framework for Community action in the field of water policy, *Official Journal L 327*, 22/12/2000, pp. 22–39.

Dir 2008:157, '*Kommittédirektiv Styrmedel för bättre vattenkvalitét*' ['Directive for the government investigative committee policy instruments for improved water quality'], accessed 15 April 2009 at http://www.sou.gov.se/kommittedirektiv/ 2008/dir2008_157.pdf.

Engelen, Ewald, J. Keulartz and G. Leistra (2008), 'European nature conservation policy making: from substantive to procedural sources of legitimacy', in Jozef Keulartz and Gilbert Leistra (eds), *Legitimacy in European Nature Conservation Policy: Case Studies in Multilevel Governance*, Amsterdam: Springer, pp. 3–21.

European Environmental Bureau (EEB) (2001), *EEB Position Paper: Making the EU Water Framework Directive Work. Ten Actions for Implementing a Better European Water Policy*, Brussels: EEB.

Gouldson, A., E. Lopez-Gunn, J. Van Alstine, Y. Rees, M. Davies and V. Krishnarayan (2008), 'New alternative and complementary environmental policy instruments and the implementation of the Water Framework Directive', *European Environment*, **18**, 359–70.

Hagberg, Lovisa (2003), 'Finding a place for green politics: political space–time, globalisation and new environmental policy concepts', PhD dissertation, Department of Political Science, Umeå University, Sweden.

Hansen, H.S. and M. Mäenpää (2007), 'An overview of the challenges for public participation in river basin management and planning', *Management of Environmental Quality: An International Journal*, **19**(1), 67–84.

Hedelin, B. (2008), 'Criteria for the assessment of processes for sustainable river basin management and their congruence with the EU Water Framework Directive', *European Environment*, **18**, 228–42.

Jägrud, Linnea (2007), *Life Forests for Water – Summary from the Final Seminar in Lycksele 22–24 August 2006, Rapport 5 2007*, Jönköping: Skogsstyrelsen.

Jöborn, A., I. Danielsson, B. Arheimer, A. Jonsson, M.H. Larsson, L.J. Lundqvist, M. Löwgren and K. Tonderski (2005), 'Integrated water management for eutrophication control: public participation, pricing policy and catchment modeling', *Ambio*, **34**(7), 482–88.

Johansson, Mats (2007), *Lokal och regional samverkan kring vatten – nu och i framtiden. Rapport om samverkansprocessen i Bottenvikens vattendistrikt* [*Local and regional cooperation concerning water – now and in the future. Report on the collaborative process in the Gulf of Bothnia Water District*], Umeå: Länsstyrelsen Västerbotten.

Jonsson, Anna (2005), 'Public participation in water resources management: stakeholder voices on degree, scale, potential, and methods in future water management', *Ambio*, **34**(7), 495–500.

Kastens, B. and J. Newig (2008), 'Will participation foster the successful implementation of the water framework directive? The case of agricultural groundwater protection in northwest Germany', *Local Environment*, **13**(1), 27–41.

Ker Rault, Ph.A. and P.J. Jeffrey (2008), 'Deconstructing public participation in the Water Framework Directive: implementation and compliance with the letter or with the spirit of the law?', *Water and Environment Journal*, **22**, 241–9.

Lanz, K. and S. Scheuer (2001), *EEB Handbook on EU Water Policy under the Water Framework Directive*, Brussels: European Environmental Bureau (EEB).

Life Forests for Water (2007a), *Erfarenheter från Projektet Forests for Water, Projekt PM*, [*Experience from the Forest for Water project*], Jönköping: Skogsstyrelsen.

Life Forests For Water (2007b), Technical final report, accessed 30 March 2009 at www.skogsstyrelsen/life.
Life Forests for Water (2008), 'Demonstration of opportunities on forest land to support the implementation of the Water Framework Directive', comparative report by Life FFW Advisory Expert Group, manuscript, Jönköping: Skogsstyrelsen.
Lundqvist, L.J. (2004), 'Integrating Swedish water resource management: a multi-level governance trilemma', *Local Environment*, **9**(5), 413–24.
McCormick, J. (2001), *Environmental Policy in the European Union*, Basingstoke: Palgrave.
Richardson, J. (1994), 'EU water policy: uncertain agendas, shifting networks and complex coalitions', *Environmental Politics*, **3**(4), 139–67.
Van Ast, J.A. and S.P. Boot (2003), 'Participation in European water policy', *Physics and Chemistry of the Earth*, **28**, 555–62.
Vernersson, L. (2009), 'Vem kan förklara vattendirektivet?' [Who can explain the WFD?], *ATL*, 14 May.
WWF/EC (2001), *Elements of Good Practice in Integrated River Basin Management: A Practical Resource for implementing the EU Water Framework Directive*, Brussels: WWF.

PART III

State and local governance

8. The deliberative turn in Swedish sustainability governance: participation from below or governing from above?

Roger Hildingsson

INTRODUCTION

The promise of 'new' modes of governance examined in this book clearly relates to contemporary efforts to promote sustainable development. The concept of sustainable development has, ever since the Brundtland Report in 1987 and the United Nations Conference on Environment and Development (UNCED) in Rio 1992, provided an overarching framework and an impetus for policy innovations and experimentation with various modes in environmental governance, in particular in developed countries. The sustainable development discourse is aligned with the post-Rio participatory mantra on bottom-up implementation and inclusion of stakeholders and with what is referred to in this book as a deliberative turn to environmental politics. Despite this, states have assumed the most prominent role in the process of achieving sustainable development. Thus, sustainability reforms have to a large extent been state-led and characterized by transforming the hierarchical forms of governance.

In this chapter such state reforms to enact modes of sustainability governance are studied in the context of Sweden. The objective is to examine how institutional reforms and policy innovations to promote broader notions of 'sustainability governance' in the Swedish context have transformed the rationalities and forms of environmental governance, and to what extent they adhere to deliberative ideals as set out in the introduction (see Chapters 1 and 3). The term 'sustainability governance' is closely associated with the normative governance tradition, as outlined in Chapter 1, which promises to resolve problems of legitimacy and effectiveness. A specific aim is to assess how such innovations have affected the deliberative quality (input legitimacy) and effectiveness (output legitimacy) of environmental governance. The chapter focuses on innovations in state-led and hierarchical forms of governance and transformations in the underlying rationalities (see Table 2.1, Chapter 2, this volume). While such forms of governance rest upon administrative rationality, policy developments have also been influenced by economic and deliberative rationalities. My argument is, however, that calls for new modes of governance have not replaced, but have rather led to innovations in hierarchical forms of governance.

First, after a brief justification of the critical role of the state in sustainability governance and of the Swedish case, the chapter sets out what in practice might indicate a deliberative ideal in environmental governance. Building on the theoretical chapters (Chapters 2 and 3), this section discusses how such an ideal might enhance the state's responsiveness to environmental concerns and improve performance in a national context, for example through more reflexive governance arrangements. Second, the empirical analysis provides an overview of the main policy developments in Sweden since the late 1980s, divided into four phases. Elaborating on the different approaches to sustainability governance present during these phases, policy innovations in state-led forms of governance are examined with a view to assess reflexivity and effectiveness. Third, the following section discusses the deliberative quality of the Swedish model of sustainability governance in particular. Finally, the concluding section discusses to what extent the efforts to promote sustainability governance in Sweden apply to the (green) quest for more effective and legitimate policies.

THE ROLE OF THE STATE IN SUSTAINABILITY GOVERNANCE

Over the last two decades we have witnessed a transformation, be it rhetorical or substantial, in environmental governance towards what could be called sustainability governance. This transformation implies a reorientation of environmental governance towards the broader agenda of economic, ecological and social sustainability, often referred to as the three pillars of sustainable development. As discussed in Chapter 1, the deliberative turn has been associated with the rise of new modes of governance for managing environmental problems and for steering societies in more sustainable directions. This strive towards more effective forms of governance can be understood as a response to both market failures in internalizing environmental externalities, and politico-administrative failures in governing environmental problems in effective and legitimate ways. In this chapter I argue that the deliberative turn has not only implied innovations in terms of market- and network-based modes of governance but also in hierarchical forms, exemplified by new forms of public regulation and new policy instruments.

The role of the state and administrative rationality has been a central issue in the environmental debate since the 1960s. Although pending over time, many green political scholars have been rather reluctant to view the state as a source of environmentally sound governance (see Chapter 1). In recent years scholars in political ecology are 'calling the state back in' in an effort to develop theories about the green state (Dryzek et al., 2003; Eckersley, 2004; Barry and Eckersley, 2005) or the ecological state (Meadowcroft, 2005; Lundqvist, 2001a). Such efforts to rethink the role of the state in environmental governance largely contrast with concerns that the state will be hollowed out in the era of globalization. Even if we admit that global economic integration has limited the scope for state control and induced a move from traditional forms of government towards new forms of governance, the state remains, as Pierre and Peters (2000) argue, at the centre as a fundamental source of authority for legitimate and effective governance. As argued by Lundqvist (2004a), states are the only authority with enough legitimacy to represent its citizens and with enough coercive powers to facilitate the structural transformations necessary for sustainable outcomes. Given the amplitude of the sustainability challenge it is, thus, 'difficult to imagine how such changes might occur on the kind of scale that is needed without the active support of states' (Eckersley, 2004, p. 6). This justifies attention to the forms of governance exercised by the state in search for more legitimate and effective environmental governance.

In Sweden environmental governance has changed considerably during the last 20 years. In international comparison, the Swedish case is often invoked as one of the most progressive examples of institutional and policy reforms towards sustainability governance (Lafferty and Meadowcroft, 2000; Eckersley, 2004; Lundqvist, 2004a; Meadowcroft, 2005). The Swedish efforts to translate the sustainability concept into governance arrangements has induced a 'renewal, and expansion, of environmental policy' (Eckerberg, 2001, p. 17) and a range of experiments with various modes of governance. For sure, such reforms have turned 'ecological sustainable development' into a key political priority and improved the problem-solving capacity of environmental governance.

A DELIBERATIVE TURN TOWARDS MORE REFLEXIVE ENVIRONMENTAL GOVERNANCE?

As discussed in Chapter 1, the promise of new modes of governance holds that new governance arrangements can strengthen both the legitimacy and effectiveness of environmental policy. Advancements in the deliberative quality of governance processes will increase the responsiveness to environmental concerns and promote more sustainable outcomes. Deliberative approaches are thought to enhance performance and effectiveness (output legitimacy) through wider inclusion of interests by means of participation or representation and through mechanisms for transparency and accountability (input legitimacy). In such a view a deliberative turn would manifest itself through greater representation of various perspectives in public deliberations, ultimately to the extent that the views of all those affected are represented as if they were present in the deliberations (Eckersley, 2004, p. 111). While traditional environmental governance hardly lives up to such ideal conditions for inclusiveness and unconstrained dialogue (see Chapter 3, this volume), normative governance approaches promise to fulfil the deliberative ideal to a greater extent through more participatory, reflective and reflexive governance arrangements.

On this point sustainability governance is interrelated with concepts about reflexive modernization (Beck et al., 1994) and reflexive governance (Voss and Kemp, 2006). In green political thought, the term 'reflexivity' represents a higher order of reflectiveness and responsiveness to socio-ecological problems and risks caused by modernity. The reflexivity of the governance system is in this view closely associated with its deliberative quality. As indicated by Voss and Kemp (2006, p. 5), reflexive governance implies that 'one calls into question the foundations of governance itself, that is, the concepts, practices and institutions by which societal development is governed, and that one envisions alternatives and reinvents and shapes those foundations'. Thus, efforts to improve participation and representation in sustainability governance contribute to the enhancement of such reflexivity through means of dialogue, contestation and critical self-reflection on ecological problems and common norms as well as on the ends and means of environmental governance. As discussed in Chapter 3, such public deliberation is thought to foster an orientation towards more systemic and structural transformations conducive to ecological sustainability and 'stronger' forms of ecological modernization (Eckersley, 2004, p. 70).

Eckersley proposes a regulatory ideal for transformations in state environmental governance against which deliberative quality and reflexivity can be assessed. This ideal proposes reforms to improve the conditions for public deliberation and thereby to ensure both input and output legitimacy. Efforts to ensure input legitimacy of state environmental governance are manifested in green constitutional design (Eckersley, 2004, Hayward, 2005) and new mechanisms for participation, deliberation and contestation. Efforts to improve output legitimacy are found in institutional reforms and policy innovations towards strategic goal formulation, choice and design of policy instruments, implementation strategies and enforcement mechanisms. For greening state governance, Eckersley refers to policy change at four levels; (i) policy instruments (for example steering rather than rowing); (ii) policy goals (for example iteratively put under scrutiny); (iii) the policy paradigm or hierarchy of policy goals (giving priority to sustainability); and (iv) the role of the state (upgrading ecological rationality to a core state imperative). Substantial transformations at the first two levels (policies and goals) do not necessitate reflexivity in a systemic sense but do rather imply reflection on a 'full range of attributes to the subject in question' (Stirling, 2006, p. 227). Transformations at the third and fourth level, however, require more reflexive approaches that go beyond the considerations of reflection. A key element in such reflexive governance might be to provide for and facilitate the interactive and iterative participatory processes deemed necessary for critical and systemic self-reflection (Voss and Kemp, 2006).

FROM ENVIRONMENTAL TO SUSTAINABILITY GOVERNANCE IN SWEDEN

Efforts to introduce models of sustainability governance in Sweden since the late 1980s offer a critical case for examining transformations in hierarchical environmental governance. The following empirical analysis, based on documentary analysis and secondary literature, provides an overview of policy developments in Sweden over four phases. These phases represent distinctly different approaches to sustainability governance and variations in the main rationalities and modes (see Table 8.1). The first phase represents the early adoption of the sustainability concept in Sweden, which spurred a reorientation towards more anticipatory environmental regulation. The second phase after the Rio summit is primarily characterized by what has been termed the local Agenda 21 movement aligned with aspirations to increase stakeholder and citizen participation. The third phase embodies a distinct shift in Swedish environmental policy induced by the launch of a new strategy for 'Ecologically Sustainable Sweden' in 1996. This strategy was implemented in the following years through a set of institutional and policy reforms such as the new Environmental Code and the Environmental Quality Objectives (EQOs). These reforms still signify Swedish environmental governance, although the particular model of sustainability governance has been challenged since the electoral turnover in 2006. The present fourth phase reflects that and an increased attention to economic rationality and more market-based forms of governance.

The Adoption of the Sustainability Concept

The sustainability concept was adopted early in Swedish environmental policy. The Brundtland Report was acknowledged and taken as a justification for policy innovation in environmental regulation by the environmental minister at

Table 8.1   Four phases towards sustainability governance in Sweden

Phase	Main feature of phase	Main rationality and mode of governance	'Deliberative approach'
1987–1992	Anticipatory pollution prevention control.	Administrative: Policy integration ('sector responsibility').	Corporatist inclusion of key societal interests
1992–1997	'Eco-cycle society' and Local Agenda 21	Deliberative: Local implementation of Eco-cycle society'. Administrative: legislative reforms (e.g. 'eco-cycle producer responsibility', new forestry act, etc) Economic: carbon tax, etc	Stakeholder involvement, cooperative arrangements (primarily at local level).
1997–2006	Ecologically Sustainable Sweden	Administrative: Steering-by-environmental-objectives; Green constitutional reform; Biodiversity protection; etc Economic: Eco-tax and LIP reforms; etc	Improved state reflexivity, but limited inclusion of key societal interests
2006–	Climate change policy	Economic: market-based policies (e.g. carbon pricing); R&D and industrial policy	Cooperative arrangements, but limited inclusion of key societal interests

the time, Mrs Birgitta Dahl. In the mid-1980s she argued for a new third way for environmental policy for the Social Democratic Party (Anshelm, 1995). In response to the increasingly strong public concern for environmental issues, policy integration and anticipatory approaches to promote sustainable development were addressed in two comprehensive Swedish environmental bills (Prop. 1987/88:85; 1990/91:90). Although targeting administrative and regulatory agencies at the central and regional level, the ambition was clearly to change the traditional policy paradigm characterized by remedial strategies towards more anticipatory pollution prevention. In order to improve environmental effectiveness and performance, and overcome problems with compartmentalization, a new environmental policy strategy for policy integration emerged during this period in terms of the renowned Swedish sector responsibility for environmental risks (Lundqvist, 2004a, p. 122). The need for a new strategy informed by the responsibility of 'different sectors of society [...] to prevent new environmental damage' had already been addressed in 1988 (Prop. 1987/88:85, p. 35; Nilsson and Persson, 2003). The benefits of an integrated and cross-sectoral approach to strengthen ecological concerns in all relevant societal sectors were, however, not fully articulated until after what have been termed the environmental elections in 1988 (Anshelm, 1995). The full extent of the new strategy became obvious in the second bill, *A good living environment* (Prop. 1990/91:90), which reproduced much of the recently adopted new social democratic environmental policy programme (Anshelm, 1995). Stating that 'the mission of the 1990s is to re-adjust all societal activities in an ecological direction' (Prop. 1990/91:90, p. 11) it proposed a coherent, cross-sectoral and decentralized approach for integrating environmental concerns in policy areas such as road, air and railway transportation, agriculture and forestry (later also energy). National authorities were given certain responsibilities for adopting sector plans and programmes for implementing environmental objectives within their respective sector. The Swedish Environmental Protection Agency (EPA) and the Chemical Inspectorate, as the central environmental authorities, were given a particular oversight and facilitating role. Although authorities were encouraged to involve private (business and industry) and civil society actors in this process, the reform mainly targeted the public environmental administration. The efforts to improve integration still remained within the realms of administrative regulation and were thus more an act of transforming the administrative rationality in environmental governance than of introducing new modes of governance. At the beginning of the 1990s 'such integration was still more of an aspiration than an actual, effective change' (Lundqvist, 2004a, p. 124; Nilsson and Persson, 2003).

Post-Rio: The Eco-cycle Society and Local Agenda 21

The Swedish model of sustainability governance is clearly associated with the post-Rio participatory and bottom-up approach to implementation. After UNCED, the new conservative–liberal government began to promote the sustainability concept to the public and a broad range of societal actors. The preparations for UNCED were already a prelude to this reorientation. A variety of stakeholders such as industry, agricultural organizations, municipalities and environmental NGOs were invited by the government to take part in the preparations as well as in the Swedish delegation to Rio. The Environmental Advisory Council, chaired by the environment minister, Mr Olof Johansson, in cooperation with the Swedish Association of Local Authorities and NGOs, organized a series of national and regional conferences to promote the idea of sustainable development and to discuss the implications of UNCED (SOU, 1992:104). Recurrent themes during this period were the eco-cycle society concept, perceived synonymous with sustainability (Prop. 1992/93:180), and the bottom-up approach to implementation at the local level. In particular, local municipalities were emphasized as having a critical role for initiating local Agenda 21 (LA21) processes that involved all key societal stakeholders (Hägerhäll and Gooch, 2002). This led to what Eckerberg (2001) and others have called a broad local Agenda 21 movement for true sustainable development (Lafferty and Meadowcroft, 2000). The response from Swedish municipalities seems outstanding in an international comparison and spurred involvement of interest organizations and grass-roots in developing local visions and strategies for sustainable development. During 1994–95 a majority of Swedish municipalities introduced activities to encourage such local processes (SALA, 1996), and in 1997 the National Committee for Agenda 21 reported that all municipalities had initiated some kind of LA21 process (SOU, 1997:105). A survey later confirmed this finding and also found that 60 per cent of the 289 Swedish municipalities had adopted LA21 strategies by 1998 (Eckerberg and Brundin, 1999). Local Agenda 21 in Sweden was, at least rhetorically, clearly associated with participatory and deliberative approaches and aspirations to open up strategic decision-making processes to a wider audience of stakeholders and citizens. These LA21 processes led to a range of experiments in local democracy and stakeholder participation and have, as Eckerberg and Forsberg (1998, p. 343) put it, brought about a 'new form of relation between the local administration and the civil society [that] can be described as a process of trial and error'.

This positive view of the Swedish LA21 process can, however, be challenged. First, it can be discussed whether these processes were truly local or bottom-up in the sense expressed in the policy rhetoric. With reference to Chapter 28 in the Agenda 21 document, local authorities were emphasized as crucial to initiate and adopt LA21 strategies to address local problems of sustainability in a bottom-up fashion through the involvement of stakeholders and citizens. However, it can be questioned whether these processes were anchored in local problems of sustainability or rather whether they were influenced by recommendations from the national government, authorities and organizations. Nordgren (2005) elucidates the striking similarities in the contents of the LA21 strategies across different types of municipalities, a finding that clearly contrasts with earlier studies concluding local Agenda 21 in Sweden as being well founded in local sets of problems.

Second, it is questionable whether the Swedish stakeholder participation approach to local Agenda 21 really improved and opened up the decision-making process to a wider set of constituencies (Hägerhäll and Gooch,

2002). At best, it broadened the participation of stakeholders in consultation processes and implementation of environmental policy through means of information, dialogue and cooperative arrangements. Alternatively, one could argue that local Agenda 21 was handled in a rather business-as-usual fashion involving only well-established interests such as worker unions, business organizations and large NGOs in order to build functioning coalitions and networks for implementation (see further Chapter 11, this volume) and to counteract potential opposition. In such a perspective, aspirations to increase citizen participation appear to have been simply an act of symbolic rhetoric to anchor local and national governmental initiatives (Hägerhäll and Gooch, 2002). Local Agenda 21 rather implied an assemblage of implementation strategies than a process for problem definition and policy formation, even if exceptions can be found in a few progressive municipalities. This is problematic from a democratic point of view. As Hedrén (2002, p. 30) has put it, if '(p)eople are invited not to take part in politics, but rather in implementation [...] that is not politics, and certainly not democracy'.

Hence, what emerges from this analysis is a picture that seriously contrasts with the dominant account of the Swedish experience where local Agenda 21 constitutes a success story in international comparison (Eckerberg, 2001; SOU, 1997:105). While these processes did lead to innovations in local public governance and experimentations in new forms for stakeholder and citizen involvement, it is questionable whether they advanced local democracy as emphasized by some observers. Later studies (for example Eckerberg and Dahlgren, 2005) conclude that local priorities on Agenda 21 were downsized with the emergence of the new reform for local investment programmes during the following phase, to which we turn in the next section.

Institutional Reforms for Ecologically Sustainable Sweden

Returning to power in late 1994, the Social Democratic government continued the previous emphasis on local Agenda 21 and stakeholder participation at the local level. However, when Mr Göran Persson was appointed Prime Minister in 1996, the national strategy started to change. He endorsed a new social democratic mission for an ecologically sustainable Sweden. He made strong symbolic reference to the Swedish welfare model in launching a vision for the Greening of the People's Home (Lundqvist, 2004b) as a Swedish account of the green welfare state. This epitomized an eco-modernist strategy for reconciling ecological concerns with economic growth and social welfare objectives by means of reconstructing and revitalizing the Swedish welfare state. But, as emphasized by Lundqvist (2004a), the consecutive institutional reforms seem to go well beyond such weak eco-modernist (Christoff, 1996) or cosmetic strategies (Meadowcroft, 2007). This is, for instance, reflected in the development of long-term environmental objectives and the focus on ecological sustainability. However, although expressed as a continuation of the support to local Agenda 21 (SOU, 1997:105), the Greening of the People's Home in effect marked the beginning of a distinct shift towards a more hierarchical top-down policy approach (Lundqvist, 2001b). The new strategy for Ecological Sustainable Sweden may even be considered a counter-discourse to the LA21 movement which caused the latter to successively fizzle out during the coming years.

The new philosophy, singled out in a couple of seminal speeches in 1996 by the Prime Minister, was based on two fundamental ideas reconciled in the sustainability concept and the vision of a green welfare state; the significance of the 'Green People's Home' and the strong state (Svenning, 2005). The new framing clearly adhered to traditional social democratic values, albeit under the guise of contemporary ecological concerns. In early 1997 the government appointed a Ministerial Delegation for Ecological Sustainable Development, led by the environmental minister at the time, Mrs Anna Lindh. In an action programme comprising a 93-point list of measures, the delegation outlined the new strategy. In particular, three major investment programmes were announced: the Ecocycle Billion; the Energy Transformation Programme (9 billion SEK); and the Local Investment Programme (LIP) for ecological sustainability (6 billion SEK, 1998–2002). In particular the LIP reform was used as a key economic policy measure to structure and steer the implementation and institutionalization of the new policy discourse (Lundqvist, 2004b). In this regard, the new strategy combined administrative and economic rationalities, although the dominant form of governance remained within the realm of hierarchy. Although these subsidy programmes as well as the post-1998 ecological tax reforms indicate greater attention to economic instruments, the hierarchical and administrative logic of top-down steering and delegation of authority remained during this period.

The new strategy also comprised a couple of institutional reforms, later implemented after the 1998 elections. The most important of these were a new set of Environmental Quality Objectives and the new Environmental Code, both introduced in 1999, as well as the ecological tax reforms implemented with political support from the Left and Green parties. While the tax reforms have been crucial for climate and energy policy, the former two institutional innovations are at the core of the Swedish model for sustainability governance. As such, they have turned out to be the most lasting features of the reorientation of Swedish environmental governance during the 1990s. These reforms have been critical for advancing the overall institutional and policy effectiveness of Swedish environmental governance and seem also to have facilitated a more reflexive approach to environmental concerns.

The Environmental Quality Objectives reform: a steering-by-objectives strategy

The main feature of the Swedish sustainability reform has been the introduction of a comprehensive management-by-objectives strategy (Lundqvist, 2004a) framed by a set of national Environmental Quality Objectives (EQOs). In 1999 the Parliament adopted 15 EQOs while outlining the new structure and strategy for their implementation (another objective on biodiversity was later introduced in 2005) (Prop. 1997/98:145). The EQOs are based on assessments of desired environmental quality resting on scientific definitions of ecological sustainability (resilience). In the 1997 Government Declaration a generational objective had already been set for the EQOs, which stated that all major environmental problems are to be resolved within one generation (Prop. 1997/98:145, p. 19). The EQOs are expressed in a highly general manner, for example 'Fresh air', 'Only natural acidification' or 'Limited climate impact'. Each objective is then operationalized in a set of interim targets to be met by 2010. These were adopted in 2001 (Prop. 2000/01:130) and revised in 2005 in connection with the first full reassessment of the EQOs (Prop. 2004/05:150).

The EQO reform has implied that a certain degree of implementation authority has been delegated to administrative national agencies, responsible for sector-specific targets and strategies, and to the governmental regional administrations. The latter are responsible for the adoption of regional EQO programmes and for monitoring and assessing regional performance (Prop. 2000/01:130, p. 16). The assessments are coordinated by the Environmental Objectives Council (EOC) and reported in accordance with a set of key indicators. The EOC is further responsible for coordination, consultation and communication in the implementation process.

The governmental EQO bills explicitly stated that achieving the EQOs is everyone's responsibility and the reform entailed elements of deliberative approaches to integrate environmental concerns and involve a broad range of stakeholders, in particular in the implementation phase (Johansson, 2008). In addition to establishing an organization for monitoring and reporting, the Swedish EPA devoted substantial resources for information and communication about the EQOs. The introduction of the EQOs was (as was the new Environmental Code (see below)) followed by a massive information campaign targeting authorities, industry, NGOs and the general public. Regional administrations have to varying degrees invited stakeholders to consultative working groups (comprising local municipalities, industry and NGO representatives) for deliberations on regional EQOs and measures for implementation. These processes have been important in obtaining acceptance and legitimacy for the objectives and in encouraging other societal actors to carry through appropriate measures. However, in a recent dissertation about the communicative conditions for implementing the EQOs, Johansson (2008) concluded that the implementation has been hampered both by communicative and structural barriers for integrated approaches to environmental governance and by diverging perceptions among affected actors. In addition, the latest full assessment (EOC, 2008) indicates that achievements thus far have been largely unsuccessful in fulfilling many objectives. A main reason for this has been limitations in resources and capacity with respect to the EQOs, in particular in a context of increased international interdependence (EOC, 2007). This indicates that the EQO reform is insufficient in promoting environmental performance, although the new hierarchical forms of administrative steering and consultative deliberation have enhanced the state's problem-solving capacity and allowed for wider inclusion of interests in the implementation process.

The Environmental Code: green constitutional designs

In 1999, after nearly a decade of inquiries and legislative preparations, a new Environmental Code was introduced to gather separate environmental and natural resource management laws under a common legal framework. The preamble stipulates the long-term objective of sustainability, environmental preservation and human health protection operationalized in five sub-objectives. In the preparatory works legislators presented the Code as a crucial mechanism for achieving the EQOs. Although not legally binding, these political objectives provide guiding principles for interpreting the objectives of the Code. Another innovation of particular interest here is the extended rule about the right of speech (12§ 16 Ch in MB). In transposing the EU Directive on Environmental Impact Assessments, the Code gives environmental NGOs legal standing in Swedish jurisdiction. Although somewhat circumscribed, the right of speech rule provides access to environmental jurisdiction for the defence of public interests (as distinct from private interests), where NGOs act as political trustees for the environment and non-human others (see Chapter 3, this volume). This has turned the Environmental Courts into new arenas for environmental NGOs to address ecological concerns and deliberate on the interpretation of sustainability objectives in legal cases (for example permit licensing). In this regard, the Swedish legislative reform entails prospects for improved responsiveness to ecological interests in terms of providing a new regulative ideal that in effect might facilitate ecological democracy and environmental justice. However, a remaining challenge is to get the judiciary to adopt the regulative ideal of sustainability as a new overarching norm. In practice, the judiciary is still caught up in the liberal conception of trials as negotiations between conflicting interests (Westerlund, 2003). For instance, contrary to the intentions of the legislators, neither the objectives of the Code nor the EQOs are normally taken into account by the Environmental Courts (SGU 2006).

In sum, the analysis brought forward here indicates how these reforms have advanced the capacity for effective problem-solving and strengthened the priority of environmental concerns, albeit not yet in parity with other state imperatives (economic, legitimation). While these innovations have been facilitated by a certain degree of input legitimacy (see next section for a discussion), they have primarily strengthened output legitimacy in terms of both institutional, policy and, potentially, environmental effectiveness (see Chapter 2, this volume). Applying Eckersley's criteria, or levels of change, these sustainability reforms have led to changes with regard to both policy instruments and policy goals as well as implying a reorientation of the policy paradigm. Taken together, state governance has thus been transformed towards enhanced reflexivity. The EQO reform, for instance, has admittedly been 'a way to augment sector responsibility' (Eckerberg, 2000, p. 217; Nilsson and Persson, 2003), at least if we consider its bias towards hierarchical forms of steering and administrative delegation. On the other hand, this reform has turned out to institutionalize an interactive and iterative process of monitoring and reassessment conducive to reflexive environmental governance.

Electoral Turnover Putting the Strategy to Test

After the electoral turnover in 2006 the Social Democratic Party lost power to a new conservative–liberal government. In opposition, the four coalition parties had been strongly critical of the Green People's Home strategy, but once in office found themselves bound to largely continue the policy approach of their predecessors. In particular, the new momentum on climate change following the Stern report forced the new government to accept carbon taxation in spite of electoral pledges to lower fuel taxes. However, in other regards there has been a change of course, for example by reforming key institutions. The Environmental Advisory Council was turned into the Scientific Council on Climate Change, while the Sustainability Council was abrogated and replaced by a new Commission on Sustainable Development comprising more business and industry representatives. More importantly, the present government reflects a less 'holistic' approach to sustainable development and tends to emphasize particularly salient and strategic issues such as climate change or the Baltic Sea environment. The EQO reform might be a case in point in this regard. The second reassessment of the EQOs from 2008 (EOC, 2008) was intended as a basis for the forthcoming Environmental Bill. However, at time of writing (June 2009), the resolution of the bill is still pending while awaiting another inquiry of the EQO structure. This process will put the Swedish strategy for sustainability governance to the test and it remains to be seen whether this will imply any recasts in the orientation towards other forms of governance. While the use of economic policy instruments has for some time been a central element of the Swedish model for sustainability governance, the present government seems more oriented towards economic rationality in its emphasis on neoliberal and eco-modernist ways of thinking about greening the economy through market-based policy instruments, R&D and industrial policy measures.

THE SWEDISH MODEL OF SUSTAINABILITY GOVERNANCE: DELIBERATIVE, PARTICIPATORY OR SIMPLY CORPORATIVE?

The Democracy Inquiry concluded, after a series of analyses of the state of the art of Swedish democracy, that Sweden ought to be described as a 'participatory democracy with deliberative qualities' (SOU, 2000:1, p. 23). It is debatable whether this is an accurate description or even if the members of the inquiry agree (Premfors and Roth, 2004, p. 7). Perhaps a statement such as 'representative democracy with participatory qualities' (or corporative qualities) would be more appropriate. The discussions in this chapter are best understood in the context of the Swedish political culture, with a corporatist tradition of inclusion of highly organized interests in state governance. Lundqvist (2004a, p. 217) argues that the Swedish model of sustainability governance represents a form of negotiated governance that seems 'to follow the maxim of minimum coercion and maximum content' typical for representative liberal democracies. Hence, 'the dominant form for ecological governance is co-operation with organised interests and persuasion of the general public' (ibid., p. 217). For example, the shift in Swedish policy discourse after 1997 has been associated with the building of discourse coalitions around the new strategy rather than improving democratic participation (Lundqvist, 2004b, building on Hajer, 1995). Local Agenda 21 processes, especially vibrant before 1998, were clearly associated with ambitions to increase participation in local politics. However, as indicated above, it is questionable whether such ambitions were informed by deliberative democratic ideals. In practice, the Swedish approach seems not to have entailed much of public deliberation in the phases of problem perception and policy design, but primarily in policy implementation (Hedrén, 2002). In such respects, Swedish sustainability governance is essentially at odds with the deliberative ideal of ecological democracy.

Having said this, the Swedish approach to participation and deliberation provides a rather mixed picture. On the one hand, democratic governance in Sweden possesses a certain degree of input legitimacy in terms of established mechanisms for inclusion and representation, transparency and accountability. For instance, Sweden has a tradition of special investigative Committees of

Inquiry and a well-established process for public consultations with organized stakeholders (see Chapter 10, this volume). These kind of ad hoc commissions, comprising political parties, public authorities and organized interest groups, are also applied in environmental governance for policy deliberation and pre-legislative investigation. In particular the Swedish Environmental Advisory Council, formed already in 1968, has played a critical role as policy adviser. After Rio, stakeholder involvement in such commissions has opened up for NGOs, business and local representatives. Furthermore, Sweden has a long-standing tradition of a high degree of transparency in political decision-making and public administration. The far-reaching transparency principle, a crucial provision in the Swedish constitution for centuries, provides a fundamental condition for public access to information about, for instance, environmental governance. This transparency is critical as an accountability mechanism and facilitates open dialogue and contestation between citizens, media and stakeholders.

On the other hand, a striking feature in Sweden is the absence of radical (green) perspectives in deliberations or open contestations in public discourse. One reason for this might be the far-reaching involvement of societal interest organizations in the operations of state governance. When comparing social movement interactions with the state in four advanced welfare states, Dryzek et al. (2003) conclude that such inclusion has been detrimental to the impact of green perspectives in the similar case of Norway. In Sweden, most established interest groups are deeply implicated in state governance through public consultations at various levels and through financial support from the state to certain NGOs and grassroots organizations. As such the Swedish EPA provides a substantial amount of support to the environmental movement. This implies that democratic governance is primarily open to those well-organized interests 'talking the right "technocratic" language' (Lundqvist, 2004a, p. 217). Thus, the above-mentioned forums for public consultation do not relate to the ideal speech situation (see Chapter 3, this volume), in the understanding of an unconstrained discourse for critical publicity and public opinion formation. There are no signs yet of such communicative ideals in Sweden, where policy deliberations are rather applied to extract policy-relevant knowledge, negotiate political compromises and to build coalitions around specific policies and their implementation. In this regard inclusion in Swedish policy-making is hardly deliberative, but is rather based on participatory mechanisms informed by liberal accounts of preference aggregation and compromise. Further, in advanced welfare states such as Sweden, the political activity of civil society tends to take place within highly organized interest groups and organizations rather than in open public discourse (Lundqvist, 2004a). This supports the line of criticism, mentioned in Chapter 1 (this volume), that deliberation runs the risk of being reduced to interest group politics.

As a consequence, the public sphere metaphor (see Chapter 3, this volume) might need to be reinterpreted in corporatist, semi-open contexts like the Swedish one, and in particular if state institutions already assume a considerably reflexive role. Rather the seemingly limited scope for unconstrained public discourse in Sweden might be better understood as constituted in semi-constrained spheres within highly organized interest groups, such as the environmental movement, and various networks. In sum, while the emphasis on greater stakeholder participation in policy-making processes and the evolutions in green constitutional design have been conducive to deliberative quality, the Swedish model rather adheres to the neo-corporatist tradition of inclusion of organized interests to inform, negotiate and anchor policy. This model is based on a rationalistic problem-solving approach clearly in contrast with the ideals of deliberative democracy. Hence, the Swedish model seems to be more preoccupied with extending dialogue and cooperation in order to ensure policy and compliance effectiveness (see Chapter 2, this volume), rather than with improving the conditions for public deliberation and open contestation deemed critical for societal self-reflection and stronger responsiveness to environmental concerns.

CONCLUSIONS

This chapter has elaborated on what might indicate a deliberative turn in the practices of state-centred environmental governance and examined to what extent the promise to resolve problems of legitimacy and effectiveness holds in an arguably progressive case. Sustainability governance in Sweden consists of state-led and hierarchical forms of governance operating under the primary condition of administrative rationality. The chapter has shown how these rationalities and forms of governance are still vibrant in environmental politics, albeit in transformation under the influence of other rationalities. Such state-sponsored policy innovations have a potential to strengthen both deliberative quality (input legitimacy) and environmental performance (output legitimacy), however not necessarily to the extent presumed in green deliberative theory. An interesting observation is how the Swedish model has fostered an orientation towards more reflective and reflexive governance and enhanced responsiveness to environmental concerns without adhering to deliberative democratic ideals (as set out in Chapter 3, this volume). This indicates that state institutions can be made more responsive to ecological problems, even if their operations are influenced predominantly by administrative rationality and the deliberative quality of the policy-making process is far from satisfactory.

In particular, the Swedish model for sustainability governance captures a degree of reflexivity in terms of handling environmental problems in a more thorough, integrative and self-reflective way. Although the implementation of sustainable development was initially associated with a bottom-up approach to increase participation, the dawning momentum for participatory approaches in the mid-1990s got lost during the following strategy of reconstructing the Green People's Home. This strategy implied a shift that was not associated with the deliberative ideal of widening participation and inclusion in public discourse and decision-making, but that was rather biased towards effective problem-solving and administrative steering. While the representation of green interests has partly improved (for example through the extended right of speech in the Environmental Code), the participatory rhetoric has mainly been symbolic and in practice circumscribed by a reluctance to open up policy-making processes to uncontrolled interests and the general public. Contrary to the dominant view, this seems true also for the earlier Swedish experience with local Agenda 21. These processes were preoccupied with local implementation of sustainable development projects rather than advancing local deliberative governance. Further, the Environmental Quality Objectives (EQOs) policy reform has been characterized by an ambition to integrate environmental concerns across key societal sectors. While conducive to more reflexive governance at the meta-level (in terms of an interactive and iterative implementation process), the reform, however, clearly represents a management-by-objectives strategy built on expertise and administrative rationality that has so far been largely unsuccessful in involving wider societal interests. In practice, sustainability governance in Sweden conforms to new public management ideals while being reluctant to embrace the deliberative ideal of (ecological) democracy. Thus, the ambitions to strengthen participation from below have rather played out in new ways of governing from above.

Above all, it is difficult to give a balanced picture of the Swedish case as far as the deliberative turn to environmental governance is concerned. On the one hand, it provides one of the most prominent cases of comprehensive policy innovations for improved institutional and environmental effectiveness. On the other hand, these advancements have not been directly linked to or informed by ambitions to improve the deliberative quality of hierarchical forms of governance. Rather, they represent efforts to enhance environmental performance and reconcile environmental objectives with other societal aims. In effect, such evolutions have contributed to a gradual transformation of the administrative rationality of hierarchical forms of governance. These transformations have been influenced by other rationalities, deliberative as well as economic, but without transcending into other governance forms. Hence, the promise of new modes of governance seems to correlate poorly with empirical evidence, at least in the Swedish case. One reason for this might be that the ideal conditions presumed in green political theory are largely incompatible with the realities of policy-making in advanced welfare states and, even more importantly, tend to ignore the key role of state institutions in the governance for sustainability.

REFERENCES

Anshelm, Jonas (1995), *Socialdemokraterna och Miljöfrågan* [*The Social Democrats and the Environmental Issue*], Stockholm: Brutus Östlings.
Barry, John and Robyn Eckersley (eds) (2005), *The State and the Global Ecological Crisis*, Cambridge, MA: MIT Press.
Beck, Ulrich, Anthony Giddens and Scott Lash (1994), *Reflexive Modernization: Politics, Traditions and Aesthetics in the Modern Social Order*, Cambridge: Polity Press.
Christoff, Peter (1996), 'Ecological modernisation, ecological modernities', *Environmental Politics*, **5**(3), 476–500.
Dryzek, John S., David Downes, Christian Hunold, David Schlosberg and Hans-Kristian Hernes (2003), *Green States and Social Movements: Environmentalism in the United States, United Kingdom, Germany, and Norway*, New York: Oxford University Press.
Eckerberg, Katarina (2000), 'Sweden: progression despite regression', in William Lafferty and James Meadowcroft (eds), *Implementing Sustainable Development: Strategies and Initiatives in High Consumption Societies*, Oxford: Oxford University Press, pp. 209–44.
Eckerberg, Katarina (2001), 'Sweden: problems and prospects at the leading edge of LA21 implementation', in William Lafferty (ed.), *Sustainable Communities in Europe*, London: Earthscan, pp. 15–39.
Eckerberg, Katarina and Pia Brundin (1999), *Svenska Kommuners Arbete med Agenda 21: en Enkätundersökning* [*Swedish Municipalities and Agenda 21: A Survey*], Stockholm: Kommentus.
Eckerberg, Katarina and Katrin Dahlgren (2005), *Status för Lokal Agenda 21 – en Enkätundersökning 2004* [*Status for Local Agenda 21 – A Survey*], Umeå: Swedish Institute for Ecological Sustainability.
Eckerberg, Katarina and Björn Forsberg (1998), 'Implementing Agenda 21 in local government: the Swedish experience', *Local Environment*, **3**(2), 333–48.
Eckersley, Robyn (2004), *The Green State: Rethinking Democracy and Sovereignty*, Cambridge, MA: MIT Press.
Environmental Objective Council (EOC) (2007), *Miljömålen i ett Internationellt Perspektiv – de Facto 2007* [*The Environmental Objectives in an International Perspective*], Stockholm: Swedish EPA.
EOC (2008), *Miljömålen – nu är det bråttom!* [*The Environmental Objectives – Now it is Urgent*], Stockholm: Swedish EPA.
Geological Survey of Sweden (SGU) (2006), *Beaktar Miljödomstolarna Miljökvalitetsmålen?* [*Do the Environmental Courts take the EQOs into Consideration?*], report to the EOC from SGU, 7 September.
Hägerhäll, Bertil and Geoffrey Gooch (2002), 'Sustainability as a centrally-induced Swedish local discourse', in U. Svedin and B. Aniansson (eds), *Sustainability, Local Democracy and the Future: The Swedish Model*, Dordrecht, Netherlands: Kluwer, pp. 49–82.
Hajer, Maarten A. (1995), *The Politics of Environmental Discourse: Ecological Modernization and the Policy Process*, Oxford: Clarendon Press.

Hayward, Tim (2005), *Constitutional Environmental Rights*, Oxford: Oxford University Press.

Hedrén, Johan (2002), 'Critical notes on sustainability and democracy', in U. Svedin and B. Aniansson (eds), *Sustainability, Local Democracy and the Future: The Swedish Model*, Dordrecht, Netherlands: Kluwer, pp. 17–48.

Johansson, Madelaine (2008), *Barriärer och Broar: Kommunikativa Villkor i det Svenska Miljömålsarbetet* [*Barriers and Bridges: Communicative Conditions within the Swedish Environmental Objectives Implementation Process*], Linköping, Sweden: Linköping Studies in Arts and Science.

Lafferty, William and James Meadowcroft (eds) (2000), *Implementing Sustainable Development: Strategies and Initiatives in High Consumption Societies*, Oxford: Oxford University Press.

Lundqvist, Lennart J. (2001a), 'A green fist in a velvet glove: the ecological state and sustainable development', *Environmental Values*, **10**, 455–72.

Lundqvist, Lennart J. (2001b), 'Implementation from above: the ecology of power in Sweden's environmental governance', *Governance*, **14**, 319–37.

Lundqvist, Lennart J. (2004a), *Sweden and Ecological Governance: Straddling the Fence*, Manchester: Manchester University Press.

Lundqvist, Lennart J. (2004b), '"Greening the people's home": the formative power of sustainable development discourse in Swedish housing', *Urban Studies*, **41**(7), 1283–301.

Meadowcroft, James (2005), 'From welfare state to ecostate', in John Barry and Robyn Eckersley (eds), *The State and the Global Ecological Crisis*, Cambridge, MA: MIT Press, pp. 3–23.

Meadowcroft, James (2007), 'National sustainable development strategies: features, challenges and reflexivity', *European Environment*, **17**, 152–63.

Nilsson, Måns and Åsa Persson (2003), 'Framework for analysing environmental policy integration', *Journal of Environmental Policy & Planning*, **5**(4), 333–59.

Nordgren, Anna (2005), 'Lokal förankring av Agenda 21 – verklighet eller vision?', [*Local Anchorage of Agenda 21 – Reality or Vision?*], Bachelor thesis, Stockholm University Department of Physical Geography and Quaternary Geology.

Pierre, Jon and B. Guy Peters (2000), *Governance, Politics and the State*, New York: Macmillan.

Premfors, Rune and Klas Roth (2004), *Deliberativ Demokrati*, Lund, Sweden: Studentlitteratur.

Prop. (government proposition) 1987/88:85, *About Environmental Policy for the 1990s*, Ministry of Environment.

Prop. 1990:91:90, *A Good Living Environment*, Ministry of Environment.

Prop. 1992/93:180, *The Eco-cycle Bill. On Guiding Principles for a Societal Development adjusted to Natural Eco-cycles*, Ministry of Environment.

Prop. 1997/98:145, *Swedish Environmental Objectives*, Environmental policy, Ministry of Environment.

Prop. 2000/01:130, *Swedish Environmental Objectives – Interim Targets and Measures*, Ministry of Environment.

Prop. 2004/05:150, *Swedish Environmental Objectives – a Common Task*, Ministry of Environment.

Swedish Association of Local Authorities (SALA) (1996), *Agenda 21 i Sveriges Kommuner* [*Agenda 21 in Swedish Municipalities*], Stockholm: SALA.

Swedish Investigatory Commission (SOU) 1992:104, *Vår Uppgift efter Rio – Svensk Handlingsplan inför 2000-talet* [Our Task after Rio – a Swedish Action Plan for the 21th Century], Environmental Advisory Council, Stockholm: Allmänna förlaget.

SOU 1997:105, *Five Years after Rio – Results and Future,* final report from the National Committee on Agenda 21, Ministry of Environment, Stockholm: Fritzes.
SOU 2000:1, *En Uthållig Demokrati! Politik för Folkstyre på 2000-talet* [A Sustainable Democracy! Politics for Democracy in the 21st Century], final report, Swedish Democracy Inquiry, Stockholm: Fritzes.
Stirling, Andy (2006), 'Precaution, foresight and sustainability: reflection and reflexivity in the governance of science and technology', in Jan-Peter Voss, Dierk Bauknecht and René Kemp (eds), *Reflexive Governance for Sustainable Development,* Cheltenham, UK and Northampton, MA, USA: Edward Elgar Publishing, pp. 225–72.
Svenning, Olle (2005), *Göran Persson och hans Värld* [*Göran Persson and his world*], Stockholm: Nordstedts.
Voss, Jan-Peter and René Kemp (2006), 'Sustainability and reflexive governance: introduction', in Jan-Peter Voss, Dierk Bauknecht and René Kemp (eds), *Reflexive Governance for Sustainable Development,* Cheltenham, UK and Northampton, MA, USA: Edward Elgar Publishing, pp. 3–28.
Westerlund, Staffan (2003), *Miljörättsliga Grundfrågor 2.0.* [*Basic issues of environmental law 2.0*], Uppsala, Sweden: Åmyra förlag.

9. Old and new forms of governance of food technologies in mid-20th century Sweden

Gustav Holmberg

INTRODUCTION

The governance of science and technology is not confined to governments alone. The Science and Technology Studies (STS) literature has for a long time highlighted how a wide range of actors, such as industry, scientific organizations, experts, pressure groups, patient groups and consumer groups contribute to techno-scientific decisions in shifting constellations and in various institutional settings. Scholars and practitioners alike have welcomed this development. In order to (re-)gain public trust and increase the legitimacy of expert and innovation processes, it is today commonly argued that this sector should be open to the input of a diverse citizenry (Jasanoff, 2005; Hagendijk and Irwin, 2006; Irwin, 2008). As pointed out by Evans and Collins (2008, p. 614), 'science and technology need to be made more accountable and responsive to the wider society, and one way to do this is through the increased participation of users, stakeholders and citizens'. Hence, both in theory and practice, the governance of science and technology seems to signify what in this book is called the 'deliberative turn'.

This chapter argues that the contemporary interest in more participatory and non-hierarchical modes of science and technology governance can be used to re-interpret governance processes in other historical contexts. In this vein, the aim of the chapter is to analyse policy processes in the governance of food technologies during the emergence of the modern Scandinavian welfare state in the 1940s and 1950s. The governance concept is suitable for the food sector, which included a multitude of actors throughout the twentieth century (Smith and Phillips, 2000). The chapter pays particular attention to the role of boundary organizations, hybrid research institutes and knowledge intermediaries in the Swedish food sector during this time period, and examines whether early processes of deliberation and stakeholder dialogues can be found in such sites. Although the boundary organization concept has a rather short history, it can be seen as an example of network governance that had already played a central role in mid-twentieth century policy-making on food technology.

The historical context for the chapter is the emerging welfare state. Was it solely defined by hierarchical steering and administrative rationality? By studying the emerging welfare state through the lens of deliberation and public–private interaction, this chapter paints a mixed picture. Examining the example of food technologies in Sweden, and in particular frozen food, the chapter draws attention to collaborative practices and softer forms of steering during a period of modernization in the post-war era, at a time when innovations both in policy mechanisms and food technologies themselves loomed large over the Swedish food sector. It especially analyses instances of deliberation where non-state organizations and scientific experts were active in reforming the Swedish food sector. As such, the chapter critically engages with the distinction between new and old modes of governance, and presents an empirical case that can work as heuristics for reflection on the deliberative turn of today.

BOUNDARY ORGANIZATIONS, DELIBERATION AND PUBLIC–PRIVATE INTERACTION

The main aim of this chapter is to identify and discuss some of the organizational and procedural factors that paved the way for deliberations on food technology in mid-twentieth century Sweden. In particular, the focus is on organizations that tried to bring together expertise, public and private actors. The concept of boundary organizations has been developed to grasp the heterogeneous nature of governance in the science and technology field. The concept refers to organizations that facilitate mediation between actors from different institutional milieux. In the governance of science and technology, boundary organizations typically offer a platform for dialogue and interaction between politicians, civil servants, scientists and industry representatives (Irwin, 2008; Guston, 2001; 1999). By including participants from both the public and private sector, boundary organizations emerge as an example of private–public partnerships. In line with Chapter 5 (this volume), boundary organizations and public–private partnerships are conceptualized as networked governance in combining different rationalities and forms of governance (see also Chapter 2, Table 2.1, this volume).

This book offers a critical assessment of the promise of new modes of governance, which has been interpreted as their alleged potential to contribute to more legitimate decision-making and to increased environmental effectiveness. In the context of the emerging welfare state this promise needs to be viewed in a different light. Issues such as lack of legitimacy, implementation problems and environmental degradation had not yet come to the fore or were interpreted in different ways during the time period examined in this chapter. Still, as will be argued, contemporary observers saw a promise in boundary organizations. Operating at the public–private frontier, these governance arrangements were generally expected to contribute to more effective policy-making attuned to the needs of industry, consumers and society at large.

In this chapter we will examine the extent to which deliberative processes took place in mid-twentieth century food technology governance, and which actors such processes involved. The literature on STS and environmental politics shares a critical perspective on deliberation and neither has bought the deliberative logic lock, stock and barrel. The environmental politics literature has critically engaged with the naive expectations levelled around new modes of governance to deliver legitimate policies. Critics highlight the problem with power asymmetries in deliberative processes, and have among other things stressed the ambivalent status of science and technology, which is indispensable for environmental problem-solving but also creates sites of immense socioeconomic and administrative power (see critical discussion in Chapter 1, this volume). Critics in the STS literature argue that the deliberative ideal as applied to science and technology idealizes social reality and the arenas and processes in which techno-science plays out (Pestre, 2007; 2008). Social, cultural and economic capital is highly unevenly distributed, and the capacity to participate in deliberations surrounding techno-science is, for large numbers of citizens, modest or non-existent. Social and economic differences and power-inequalities, either inside states or globally across the North–South divide, make for highly different opportunities for participation.

Pestre has also criticized the notion that deliberation will lead to more optimal technical choices. By looking exclusively at optimal governance forms for democratic deliberation, he claims that the attainment of 'real democracy' is hampered (Pestre, 2007; 2008). It is important to actively maintain 'the protection of alternative ways of making worlds [… and] the defence of "dissident groups" (able to go on with their expertise and publicize it)' (Pestre, 2007, p. 417f.). Following Pestre's suggestion that alternative discourses can be important in steering technologies around environmentally sensitive and potentially dangerous side-effects, this chapter looks for instances of interaction between the formal modes of deliberation and such alternatives. Ultimately, the chapter attempts to answer the question: how sensitive was the food technology governance system to such criticism in the emerging Swedish welfare state?

MID-20TH CENTURY SWEDEN AND THE FOOD TECHNOLOGY SECTOR

The 1940s and 1950s have been described as a period when governments in many countries sought to manage capitalism in an attempt to protect society from what were seen as its negative side-effects. In several countries such an appeal to a more planned economy was not limited to the political left (Berman, 2006). The economic crisis of the 1930s and the Second World War paved the way for increasingly active state planning, without resorting to a full-blown centrally planned type of economy. Rationalization of the economy and industrial production became a leading idea. In Sweden, influenced not least by developments in the US, several organizations took up the task of rationalization, notably the Academy of Engineering Sciences (IVA) and the Royal Institute of Technology (KTH) (De Geer, 1978). Also, the Swedish research system saw fundamental changes. Several research councils were set up, following the proposals of a government committee (the 'Malm' Committee) (Nybom, 1993; 1997; Weinberger, 1997). In the following, the suggestions of the 'Malm' Committee for the food technology sector will be discussed in some detail, as it gave vital impetus to public–private partnerships and boundary organizations built up in the Swedish food technology sector.

The drive to rationalize production, distribution and consumption of food took several forms. A glorious future of hassle-free and time-saving modern cooking and kitchen culture was often presented to consumers. Epitomized in three full-size kitchen mock-ups, which under the banner of 'the Day after tomorrow's kitchen' toured American department stores in the later stages of World War II, the display of the future of food and consumption in the Western world was, in the words of one historian, 'a tantalizing display, conditioning an eager body of consumers for the glittering prizes that awaited them at war's end' (Horrigan, 1986, p. 158). Some food technological projects did not lead anywhere. Instead they more or less fizzled out after a period of initial futuristic technological hype, as when the food sector entered the atomic age with the hope of using radiation as a new technology for preservation (Buchanan, 2005). Frozen food was initially something of a luxury product and did not, even in the technologically and economically prosperous US, take off properly until the late 1940s.

However, frozen food eventually entered the group of mass-market technologies, supplementing canning and other ways of preserving food. It was born in a period of expansion of the American food processing industry, a period that also saw food processing technologies being developed in heterogeneous environments. Public–private networks were formed spanning food technology research in the universities, the food processing industry and other parts of the industry (and, in some cases, the military). In these networks, people, ideas, funding and material objects mingled. Complementing developments in the industrial supply-side part of the equation, transformed consumer preferences and shopping patterns in large parts of the American population also drove developments. Supermarkets flourished, people increasingly began using freezers in their homes, and consumption of processed food generally increased (Josephson, 2008; Hamilton, 2003a; 2003b; Levenstein, 1993). The US was ahead, but other countries soon followed (Pantzar, 1998; Shove and Southerton, 2000).

In the Swedish food sector, national issues loomed large over the policy process. Public health and national security issues, which can be conceived as self-sufficiency in food production in times of war, were important (Holmberg, 2005). It is worth noticing that the food technology sector was seen as so important that it warranted its own special report by the 'Malm Committee'. Surveying the Swedish food sector, the 'Malm' government committee identified a combination of state and industry activities as an important remedy to key national problems (SOU, 1945:6). Public health would improve with better quality of food, which would give economic benefits, such as workers' health, which figured prominently in the debates. The 'Malm' committee's special report on food technology research came at a very technocratic period in the modern history of Sweden. The bulk of the government report was written by Henry Brahmer. He was an engineer and manager at the Swedish Yeast Company (Svenska Jästfabriks AB), a company with a near-monopoly in the industrial production of yeast in Sweden. Close state–industry collaboration, as will be shown below, was not unusual in this period.

Other parts of the report were written by Edy Velander, an engineer and the director of the Academy of Engineering Sciences, who was a key actor in and a driving force behind the academy's efforts to act as a broker of heterogeneous research and state–industry collaborations. This report was symptomatic of the far-reaching collaboration between state and industry inherent in the governance of science and technology in the era. Not only did people connected with stakeholder interests write the text to a large degree but the recommendation of the committee was in favour of an increase in state–industry–science collaboration. Pressure groups from industry and the technological establishment successfully took part in the re-shuffling of the Swedish research system during the 1940s, and the food sector was no exception (Nybom, 1993). The promise of modernizing the Swedish food sector was improved public health, society-wide economical benefits and security in times of conflict and a safer and more rational food supply. Such modernization was to be achieved through a more rational and technologically advanced production of food.

The policy documents also called for increased collaboration between state, industry and organizations, which represented citizens, scientific and technological experts. Perhaps the most important of the committee's suggestions was the formation of a research institute jointly financed by the state and a foundation made up of companies in the food sector. The committee's suggestions were accepted and its main policy recommendation was implemented subsequently when the Swedish Institute for Food Preservation Research (SIK) was established in 1946. The SIK was one of several industry-research institutes where the state, academia and industry collaborated. Jointly financed by state and industry, it represented a mode of research funding and private–public research organization that had a long tradition in Sweden (Tunlid, 2004; Widmalm, 1999). The stated goal of the SIK to bring academia and industry together to cooperate with a range of actors turned it into a kind of boundary organization or public–private partnership.

Boundary Organizations and Expertise

Boundary organizations and research institutes with hybrid public–private identities can facilitate meetings across socio-cultural boundaries, where scientific experts often play important roles. Such 'knowledge intermediaries' have been a staple of the academy–state–industry system in Sweden for a long time (Kaiserfeld, 2008). Sector-type organizations and professional interest groups that formed around a particular type of technology were also important. They functioned as 'ambassadors' for the technology in question by organizing meetings between scientific and technological experts, politicians and other state officials and industry representatives. Below we will discuss three examples of such organizations, which aimed at facilitating private–public dialogue and thereby functioning as knowledge intermediaries to expand frozen food technology.

In 1944, the Home Research Institute (HFI) was inaugurated. The HFI was a research institute aimed at rationalizing domestic work, and was jointly financed by the government as well as other actors. The amount of funding from the state was determined by funding from non-state organizations and individuals. In its first year, such matching grants came from, among others, the Cooperative federation (KF) and the Swedish Association of Mechanical Manufacturing. In the HFI laboratories, domestic technologies were studied. What was the optimal layout of a kitchen; how could dishwashing be made more efficient? The research also took place outside the institute in interaction with 'advisory boards' through the formation of committees of housewives testing out appliances in their homes, thus consulting with the experts at the institute. The rationality of governance at HFI was partly of a deliberative kind. Experts worked together with citizens interested in how to run a household (a field, at the time, framed as the domain of women) in a hierarchical form.

The institute collaborated with other organizations such as the State Institute of Public Health, the State Commission on Standardization, the Swedish Association of Shopkeepers, the Swedish National Testing Institute and the Society for the Rational Use of Electricity. The results of its research into a more rational home for Swedish citizens were widely disseminated. The institute's personnel often appeared in the media with articles and radio features on topics ranging from the best way to mash potatoes to large-scale public health issues. Interacting with society also meant inviting groups of citizens/housewives for study visits at the institute, giving courses and appearing at exhibitions as well as holding public lectures. In 1950, personnel at the Home Research Institute held 100 public lectures (Lövgren, 1993). Its production of a popular series of 'Housewife's movies' soon reached half a million viewers per year. The films extolled the virtues of frozen fish and the wizardry of chemical industry that shaped modern cleaning practices as well as other parts of the modern kitchen and home technology (Berner, 1996).

While the experts on home economics at the HFI worked on finding ways of modernizing the Swedish kitchens, the Academy of Engineering Sciences also took on domestic technologies and worked on making them fit into Swedish life. The Academy acted as a liaison with international developments, especially in the US, organizing meetings and talks where international experts, such as the director of the US General Foods Corporation, visited and presented information on the developments in the US frozen food industry (Anon., 1948a). The US was a leader in this area. Trade publications such as *Livsmedelsteknik*, a joint IVA–SIK project, and *Kylteknisk tidskrift* from the 1940s and 1950s, often contained articles about developments across the Atlantic, either derived from the American literature or built upon US study visits by Swedish engineers and experts.[1]

The IVA was instrumental in introducing new technologies such as frozen foods into the Swedish system of food production and consumption. The IVA's key spokesperson, Edy Velander, had spent six months in the US during the Second World War, studying the country's food processing industry (Holmberg, 2005). The organization also took the initiative to a Nordic committee on frozen foods that was founded in 1946, and organized visits by experts from the OEEC (the Organization for European Economic Co-Operation, the precursor of the OECD) to Swedish institutes and organizations dealing with refrigeration technologies (Anon., 1948b). The academy thus worked actively to facilitate networking between scientific and technical experts at national and supra-national levels.

The Swedish Society of Refrigeration was formed in 1942, with the aim of promoting frozen foods and related technologies. Complementing the research institutes such as the SIK and the HFI and the official state regulatory bodies, it played a significant role in developing, promoting and spreading knowledge about this technology as well as developing regulation pertaining to frozen food technologies. Thus, it played a role similar to the IVA in furthering the interests of the industry in this area. All the research institutes, boundary organizations, and knowledge intermediaries studied in this chapter represent several of the qualities normally associated with 'new modes of governance', albeit not always in a clear-cut way. As noted in Chapter 2 (this volume), hierarchy can co-exist with other forms of governance in a hybrid manner; mixed or hybrid forms of governance can also be informed by different governance rationalities. Along these lines, the organizations, people and processes discussed in this chapter inhabit several parts of the spectrum of governance delineated by the shaded areas of Table 2.1 (Chapter 2, this volume).

The work performed at the Home Research Institute (HFI) was organized in a hierarchical form, but informed by a deliberate rationality (Box 3 in Table 2.1). The HFI summoned a diversity of actors interested in the development of new kitchen and food-related technologies. Public panels tested and debated new kitchen norms and home technologies, and gave input to the institute's experts. Work at the SIK institute was organized in a way as to make the experts more attuned to the needs of industry. Jointly funded by state and companies in the Swedish food technology sector, teaming together in an industry foundation, the research institute took the form of a private–public partnership informed by an administrative rationality (Box 7 in Table 2.1). Many of the actors studied in this chapter were involved in several organizations at the same time, Matts Bäckström and Edy Velander being just two examples. Sweden was a fairly small country, and one can thus envisage the emergence of a 'freeze technology culture' where experts and civil servants moved between various milieux of importance to the development of policies, technologies, and regulation that were relevant to the development of food technologies.

Deliberation

The Academy of Engineering Sciences (IVA) organized processes of deliberation and promoted collaboration between makers of cooling equipment, food processors, experts, the Swedish Society for Refrigeration and other organizations. For example, the IVA was active in developing security regulation for refrigerating technologies, in which engineers from various stakeholders were invited to give input in a deliberative process, before the IVA's proposal was forwarded to the government. Standardization of packages and the proper ways to handle frozen foods in the Swedish railway system was one area of study. The IVA also organized several large-scale events aimed at spreading the gospel of new food technologies and bringing together actors from various parts of the food technology system. Drawing hundreds of experts together, these events were important in forming a kind of deep freeze and modern food technology culture, sometimes finishing the proceedings with dinner receptions. One menu proudly stated that the main course, which was turkey delivered from Hungary, had been kept in deep freeze for one year before being cooked, while the entrée, turtle soup, had been frozen for a month. The industry journal, *Kylteknisk Tidskrift*, did not venture to put forward an opinion on the culinary qualities of the dinner, but it was clear that the meeting of these various types of actors was an important event (Velander, 1944; Haglund, 1946).

The Society of Refrigeration Technologies organized several activities and forums with the aim of discussing and developing knowledge about frozen foods, among them food safety issues (Anon., 1946a) and to organize freezing, in which experts representing both the engineering side (Velander from IVA) and the home economics/consumers side (Neymark from the Home Research Institute), took part (Anon., 1946b). These activities can be illustrated by a deliberative process held in 1956 under the auspices of the Society of Refrigeration Technologies concerning the question of the proper minimum temperature in the cold chain. This was a time when the system for production, transport, mass storage, retailing and home storage was still in development. Questions concerning food safety, such as at what temperatures frozen foods should be stored throughout the cold chain and for how long in order for them both to retain sufficiently good taste and to be safe for consumers, had not yet become the subject of state regulation.

Included in the discussion was a professor of cooling technologies at the Royal Institute of Technology, representatives from Swedish companies such as STAL and Elektrohelios (manufacturers of freezing and cold storage equipment), experts from the State Board of Medicine and the State Veterinary Board, engineers and scientists working in large Swedish food companies such as Findus and Marabou, scientists from the Swedish Farmers' Meat Marketing Association (one of several organizations in the sector that ran its own lab with PhD staff), engineers working with frozen foods issues at the Union of Co-operative Societies, and representatives from the State Institute for Consumers. The viewpoints were sometimes divergent. For instance, the experts Gösta Tegnér and Matts Bäckström debated whether the current state of knowledge suggested that $-12°$Celsius was sufficient, or if a lower temperature was needed in order to uphold adequate public health standards and sustain consumers' trust in the still rather new technology (Bäckström, 1956; Anon., 1957).

Such broad set-ups of actors were typical of regulative procedures of importance to the Swedish food technology sector during this period. The SIK, the main research institute in the sector, was funded both by the industry and the government. This co-financing was informed by the idea that research should be geared towards industry interests, which would simultaneously give positive societal effects. Companies and organizations also built up competencies in the field, either through financing in-house lab facilities or collaborating

closely with academics. The Johnson shipping line ran its own research institute, the IVK, which specialized in cold storage technologies, manned by
PhDs from the biological sciences. People working at the IVK moved between
academia, industrial research organizations and hybrid research organizations.
Georg Borgström, for example, moved from Lund University to the IVK and
then to the SIK (Gustafsson, 1995). The Elektrolux corporation, which was
Sweden's premier producer of cold storage technology for mass markets, had
close contacts with a department for refrigeration technologies at the Royal
Institute of Technology, financing a professorship among other things. Matts
Bäckström, professor at the department, had previously worked at the
Electrolux labs and was also one of the leading people in the Society for
Refrigeration, and he published a central textbook on the subject. Thus,
besides boundary organizations, other networks of expertise also represented
an important governance arrangement in this field.

Critical Perspectives

While the main aim of this chapter has been to explore the activities and
processes in and around boundary organizations and 'knowledge intermediaries' in mid-twentieth century food technology governance, and to identify
the deliberative processes they fostered, some critical notes will also be made
regarding the governance of food technologies in the emerging Swedish
welfare state. Although this study has not focused on the history of consumer
activities, it can be noted that consumers were often present in the process
through representation by a range of organizations that existed in Sweden at
the time. The Home Research Institute tried to involve citizens in the production of knowledge and the processes of regulation surrounding kitchen technologies and housing norms. Consumer groups were sometimes invited to
contribute to the process. In hindsight it is, however, rather difficult to see
them as being on an equal footing with companies and state interests during
this period. The coupling of company interests and a strong national hege-
monic idea of self-sufficiency, which was present in food policy in many
countries, then and now, was a strong tie.

When passing judgement on history (if historians should engage in that at
all), one has to be aware of power asymmetries in the system. Not all participants were given equal voice, nor were they equal in terms of social capital,
nor did they have the same access to knowledge. This asymmetry can either
be explained by clear-cut economic factors that affected the participants'
perceived expertise, such as the size of research grants for example, or by non-
tangible but important ways of regulating access to the inner sanctums of
deliberation and knowledge-making. As has been implied by this study, 'old-
boys'' networks between influential actors across the public–private divide

seem to have played a role in the Swedish governance of food technology. Consequently, the public–private collaboration in this field resonates poorly with the ideal deliberative procedures discussed by Lövbrand and Khan in Chapter 3 (this volume).

Moreover, the opportunity for deliberation *within* expertise and the maintenance of pluralism among experts is important for the ability for a society to steer around emerging problems. A case in point was the Georg Borgström affair. When Borgström began lecturing about world poverty and neo-Malthusian world-views while being the director of the SIK, a research institute that was supposed to help the Swedish food industry in producing better and cheaper food, he was fired (Linnér, 1998, pp. 165–81). Industry representatives on the board of the SIK claimed that Borgström had been too interested in broader issues instead of running the daily scientific work at the institute. Another interpretation of this event (offered by Borgström himself) is that PLM, a dominating firm in the tin can manufacturing business and a source of funding for the SIK, had become increasingly uneasy about the SIK's investments in frozen food technologies research, which was seen as a rival product category.

The Borgström affair helps us to reflect upon procedural qualities of deliberation beyond the involvement of non-experts. Following Pestre's (2007; 2008) critical account of deliberations in science and technology, one can ask what room there was for opposing schools of thought and counter-expertise in the expert deliberations studied here. In order to secure legitimate governance of science and technology, Pestre has argued that we have to actively maintain and protect parallel modes of expertise and defend techno-scientific dissidents. Although Swedish mid-twentieth century food technology governance was a collaborative exercise between a number of public and private actors, it offers few examples of such diversity and dissent.

CONCLUDING REMARKS

Is it just a play on words to include a study of collaborations between state and non-state actors in the food sector in the 1940s and 1950s in an anthology on new modes of governance? After all, this was a period when not only Sweden but also the rest of Scandinavia implemented far-reaching programmes in eugenics, signs of a strong and coercive state policy towards citizens, to say the least (Broberg and Roll-Hansen, 2005). On the other hand, the period saw several collaborative ventures between state, scientific experts, companies and other organizations. The power emanating from the state was clearly not absolute. Rather, the widespread collaboration between actors from industry, organizations representing consumers and housewives and experts from science and technology in the food technology sector, points to the existence of multiple forms of governance informed by both administrative and deliberative rationalities. Time and again the state ceded control over parts of the policy process, giving ample room for non-state actors to manoeuvre. These examples of network governance are rather common in the Scandinavian states (Hagendijk and Irwin, 2006).

A main conclusion of this chapter is thus that what have been called new modes of governance, may in fact not be so new after all. We have seen examples of hierarchies and network forms of governance with administrative and deliberative rationalities engaging non-state actors from industry and consumer groups. The mid-twentieth century was a period of mixed, 'hybrid' modes of governance in the food technology domain. Even during what could be seen as the heyday of hierarchic governance, that is in the era of the emerging welfare state, we find that public–private partnerships and, to some extent, deliberative processes, were common aspects of governance, though often far from a Habermasian or a citizen panel-type of exercise that tried to reach outside of organized expertise and industry stakeholder interests (with the Home Research Institute as one possible exception).

Rational handling of food would, it was hoped, simplify life and save time and money for everyone, from the individual citizen to the aggregated societal economy. Modernization of food technology was attuned to a changing place for women in society. Some commentators stated that a more efficient handling of food would help women enter the job market (Holmberg, 2005). Those who argued for a more technologically advanced mode of production, distribution and consumption of food could, thus, adhere to a central tenet of modern Swedish politics. It was sometimes argued, for example in the 'Malm' Committee report, that if modern nutritional science could be better utilized in a more modern and technologically advanced production of food, Swedes would become healthier. Food safety was at hand and new technologies for preserving, storing and transporting food required critical scrutiny by experts with sufficient care. The work of boundary organizations, such as the SIK, was to a substantial degree tied to these kinds of questions.

Finally, it is worth noting the virtually absent question of the environmental effects of a large and modernized food technology system analysed in this chapter. Interestingly, such a discussion was in fact beginning during this period but it did not take place within the systems of deliberation discussed. Sten Selander, who was an author, biologist and environmentalist at the time, argued against the use of pesticides in modern food production and highlighted the fact that short-term economic gains had negative environmental consequences. He published widely on environmental issues during the 1950s (Kylhammar, 1990, pp. 177–200). The food technological system was geared toward central socio-political concerns such as public health, the need for technological rationalization and national security, questions harbouring a broad consensus-like quality. However, environmental issues were more or less outside the loop, and were instead raised in other arenas such as the media. There were, at least then, limits to the issues that could secure a place on the agenda of networked governance arrangements.

NOTE

1. Important sources for this book chapter are an extensive literature survey and analysis, particularly of *Kylteknisk Tidskrift* and *Livsmedelsteknik*.

REFERENCES

Anonymous (1942), 'Säkerhetsanvisningar för installation och skötsel av kylanläggningar och kylskåp. Utarbetade av IVA's kyltekniska kommitté' ['Safety regulations for the installation and support of cooling plants and refrigerators developed by the cooling technologies committee of IVA'], prepared in June, 1942, *Kylteknisk Tidskrift*, no.3.
Anonymous (1946a), 'Normer för kyl- och fryshus' ['Norms for Cold Storage Plants'], *Kylteknisk Tidskrift*, no. 6.
Anonymous (1946b), 'Svenska kyltekniska föreningens möte den 5 juni' ['Meeting of the Swedish Society for Refrigeration Technologies on 5 June'], *Kylteknisk Tidskrift*, no. 6.
Anonymous (1948a), 'Metoder för livsmedelsförvaring, speciellt genom köldbehandling' ['Methods of food preparation, especially deep freeze'], *Kylteknisk Tidskrift*, no. 11, 169–73.
Anonymous (1948b), 'Nordiskt frysmöte i Oslo' [The Nordic meeting for cold technologies in Oslo'], *Kylteknisk Tidskrift*, no. 11.
Anonymous (1957), 'Lagrings- och transporttemperaturer för frysta varor: Diskussionssammanträdet med Svenska Kyltekniska Föreningen den 26 oktober 1956' ['Temperatures for storage and transport of frozen foods: discussion meeting with the Swedish Society for Refrigeration Technologies on 26 October 1956'], *Kylteknisk Tidskrift*, 1.
Bäckström, Matts (1956), 'Frysta varors lagringstemperatur' ['Storage temperature of frozen goods'], *Kylteknisk Tidskrift*, (5), 55–8.
Berman, Sheri (2006), *The Primacy of Politics: Social Democracy and the Making of Europe's Twentieth Century*, Cambridge: Cambridge University Press.
Berner, Boel (1996), *Sakernas tillstånd: kön, klass, teknisk expertis* [*The State of Things: Gender, Class, Technological Experts*], Stockholm: Carlssons.
Broberg, Gunnar and Nils Roll-Hansen (eds) (2005), *Eugenics and the Welfare State: Sterilization Policy in Denmark, Sweden, Norway, and Finland*, East Lansing, MI: Michigan State University Press.
Buchanan, Nicholas (2005), 'The atomic meal: the Cold War and irradiated foods, 1945–1963', *History and Technology*, **21**(2), 221–49.
De Geer, Hans (1978), *Rationaliseringsrörelsen i Sverige: Effektivitetsidéer och socialt ansvar under mellankrigstiden* [*The Rationalization Movement in Sweden:*

Efficiency Programs and Social Responsibility in the Inter-War Years], Stockholm: Studieförbundet Näringsliv och Samhälle.

Evans, Robert and Harry Collins (2008), 'Expertise: from attribute to attribution and back again?', in Edward J. Hackett, Olga Amsterdamska, Michael Lynch and Judy Wajcman (eds), *The Handbook of Science and Technology Studies*, 3rd edn, Cambridge, MA and London: MIT Press, pp. 609–30.

Gustafsson, Nils (1995), *IVK 1942–1992: 50 ars verksamhet i potatisodlingens tjänst vid Institutet för Växtforskning och Kyllagring och IVK Potatis AB.* [*IVK 1942–1992: 50 Years of Serving the Growing of Potato at the Institute for Plant Research and Cold Storage and IVK Potatoes Inc.*], Umeå: IVK Potatis.

Guston, David H. (1999), 'Stabilizing the boundary between US politics and science: the role of the office of technology transfer as a boundary organization', *Social Studies of Science*, **29**, 87–111.

Guston, David H. (2001), 'Boundary organizations in environmental policy and science: an introduction', *Science, Technology, and Human Values*, **26**, 399–408.

Hagendijk, Rob and Alan Irwin (2006), 'Public deliberation and governance: engaging with science and technology in contemporary Europe', *Minerva*, **44**, 167–84.

Haglund, Folke (1946), 'Kölddagen' ['Cold Storage Day'], *Kylteknisk Tidskrift*, (4).

Hamilton, Shane (2003a), 'The economies and conveniences of modern-day living: frozen foods and mass marketing, 1945–1965', *Business History Review*, **77**, 33–60.

Hamilton, Shane (2003b), 'Cold capitalism: the political ecology of frozen concentrated orange juice', *Agricultural History*, **77**, 557–81.

Holmberg, Gustav (2005), 'Vetenskap och livsmedelsindustri: Svenska Institutet för Konserveringsforskning' ['Science and the food industry: The Swedish Institute for Food Preservation Research'], *Lychnos: Årsbok för Idé- och Lärdomshistoria*, pp. 199–218.

Horrigan, Brian (1986), 'The home of tomorrow, 1927–1945', in Joseph J. Corn (ed.), *Imagining Tomorrow: History, Technology, and the American Future*, Cambridge, MA: the MIT Press, pp. 137–63.

Irwin, Alan (2008), 'STS perspectives on scientific governance', in Edward J. Hackett, Olga Amsterdamska, Michael Lynch and Judy Wajcman (eds), *The Handbook of Science and Technology Studies*, 3rd edn, Cambridge, MA and London: MIT Press, pp. 583–607.

Jasonoff, Sheila (2005), *Designs on Nature: Science and Democracy in Europe and the United States*, Princeton, NJ: Princeton University Press.

Josephson, Paul (2008), 'The ocean's hot dog: the development of the fish stick', *Technology and Culture*, **49**, 41–61.

Kaiserfeld, Thomas (2008), 'From Royal Academy of Science to Research Institute of Society: long term policy convergence of Swedish knowledge intermediaries', accessed 16 May at http://econpapers.repec.org/paper/ hhscesisp/0121.htm.

Kylhammar, Martin (1990), *Den okände Sten Selander: En borgerlig intellektuell* [*The Unknown Sten Selander: A Non-Socialist Intellectual*], Stockholm: Akademeja.

Levenstein, Harvey (1993), *Paradox of Plenty: A Social History of Eating in Modern America*, Oxford: Oxford University Press.

Linnér, Björn-Ola (1998), *The World Household: Georg Borgström and the Postwar Population–Resource Crisis*, Linköping Studies in Arts and Science, 181, Linköping, Sweden: Department of Water and Environmental Studies.

Lövgren, Britta (1993), *Hemarbete som politik: Diskussioner om hemarbete, Sverige 1930–1940-talen och tillkomsten av Hemmens Forskningsinstitut* [*Housework as*

Politics: Discussions on Housework in Sweden during the 1930s and the 1940s and the Establishing of The Home Research Institute], Stockholm: Almqvist & Wicksell International.

Nybom, Thorsten (1993), 'The socialization of science: technical research and the natural sciences in Swedish research policy in the 1930s and 1940s', in Svante Lindqvist (ed.), *Center on the Periphery: Historical Aspects of 20th-Century Swedish Physics*, Canton, MA: Science History Publications, pp. 164–78.

Nybom, Thorsten (1997), *Kunskap, politik, samhälle: Essäer om kunskapssyn, universitet och forskningspolitik 1900–2000* [*Knowledge, Politics, Society: Essays on Perspectives on Knowledge, the University and Research Policy 1900–2000*], Hargshamn, Swedden: Arete.

Pantzar, Mika (1998), 'What do we need a freezer for? The social construction of the freezer use(r) in Finland from the 1950s to the 1980s', conference paper accessed 15 August 2007 at http://web.archive.org/web/20051220214642/http://www.lancs.ac.uk/users/scistud/esf/pantz.htm.

Pestre, Dominique (2007), 'The historical heritage of the 19th and 20th centuries: technoscience, markets and regulations in a long-term perspective', *History and Technology*, **23** (4), 407–20.

Pestre, Dominique (2008), 'Challenges for the democratic management of technoscience: governance, participation and the political today', *Science as Culture*, **17** (2), 101–19.

Shove, Elisabeth and Dale Southerton (2000), 'Defrosting the freezer: from novelty to convenience', *Journal of Material Culture*, **5** (3), 301–19.

Smith, David F. and Jim Phillips (2000) (eds), *Food, Science, Policy and Regulation in the Twentieth Century: International and Comparative Perspectives*, London and New York: Routledge.

SOU 1945:6, *Utredning rörande den tekniskt-vetenskapliga forskningens ordnande. VII. Förslag till åtgärder för livsmedelsforskningens oordnande* [*Government Committee on the Organization of Technical-Scientific research. VII. Recommendations for Reorganizing Food Research*].

Tunlid, Anna (2004) *Ärftlighetsforskningens gränser. Individer och institutioner i framväxten av svensk genetik* [*The Limits of Hereditary Research: Individuals and Institutions in the Emergence of Swedish Genetics*], Lund, Sweden: Avdelningen för idé- och lärdomshistoria.

Velander, Edy (1944), 'Konferens om fryskonservering' ['A conference on cold storage'], *Kylteknisk Tidskrift*, (9).

Weinberger, Hans (1997), *Nätverksentreprenören: En historia om teknisk forskning och industriellt utvecklingsarbete från den Malmska Utredningen till Styrelsen för Teknisk Utveckling* [*Network Entrepreneur: A History of Technological Research and Industrial Development from the Malm Investigation to the National Board of Technical Development*], Stockholm: Department of History of Technology and Science, KTH.

Widmalm, Sven (1999), 'Den stora växtförädlingsanstalten: Svalöf, Weibullsholm och vetenskapens samhällsroll under mellankrigstiden' ['The great institute for plant breeding: Svalöf, Weibullsholm and the role of science in Swedish society between the wars'], in Sven Widmalm (ed.), Vetenskapsbärarna: naturvetenskapen i det Svenska Samället, 1880–1950, Stockholm: Gidlunds.

10. Regulatory challenges and forest governance in Sweden

Peter Schlyter and Ingrid Stjernquist

INTRODUCTION

In recent years there has been an interest, both theoretical and practical, in what have been designated as new modes of governance and it is often claimed that environmental governance has taken a deliberative turn (see Chapters 1–2, this volume). Deliberative democracy, though, comes in many forms and there is no single universally accepted definition of the concept. Indeed there is considerable disagreement 'about value, status, aim and scope of deliberation' among the theory's proponents (Gutmann and Thompson, 2004, p. 21). A core argument of this book is that contemporary environmental governance practice has been influenced by deliberative democratic ideals, reflecting a move from hierarchical steering towards more deliberative and participatory modes of governance (see Chapter 1, this volume).

This chapter investigates this claim through a case study of Swedish forest governance seen from a historical perspective. Is there an identifiable trend away from traditional forms of environmental governance towards new modes, whether they are market-oriented or deliberative? Or could one argue that the rise of new modes of environmental governance is a reflection of the intrinsic characteristics of particular (environmental) problems that bias for particular governance forms? Alternatively, is the current trend just a chance fit between relatively young policy areas and synchronous governance fashions and ideals? Clearly, it is methodologically hard to assess whether there really is a deliberative turn based on contemporary policy issues with a short history and therefore synchronous with the suggested change. Given the relative youth of several policy areas of environmental governance, such as GMOs and climate change, it is difficult to disentangle these and other associated questions. Swedish forest governance, on the other hand, is a regulatory arena with a considerable history and with a century-long aim of sustainability. This relatively long time-line enables an assessment of how governance has varied over time and to what extent alleged new modes of governance really are all that new. Forest governance is an often-cited example of an area where non-state market-driven governance forms, such as different types of certification schemes, have been successfully established following deliberation between stakeholders (cf. Cashore et al., 2007; Boström, 2003; Guldbrandsen, 2004; Schlyter et al., 2009). However, early studies of Swedish forest governance, like Stjernquist (1973), clearly illustrate that more or less deliberative and participatory forms of governance have a long tradition. Indeed, the development of Swedish forest governance over the last century provides an example of shifting aims and governance rationalities (cf. Stjernquist, 1973; 1983; 1992; Appelstrand, 2007; Schlyter et al., 2009).

In this chapter we will examine the extent to which a deliberative turn can be identified in Swedish forestry governance. We analyse the texts and processes around a number of official government inquiries (SOU) from 1925 until 2006. We ask if deliberation is a new phenomenon or whether it has been here all along. To this end we will combine the analytic framework employed throughout this book with information from official inquiries preceding Swedish forestry legislation, subsequent legislation and policy implementation, as well as information on contemporary environmental debates and development. Our analysis of governance forms and rationalities evident in Swedish forest governance is chronologically based. Through our analysis we note that change in governance over time, by itself does not provide an explanation as to why certain forms of governance are chosen or why they change over time. Hence, in the final section we also examine whether the properties of a problem and the characteristics of the regulatory challenge can explain such change.

THE SWEDISH LEGISLATIVE CONTEXT: PRE-LEGISLATIVE AND POST-LEGISLATIVE DELIBERATION

Sweden has a long tradition of formal multi-stakeholder deliberations in the legislative process. Stakeholders are consulted both in (i) the identification and analysis of policy problems and in the development of policy proposals through governmental public inquiries; and (ii) through an open consultation and review processes that precede proposals for legislation and reform in parliament. This Swedish public inquiry system is a far-reaching example of political–constitutional deliberation in the legislature (Meadowcroft, 2004). Against this background we would hesitate to designate multi-stakeholder deliberation as a *new* mode of governance, if by 'new' we were to mean a relatively transparent and deliberative process preceding legislation. However, openness is relative. For example, it is the government who appoints the inquiry, defines its mandate and decides which stakeholder groups are allowed to participate. Clearly, the choice of stakeholders affects the problem defini-tion, interpretation, analysis and subsequent policy recommendations. The stakeholders who are regarded as significant, reasonable and politically neces-sary or expedient – that is the groups that are given standing in the inquiry process – have varied over time.

While the Swedish public inquiry system clearly does not satisfy a deliber-ative democratic ideal of engagement on equal terms, free of manipulation and the exercise of power, it does include (major) stakeholders, it provides a high degree of transparency, and during the later review phase, it allows input from stakeholders and the public (including individual citizens). While the process above may be described as a form of multi-stakeholder deliberation, the outcome in the form of legislation may or may not provide for harder or softer regulation, enforcement or education in the post-legislative (implementation) phase. The resulting regulatory strategy can in itself be more or less delibera-tive. In other words, in the Swedish context we need to differentiate between the pre- and post-legislative deliberation phases in our analysis of the deliber-ative turn.

In Sweden there has been a century-long, but geographically varied, tradi-tion of regulating the use of forest-related resources – whether for grazing, timber, early mining or energy use. In this chapter we take the year 1896 as our starting point. In many respects the 1896 Forest Inquiry, which delivered its report in 1899 (Anon., 1899), can be seen as the first attempt to regulate forestry as supplier of resources within a modern industrial context.

The Early Deliberative Period in Modern Swedish Forestry Governance

Forest policy discourse during the end of the nineteenth century focused on the threat to long-term forest production from lack of replanting after harvest. This threat was particularly evident in the northern part of Sweden. In 1896, a Forest Inquiry was given the mandate to identify measures to improve forest rejuvenation and the management of young forest stands in order to secure the long-term productivity of private forests without imposing restrictions on the right of ownership. The committee members represented private forest owners (farmers and owners of big estates), forest scientists and civil servants. The committee was guided by a deliberative rationality and travelled widely across the country to gather input from forest owners, the timber industry and forest officers. The Committee's report (Anon., 1899) noted that while there was no lack of knowledge on how to rejuvenate the Swedish forest stand, local adap-tation and participation was needed to achieve this goal. The resulting rejuve-nation regulations in the 1903 Forest Act were by necessity administrative and regulatory (as current non-regulation obviously had not sufficed), but in other respects the policy-making and its implementation can be characterized as soft and deliberative in its approach as it depended on the perceived legitimacy by the forest owners, and their knowledge and willingness to enact it.

One result of the 1903 Forest Act was the establishment of regional forestry boards. These boards were to work independently, outside the established county administration, which otherwise was a tool for state oversight at the regional level. This set-up allowed forestry boards to work more through influence and education and on a more equal footing with the private forest owners, as compared to traditional state authorities (Stjernquist, 1973; Ekelund and Hamilton, 2001).

Rejuvenation problems remained, however, and further legislation was introduced in 1923 in order to promote mandatory rules on forest rejuvenation after felling, natural disasters and in situations where forest grazing affected rejuvenation. The 1923 Forest Act also contained rules against too early and speculative felling. During the period several inquiries investigated the ecological, social and economical conditions for forestry in different parts of Sweden, all based on the premise that the policy should be economically viable for the individual property. Resource use at different sizes and types of properties, as well as the close relationship between forestry and farming, were reviewed. At that time, 60 per cent of the Swedish private forestland was owned by farmers, and most farmers viewed their forests as natural resources for long-term sustainable and multiple use (SOU, 1925:11; SOU, 1925:12). However, on the national level the only consideration of importance was to safeguard the long-term forest sustainability. Hence, government steering involved rejuvenation and cutting, while other parts of the forest management cycle were based on voluntary measures. During the next two decades, the forest inquiries were focused on further measures to increase the timber and biomass production through support for draining, ditching and road building (SOU, 1929:34; 1933:2; 1934:32; 1938:38). This goal was largely accomplished through information and various economic subsidies, and, during the depression, also by relief work.

In the forest legislation leading up to and including the 1948 Forest Act, forestry, outside corporate forestry, was seen as a component in the livelihood of a large number of traditional, non-industrial, forest owners, often in combination with agriculture (Stjernquist, 1973). The inquiry, presented in 1946 (SOU, 1946:41), was informed by the same rationale, but introduced more state steering in order to make better use of the potential productivity at each property. The inquiry was carried out by a committee with representatives from major stakeholder groups and included the forest administration, forest owners, the forest industry, parliamentarians, the county council and forest researchers. The directives highlighted a dual problematization: 1) the need for a higher production per unit area; and 2) regulations in tune with existing social, economic and ecological conditions. Nevertheless, despite the increased emphasis on forest productivity, forestland could still be used for grazing, meadows, arable land or recreation areas if the owner so decided. No uncertainties were associated with this policy, nor was there any urgency underlying the reform. The ambitions for national or regional cross-sectoral coordination were negligible; the balance between agriculture and forestry was dependent on the owner striking the balance at the holding level. Successful implementation was dependent on forest owner participation and the need to allow for local conditions, and this was widely recognized.

Hierarchical Forms of Governance to Conserve Forest Ecosystems

Under the pressure from a poor economy and government subsidies for coniferous plantations, natural beech forests were being replaced at a high rate in southern Sweden during the 1960s. The loss of beech forest ecosystems impacted negatively on biodiversity, landscapes, cultural heritage and recreation values. The process faced considerable criticism from the public, and a government inquiry was instigated to find ways to preserve beech forests. Change in the beech forest was monitored through a beech survey conducted by the forest agency. The inquiry delivered its proposal in 1971 (SOU, 1971:71). The policy issue was straightforward but went counter to the economic rationality underlying forest policy aims at the time. Its aims were to preserve an otherwise non-economic forest type through a combination of hard regulation and economic subsidies. In order to secure the preservation of beech forests, hierarchical state steering was introduced. The resulting Beech Forest Act (SFS, 1974:434) included mandatory felling permits, powers to refuse fellings, and mandatory rejuvenation after fellings.

The work of the inquiry in preparation for legislation had been carried out with a high degree of deliberation. The members of the committee and the experts came from the forest authorities, the environmental agency, and from the biodiversity and soil sciences and recreation research community. The committee also invited other stakeholders to the deliberations, such as municipalities, the county administration, tourist organizations and forest companies. Despite these deliberations, the Beech Forest Act generated conflicts with forest owners, in particular about the loss of expected future value of spruce plantations, evident in a large number of court cases about economic compensation. At the same time the legislation's long-term output effectiveness depended upon a long-term cooperation between the forest owners and the forest authorities (and to some extent compliance monitoring by the public and environmental NGOs). The law was, by and large, successful. It inspired and was later replaced by, the Valuable Hardwood Forest Act (SFS, 1984:119). Perhaps as a way to eliminate conflict, this Act was preceded by minimal deliberation and was based on the input of only two distinct positions in the form of memoranda from the Swedish Environmental Protection Agency and the Swedish Forest Agency.

The Heyday of Hierarchical Governance: the Period from 1979 to 1993

By the 1970s, major changes had occurred in Swedish forestry. These changes prompted a review of the 1948 Forest Act, and a new forest policy inquiry was presented in 1973 (SOU, 1973:14). The inquiry was small and primarily involved civil servants and experts. The policy goals for the first 1973 inquiry, 'Aims and Means in Forest Politics' (SOU, 1973:14), were well defined. The committee members and experts were mainly recruited from the forest industry, the unions and among civil servant experts. All deliberation took place in a small circle of administrative experts and representatives that emphasized the economic interests of forestry. The forest industry argued that they needed a cheap, reliable resource input and the volume was to be defined by the industry's capacity and needs. At the time, there were considerable concerns about a forest resource deficiency gap between what was available and deliverable from cuttings, and the processing capacity (demand) of an expanded forest industry. The stakes were also seen as significant; in particular, the threat from industry for not receiving enough forest resources was a strong driver. Hence, the forest policy goals were guided by an economic rationality with a national focus. According to its directives, the aims of the inquiry were: (1) to analyse the forest management methods in relation to the size of the forest estates; (2) to change the principles guiding the governmental subsidies; and (3) to change the organization of the state involvement in forest management. Small-scale, non-industrial forest holdings were also seen as non-viable in the long term, and their inclusion in state or forest industrial ownership was regarded as more appropriate. This group of actors was also marginalized in the policy process. The long-term sustainability production perspective was seen as irrelevant and, in the light of industry needs, it was thought that production ought to focus on economic optimization even if that meant reduced generation times in the forest and the cutting of non-mature forests. These problems were to be overcome by a combination of physical and fiscal monitoring and hierarchical administrative and economic governance. The inquiry consequently proposed a yearly tax on the assessed growth of the forest stock at holding level, which was easy to monitor, in order to make retention of older or mature forest uneconomical and to provide incentives for increased cuttings. The need for cross-sectoral compromise, let alone optimization, was seen as negligible as production was defined as the overriding goal. The degree of local participation and adaptation needed to reach this goal was also seen as insignificant, and it was to be reached through a mixture of hierarchical means such as legal and administrative regulation of production, and through taxation. What we observed is that with the emphasis on forest productivity and economic rationality on the national level, the committee delivered recommendations that turned out to be a clear break with previous forest policy. The proposals faced considerable criticism, and as a result another inquiry was set up in 1973. The proposals of the new inquiry (SOU, 1978:7) and the subsequent Forestry Act (SFS, 1979:429) did not break with the governance trend outlined above.

The directives of the second 1973 inquiry, which was called Future Forests, were also focused on increasing forest production. To achieve a high and even output for the expanded forest industry was the central aim (SOU, 1978:6). The committee was asked to consider the effects the forest sector expansion would have on recreation activities. The committee members were mainly selected from the forest industry and among civil servant experts. Its 1978 proposals were directed towards an intensified large-scale schematic forest management, mainly for bulk production, to be achieved by hierarchical administrative and economic means, that is more detailed regulation and taxation. Environmental issues were not included in the inquiry directives. Cross-sectoral concerns were negligible and the reform was focused on production. The environmental considerations were on the whole limited and mainly concerned a *pro forma* application before clear cutting. Directions on the age for final felling, allowed species for rejuvenation, and demands for the removal of birch in spruce stands (with the right to order this against the owners' wish), the number of plants per unit area and so on were delegated by the legislators to the forest authorities (cf. Stjernquist, 1992).

Hierarchical control over non-industrial forestry was further strengthened through amendments to the Forestry Act in 1983 (SFS, 1983:427), which aimed at increasing wood supply, for example by allowing the government or the forestry board to mandate the cutting of mature forest on private land. On the whole, the legislation over this period represents a clear break with previous governance traditions that were more inclusive, participatory and deliberative. In general, it relied less on information, dialogue, training and education, and more on hierarchical monitoring, control and rule enforcement. Indeed, the 1979 Forestry Act with the 1983 amendments can be seen as effecting a near de facto nationalization of the non-industrial forestry base with the owners responsible for policy implementation, cf. Stjernquist (1983). The legislation represented not only a policy shift aiming towards a large-scale, highly mechanized, schematic and 'rational' forestry; it also reflected something of the political *zeitgeist* at the time with a strong penchant for centralized economic policy, planning and socializing ambitions (Sundström, 2005). When economic goals in the strict sense of national large-scale forest productivity were defined as the overarching goal, only the actors who supported that view were listened to.

The Deliberative Return: the Period from 1993 till Today

The emerging environmental awareness and concerns during the 1980s increasingly clashed with the realities of the new Swedish forest policy. Indeed, many of the issues of concern to the environmental movement related to the effects of the economic and administrative governance rationalities of the 1970s. Consequently, the Swedish forestry legislation faced increasing criticism from the environmental movement, non-industrial owners, industry, as well as critics of centralized planning and detailed state control of private property. In response to this widespread criticism, the government commissioned two forest policy evaluations that drastically changed the Swedish forest governance landscape. The resulting 1993 Forest Act (SFS, 1993:553) was a revision of the 1979 Forest Act, but can for all purposes be seen as a new Act.

The departmental inquiry 'Forest policy for a new century' (Ds. 1991:31 (1994)) was an evaluation of the effects of the forest policy by two experts from the Swedish University of Agriculture. It concluded that the regulations in the 1979 Act had been inefficient and directed criticism at the dominance of the hierarchical form of governance. The inquiry proposed that the role of the state should be limited to correcting or compensating the market where it fails and that is should become less focused on national issues. An important role for the state in this perspective was to reduce transboundary air pollution through the 'polluter pays' principle and international negotiations, to safeguard nature protection, secure carbon storage in forest biomass and soils, and to secure other overarching public interests. Other forestry objectives were to be left to the market. The evaluation argued for much less as well as less detailed regulation. Indeed, too much regulation was seen as the main policy problem. The notion of a resource deficiency between industry needs and delivery from forestry had disappeared as Sweden had more forest resources than ever before in historic times; also forest owners were seen as competent to handle both production and environmental concerns. While there was no lack of knowledge about how to maintain the forest resource, the inquiry identified significant knowledge gaps in nature conservation in a landscape perspective. Needs for benchmarking and for management for multiple-use were also identified.

The inquiry advocated for deliberative rationality in governance by stating that the regulation process must be open, and that routines for stakeholder participation and supervision must be included. The importance of employing various voluntary agreements for nature protection was highlighted. The inquiry had high ambitions with regard to cross-sectoral integration and compromise. The forestry sector needed to cooperate with municipalities, the county administrations, forest owners, NGOs and the public.

The 1990 Forest Political Inquiry, 'Forest policy in the 21st century' (SOU, 1992:76) delivered its proposals in 1992. It was based on an evaluation of the long-term future use of the forest resource in a wide sense including: a systems perspective of biomass production, the sustainable use of forest soils, the impact of the deposition of transboundary air pollution, biodiversity conservation, a living countryside and assessments of the national and international importance of the forest industry. The directives focused on developing a forest management based on the ecological conditions at the forest stand level. The need to harmonize forest regulation across sectors (namely nature protection regulations) and to balance different sectoral demands on the forests, were also highlighted. The proposed modes of governance ranged from legal to voluntary measures. The former should define the minimum obligations of the forest owner. Information, guidance, education and training were seen as central for attaining policy goals and as a way of communicating and implementing forestry research. The proposals represented a return from detailed hierarchical control and enforcement towards softer and more delegated and deliberative modes of governance.

In addition to proposing deliberative ways for policy-making, the inquiry was in itself much more inclusive than previous ones and it was organized around a parliamentarian committee with experts from the forest authority, stakeholder groups representing the Sami people, forest industry and unions, forest owners, environmental NGOs, as well as representatives from a number of government departments, including agriculture, environment, finance, industry and enterprise. Problem definitions articulated were in many respects vague, for example regarding the balance between different sectoral and actor interests, and the proposed governance strategies. The proposals of the inquiry reflect an uncertainty about whether suggested measures to safeguard biodiversity, the long-term sustainable production and different habitats would work. The difficulties of monitoring these aspects are considerable and the inquiry skirted around the associated uncertainty issues, in relation to output effectiveness of the proposals, by claiming that the outcome should be less regulation, which in turn would deliver greater variation in the forest management and less bureaucracy. In this respect, the means were to some extent an end in themselves. The inquiry was distinctly deliberative in its approach, not only by involving a diverse set of actors and experts but also through its extensive consultations with stakeholders outside the traditional forestry sector, for example organizations working with biomass for energy. The committee recognized the importance of, and the need to cater for, the diversity of ownership by including a report about the decision-making processes among different forest owner categories. The importance of continuous consultations between forest owners and the local staff of the Swedish Forest Agency to reach both the production and the environmental goals was emphasized. Local action and adaptation was seen as a prerequisite for effective environmental protection.

The 1993 Forest Act represents a change of governance modes but, more importantly, also a paradigm change in goals in so far as the production and environmental goals were explicitly given equal weight. At this point in time, state steering was at a minimum and the forest owner was identified as the key actor for protecting biodiversity and habitats. The voluntary measures to reach the production and environmental goals depended on the forest owners' knowledge about local ecological and silvicultural conditions. The forest agencies' role was largely to build trust and provide a platform for information and education. Forestry agency campaigns such as 'A Greener Forest', 'Good Balance between Soil and Water' and 'Conservation of Cultural Heritage in the Forest', and the new voluntary measures to conserve areas or sites of biodiversity value such as environmental agreements have been very effective for nature conservation (Perhans, 2008). They also represent a successful reinvention of the forest authority as an educational and deliberative organization, as opposed to a mainly controlling and enforcing one. Accordingly, the policies at the beginning of the twentieth and the twenty-first centuries show large similarities in their focus on deliberative and participatory approaches as well as in their emphasis on local adaptation and action.

The Swedish EU membership in the mid-1990s, the development of a scheme of cross-sectoral national environmental quality objectives, decisions to assemble all environmental legislations into one environmental code in 1999 as well as other changes called for an updated forest legislation. The directives were to: analyse the responsibility of the state and the forestry sector for the implementation of the forest policy; evaluate the latter in a societal perspective; evaluate the effects on the forestry sector coupled to EU regulations and international accords. Furthermore, the aim was to analyse the impacts of an increasingly international timber market, environmental and consumer demands, and global environmental threats such as climate change. The role of the inquiry was also to assess the forestry sectors' contribution to increased health and welfare in society, and to the national environmental quality objectives. The inquiry 'Additional Values in Forests' presented its conclusions in 2006 (SOU, 2006:81).

A parliamentarian reference group supported the investigator. No formal group of experts was appointed but an ad hoc advisory group was formed with representatives from the forest industry, the Swedish Forest Agency, the Ministries of Environment, Finance and Enterprise, NGOs and one forest owner organization. In contrast to the committee and the expert group of the 1991 inquiry, the 2006 inquiry had no representative from the Sami people, the forest workers unions, the Swedish Environmental Protection Agency, the Swedish Forestry Association or the Federation of Swedish Farmers. The degree of deliberation was thus significantly lower and informal compared to the work preceding the 1993 Forest Act. Transparency thus became greatly reduced as different stakeholder groups had little idea of who had been approached during the process. The inclusion and participation was lower and was dependent on the commissioner's appraisal of whom to include.

While there was political urgency to adjust to new EU regulations and other legal changes, other issues were less clear and politically urgent. The issues to be investigated varied greatly in clarity. The issue of including EU regulations and the international accords with relevance to Swedish forest policy was reasonably straightforward, whereas the task of striking a balance between different sectoral and stakeholder interests in forests was a considerably more difficult task, open to much more conflict between numerous and potentially incompatible interests (cf. Andersson, 2007). To strike a balance between industrial forest demands and expected demands for bioenergy to mitigate climate change is one such example. Others involve potential trade-offs between biodiversity conservation, reindeer herding, recreational needs close to urban areas, forest owner livelihoods *and* carbon storage. These multiple goals represented a tall order that neither provided for easy problem definitions nor for clear policy proposals. Nevertheless, the current 2008 Forest Act (SFS, 2008:662) retains much of the 1993 Forest Act, especially concerning the need for local participation and adaptation to reach production and environmental goals.

IS THERE A DELIBERATIVE TURN?

Three things are clear from our analysis. First, deliberation that includes stakeholder interests both in pre- and post-legislative phases has occurred since the beginning of the studied period. Multi-stakeholder deliberations have been an institutionalized feature in the phases prior to legislation. The nature, aim and outcome of these deliberations have varied over time. It is also apparent that, for most of the time, a mixture of modes and rationalities had been a part of the regulatory palette of forest governance.

Secondly, the range of interests/stakeholders included in these deliberative processes has also varied and expanded over the studied period. This expansion does not represent a systemic increase over time. Early stakeholder deliberations included, apart from parliamentarians and experts, industry and landowner interests. Later other stakeholder interests such as the forest workers and the pulp and paper workers unions were included. To some extent, the environmental debate can be seen as a discursive struggle over problem definitions and issues. It is noteworthy that environmental NGOs, through the Swedish Society for Nature Protection, and Sami representatives, through

NGOs organizing the indigenous reindeer herders, were only given stakeholder standing in the 1990 Forest Political Inquiry (SOU, 1992:76), preceding the 1993 Forestry Act. We should, however, note that in the latest inquiry, the deliberative process was less open and transparent than in the 1990s.

Thirdly, the degree and quality of deliberation in the implementation phase has varied, and has shown considerable swings over time. Implementation of early forest policy, as well as enforcement of legislation, was largely based on deliberation directed towards small-scale forest owners through information campaigns, education and advisory services through the regional Forestry Commissions (c.f. Stjernquist, 1973). Nevertheless, one has to qualify this description of deliberation by pointing out that it did not occur between equal parties. Furthermore, it always occurred in the shadow of hierarchy in the sense that the forest authorities could potentially play the legal card. Following the 1979 Forestry Act, government monitoring, control and enforcement were given clear prominence over deliberation, and forest policy was defined narrowly as a matter of timber production. The power over the operative management was in many respects wrested from the non-industrial forest owners. With the 1993 and 2008 Forest Acts, empowerment of the forest owner, participation, local adaptation and deliberation are words that have gained renewed resonance. Deregulation created the opportunity for the development of new modes of governance such as voluntary green forest plans, forest certification and environmental agreements currently in use. But, while the legislation formally (rhetorically, some might say) put production and environmental concerns on an equal footing, they are incommensurable entities. No guidance was provided as to how to operationalize this new balance. Further, the law provided no enforcement capabilities in this respect to the forest agencies and the only way for this was to influence forest owners through educational campaigns, like Green Forestry Plans, advice and other information campaigns (SNAO, 1999:31).

Summing up, with regard to Swedish forest governance, deliberations have been there all along but varied over time, both in its pre- and post-legislative phases. Contemporary forest governance practice merely suggests that it now includes a greater number of, and more varied, stakeholders. Our study of Swedish forest governance suggests that we are witnessing a deliberative return.

WHY HAS DELIBERATION VARIED OVER TIME?

Based on our empirical analysis we suggest that the contemporary rise of new modes of environmental governance is neither driven by the retreat of the state, nor by political efforts to democratize environmental governance through multi-stakeholder deliberation. Rather, deliberation and softer forms of governance occur not only in the shadow of hierarchy, as often suggested, but probably at the mercy of what is deemed possible, expedient and effective by government and central authorities. The balance between traditional hierarchical forms of governance and more deliberative forms seems to reflect the character of the perceived regulatory challenge. According to our study, the choice of environmental governance modes varies according to aspects such as the definition of the problem at stake, technical/scientific uncertainty, size of stakes and urgency of threat (the need to act), the ease of monitoring important aspects (like problem development, compliance, policy effects), the need to accommodate different sectoral interests, the need for participation in policy enactment, as well as the need for local adaptation of the policy.

Based on this analysis of forest governance in Sweden we propose some general insights into why governance may vary over time. First, a clear problem definition is needed for traditional hierarchical regulation to be effective. Conversely, in situations where the problem definition is vague, soft steering, and in particular, voluntary measures are likely to be favoured, such as more deliberative modes of governance. Secondly, hierarchical steering is less likely to be chosen as a governance mode in situations of significant uncertainty, either with regard to the complexity of the issue or the efficacy of potential policy alternatives. On the other hand, if the perceived stakes and costs of non-action are high, hierarchical steering is likely to be favoured. Similarly, if a problem is perceived as an urgent and clear threat it is more likely to be handled through command-and-control regulation than by deliberative or voluntary measures, other characteristics allowing.

We learned from forest policy that the ability to monitor problem development and policy compliance is central to any hierarchical enforcement-directed governance strategy. However, in situations where policy-makers strive to attain multiple, and potentially conflicting, sectoral goals that require coordination between different governmental agencies or societal actors, hierarchical steering risks becoming difficult, in particular if problems and policy aims are vaguely defined. Hence, softer steering or voluntary agreements may appear as more feasible ways forward. Finally, in situations when implementation is more or less dependent on cooperation with local actors (due to difficulties of monitoring or dependence on local decision-making and action, etc.), or on local adaptation (to local traditions, situated knowledge, tree stand conditions, etc.), we may expect hierarchical forms of steering to be less effective and less favoured. In the latter case deliberative modes of governance will probably be favoured in order to achieve sufficient legitimacy and acceptance for the delivery of output effectiveness.

Faced with complexity and uncertain problems, conflicting interests, unclear voter constellations and preferences, deliberation emerges as an economically and politically safe stop-gap strategy, awaiting clearer problem definitions and voter preferences, reduced scientific uncertainty and better identified stakes and hazards.

Along these lines, we propose that areas for environmental policy-making that include well-defined and clear risks, in particular for humans, or significant uncontroversial costs, tend to be subject to hierarchical government steering. Examples are toxicity or carcinogenic risks in the work environment, waste disposal, and food and construction safety. Here we should note that the hierarchical forest governance in the 1970s was not targeting environmental issues but was directed at forest resource production and delivery (as a response to a perceived future shortfall of forest resource) at the expense of owner influence, local adaptation and environmental quality. Policy issues that are poorly defined, or more contentious, lend themselves better to steering by goals and deliberation; so do areas where environmental monitoring or monitoring of compliance may prove difficult. The Swedish environmental objectives provide an example (see Chapter 8, this volume). However, well-defined policies that need to be adjusted for local conditions for their success, and that hinge upon the willingness of multiple actors for implementation, are likely to be more dependent on deliberation both as a legitimizing, educational and mobilizing force. The success of official campaigns such as Greener Forests and Green Forestry Plans, as well as the widespread adoption of forest certification in Sweden (cf. Schlyter et al., 2009), illustrate the output effectiveness of more deliberative approaches in such situations.

CONCLUSIONS

The development of Swedish forest governance over the last century provides an example of shifting goals as well as shifts in emphasis on different governance strategies, that is, command–control–enforcement, multi-stakeholder deliberations, information–education–training, self-regulation and market-driven regulation. The change of emphasis in the chosen regulatory strategies over time reveals that multi-stakeholder deliberation and self-regulation are by no means new tools in the regulatory toolbox. There has been stakeholder representation in formal deliberation prior to legislation during the whole period studied. Hence, if we intend to speak about a deliberative turn, it would be more accurate to call it a deliberative *return* and to investigate the qualitative process of deliberation in more detail. In our case we noted that the number of stakeholder interests included in deliberations has increased over time as more ecosystem services are subject to policy considerations. The degree of transparency in the process has also varied and, surprisingly, has been reduced in the process leading up to the latest, 2008, forest legislation. There is no clear trend towards softer or voluntary approaches as opposed to hard regulation over time; rather there have been swings between softer, more deliberative/participatory and harder, hierarchical modes. Hard legal regulation has always been present to set minimum standards of behaviour. We interpret the renewed use of softer steering through deliberation, information and self-regulation in recent years as a way to accommodate current multiple, partly incompatible, interests/goals in a situation where the state as regulator is unable or unwilling to favour a single actor or interest awaiting greater clarity about the biophysical, economic *and* political risks involved.

To a large extent the perception and character of the regulatory problem as such, appears to influence the choice of governance strategy. There seems to be a relatively good fit between hard, hierarchical administrative and economic regulation and clear problem definitions, perceived high degree of knowledge about the issue to be regulated and urgency to act, and a low need for cross-sectoral compromise and participation. Conversely issues with vaguer problematization and greater uncertainty with regard to knowledge or risks, poor ability to monitor and/or a need for cross-sectoral compromise and dependence on local adaptation and participation are likely to be handled with deliberation, softer regulation or voluntary measures. Our analysis suggests that the deliberative turn in Swedish forestry governance in recent years reflects steering problems in a more complex world with less well defined issues and competing sectoral claims, rather than an imperative from deliberative democracy theories to decision-making and governance per se. We propose that the purported deliberative turn in forestry governance, which includes previously marginalized stakeholders and disenfranchised groups in policy-making and implementation probably is a reflection of the perceived intrinsic properties of the regulatory challenge and a need to handle more visibly conflicting interests as such. Nor has, in our analysis, the state retreated with regard to governance. Indeed, one may argue that the deliberations in different forums, exemplified by the various forest certification schemes, operate very much in the shadow of hierarchy (Schlyter et al., 2009). However, in a situation with competing stakeholder interests, often considerable scientific uncertainty with regard to the kind and scale of problems as well as solutions and, for many issues, difficulty in defining parameters to be monitored, the operationalization of a balance between different interests (for example production and environmental objectives, national environmental objectives and the host of other issues supposed to be handled by the 2006 inquiry) becomes rather difficult.

REFERENCES

Andersson, Therese (2007), 'En gemensam skogspolitik? En integrationsteoretisk studie av ett politikområde på tillväxt' ['A common forest policy? A theoretical study on European integration, an expanding political field']. Statvetenskapliga institutionens skriftserie 2007:4, thesis, Department of Political Science, Umeå University.

Anonymous (1899), 'Underdånigt betänkande av den för utredning angående lämpliga åtgärder för främjande av den enskilda skogshushållningen av Kungl. Maj:t den 6 oktober 1896 förordnad kommitte' ['A respectful report concerning suitable measures for the benefit of the private forest husbandry by the inquiry commissioned by His Majesty's Government'], Stockholm.

Appelstrand, Marie (2007), *Miljömålet i skogsbruket – styrning och frivillighet* [*The Environmental Goal in Forestry – Steering and Voluntariness*], Lund Studies in Sociology of Law 26, Lund, Sweden: Lund University.

Boström, Magnus (2003), 'How state-dependent is a non-state driven rule-making project? The case of forest certification in Sweden', *Journal of Environmental Policy and Planning*, **5**(2), 165–80.

Cashore, Benjamin, Elizabeth Egan, Graeme Auld and Deanna Newsom (2007), 'Revising theories of nonstate market-driven (NSMD) governance: lessons from the Finnish forest certification experience', *Global Environmental Politics*, **7**(1), 1–44.

Ds. 1991:31 (1994), *Skogspolitik för ett nytt sekel* [Forest policy for a new century], Stockholm: Finansdepartementet ESO.

Ekelund, H. and G. Hamilton (2001), *Skogspolitisk Historia* (The History of Forest Politics), report 8A 2001, Jönköping: Swedish Forest Agency.

Gulbrandsen, Lars H. (2004), 'Overlapping public and private governance: can forest certification fill the gaps in the global forest regime?', *Global Environmental Politics*, **4**(2), 75–96.

Gutmann, Amy and Dennis Thompson (2004), *Why Deliberative Democracy?*, Princeton, NJ and Oxford: Princeton University Press.

Holmberg, L.-E. (2005), *Skogshistoria år från år 1177–2005* [*The Swedish Forest History 1177–2005*], report 2005:5, Jönköping: Swedish Forest Agency.

Meadowcroft, James (2004), 'Deliberative democracy', in Robert Durant, Daniel Fiorini and Rosemary O'Leary (eds), *Environmental Governance Reconsidered: Challenges, Choices and Opportunities*, Cambridge, MA: MIT Press, pp. 183–217.

Perhans, J. (2008), 'Cost-efficient conservation strategies for boreal forest biodiversity', doctoral dissertation, Department of Ecology, SLU, Acta Universitatis Agriculturae Sueciae, vol. 208: 39, Uppsala, Sweden.

Schlyter, Peter, Ingrid Stjernquist and Karin Bäckstrand (2009), 'Not seeing the forest for the trees? The environmental effectiveness of forest certification in Sweden', *Forest Policy and Economics*, **11**(5–6), 375–82.

SFS 1974:434, *Beech Forest Act*, Stockholm.

SFS 1984:119, *Valuable Hardwood Forest Act*, Stockholm.

SFS 1979:429, *Forest Act*, Stockholm.

SFS 1983:427, *Forest Act*, Stockholm

SFS 1993:553, *Forest Act*, Stockholm.

SFS 2008:662, *Forest Act*, Stockholm.

SOU 1925:11, *De Biologiska, Historiska och Ekonomiska Förutsättningarna för det Svenska Skogsbrukets Bedrivande* [The Biological, Historical and Economical Conditions for Forest Management in Sweden], Stockholm.

SOU 1925:12, *Sveriges Enskilda Skogar* [Sweden's Private Forests], Stockholm.

SOU 1929:34, *Förslag till Lag om Virkesmätning* [Proposal about a Timber Measurement Act], Stockholm.

SOU 1933:2, *Åtgärder för ett Bättre Utnyttjande av Landets Skogstillångar* [Measures for a Better Use of the Forest Resources], Stockholm.

SOU 1934:32, *Betänkande med Förslag till Lag om Virkesmätning* [Inquiry with Proposal on a Timber Measurement Act], Stockholm.

SOU 1938:38, *Främjande av en Bättre Virkesproduktion* [Promotion of a Better Timber Production], Stockholm.

SOU 1946:41, *Betänkande med Förslag till Skogsvårdslag* [Proposal for a New Forestry Act], Stockholm.

SOU 1971:71, *Bokskogens Bevarande* [Protection of the Beech Forests], Stockholm.

SOU 1973:14, *Mål och Medel i Skogspolitiken* [Aims and Means in Forest Politics], Stockholm.

SOU 1978:6–7, *Skog för Framtid* [Forest for the Future], Stockholm.

SOU 1984:119, *Ädellövskogslag* [Proposal for an Act on the Protection of Valuable Hardwood Forests], Stockholm.

SOU 1992:76, *Skogspolitiken inför 2000-talet* [Forest Politics in the 21st Century], Stockholm.

SOU 2006:81, *Mervärdesskog* [Added Values in the Forest], Stockholm.

Stjernquist, Per (1973), *Laws in the Forest: A Study of Public Direction of Swedish Private Forestry*. Lund, Sweden: Acta Regiae Societas Humaniorum Litterarum Lundensis LXIX.

Stjernquist, Per (1983), 'Från enskild till offentlig förvaltning i skogspolitiken' ['From individual to state management of the forest policy'], *Statsvetenskaplig Tidskrift*, **86**(4), 297–307.

Stjernquist, Per (1992), *Forest Treatment: Relations to Nature of Swedish Private Forestry*. Lund, Sweden: Scripta Minora Societas Humaniorum Litterarum Lundensis 1991–1992:1.

Sundström, Göran (2005), *Målstyrningen drar åt skogen. Om government och governance i svensk skogspolitik* [Steering-by-Objectives Goes to Blazes. On Government and Governance in Swedish Forest Policy], SCORE Report 2005:6, Stockholm: Stockholms centrum för forskning om offentlig sektor [Stockholm Centre for Research on the Public Sector], Handelshögskolan i Stockholm and Stockholms Universitet.

Swedish National Audit Office (SNAO) (1999), *Skogsvårdsorganisationernas arbete med att jämställa miljömålet med produktionsmålet* [*The Forestry Authorities Work to Equate Environmental Objectives with Production Goals*], Effektivitetsrevisionen RRV 1999: 31, Stockholm: SNAO (Riksrevisionsverket).

11. Local climate mitigation and network governance: progressive policy innovation or status quo in disguise?

Jamil Khan

INTRODUCTION

Many municipalities around the world have taken a pioneering role in tackling climate change, making the local level an important political arena for climate governance (Bulkeley and Betsill, 2003; Coenen and Menkveld, 2002; Collier, 1997). The proliferation of transnational climate networks between municipalities has led to a diffusion of autonomous local climate governance that is independent of states or international institutions (Kern and Bulkeley, 2009). Although the climate goals of pioneer municipalities are often more ambitious than those enacted by national governments or international organizations, these municipalities face great challenges since they lack authority to enforce policy compliance (Betsill and Bulkeley 2007). In order to attain effective implementation of mitigation measures, it is therefore necessary to forge consensus among different municipal actors around ambitious climate policy goals.

Against this background, this chapter examines network governance as an important aspect of local climate politics. In line with Chapter 5, network governance can be understood as a 'new' mode of governance since it involves the participation of private actors (business, NGOs) in the policy and implementation process, and is based on a mix of hierarchical and non-hierarchical forms of steering (Bogason and Musso, 2006; Koimann, 2003; Pierre and Peters, 2000). In network governance, the municipality is a facilitator rather than commander and implementer. As such it does not replace hierarchical forms of steering based on administrative rationality, but exists alongside these more traditional modes of governance.

This chapter pays particular attention to the 'promise' of network governance in local climate politics, namely the capacity to achieve effective policy results in a situation where traditional modes of governance are not available or have proved ineffective (Aars and Fimreite, 2005). Beyond this focus on policy performance, network governance also holds the promise to include new actors in the policy process and thereby enhance the deliberative and participatory quality of environmental policy-making (Bogason and Musso, 2006; Sørensen, 2002). The assessment of this dual promise is, in this chapter, based on a review of existing research on municipal climate governance, and on an in-depth case study of climate governance in the municipality of Växjö, Sweden.[1] The focus is on climate mitigation policies, which have been the subject of a fairly large body of research. Climate adaptation, which is a growing research field (Storbjörk, 2007; Næss *et al.,* 2005) as municipalities are increasingly adopting adaptation policies, is not addressed here.

This chapter starts with a discussion of the concept of network governance and argues that climate change has led to institutional innovations in municipalities. Four different types of network are addressed: city-to-city networks, internal municipal networks, policy formation networks and policy implementation networks. In the remaining sections the promise of network governance is critically explored. Although developments in climate change cities can give valuable lessons on how to revitalize the democratic system and increase the effectiveness of environmental governance, network governance is not unproblematic. The chapter thus ends with a critical debate on the limits of network governance and the sceptical claim that institutional innovations neither increase participation or deliberation, nor environmental effectiveness.

NETWORK GOVERNANCE

Network governance refers to a shift from traditional hierarchical governance forms where the state is the regulator, to looser forms of governance where private actors such as business and NGOs increasingly participate in policy-making (Bogason and Musso, 2006; Koimann, 2003; Sørensen, 2002; Pierre and Peters, 2000). The shift to network governance is explained by the increasing policy dependency of governments on other actors in face of complex modern societal problems (Pierre and Peters, 2000). Research shows that network governance is also relevant in the local context (Bogason and Musso, 2006; De Rynck and Voets, 2006; Sørensen, 2006; Aars and Fimreite, 2005).

In Chapter 2, Bäckstrand and Kronsell identify networks as a governance form along with hierarchies and markets. Hierarchy is based on strong chains of command in a top-down fashion, while the market is a self-organizing governance form based on free transactions between actors. Networks, by contrast, rely on links between public and private actors, which can be both organizations and individuals. A key feature of networks is that actors are interdependent and cannot carry out their decisions alone. Cooperation and trust are thus essential traits of network governance. In Chapter 2 it was argued that governance forms can be combined with different governance rationalities. Deliberative rationality is particularly relevant for networks since the interdependence between actors calls for deliberation and consensus to reach common solutions. However, networks can also be based on administrative rationality (networks between experts) and economic rationality (networks between business actors) and combinations of these. Still, the need for deliberation between actors exists in all types of networks. As will be discussed in further depth in this chapter, network governance in local climate politics signifies a mix between administrative, economic and deliberative rationality.

Network governance also covers a broad range of organizational forms from public–private partnerships and stakeholder participation to informal personal interactions between individuals. A key feature of all network governance is that participants are bound together by a common problem that needs to be collectively solved. Actors will have various motives for joining the network and differing opinions on the preferred outcome. Interdependency between actors does not preclude asymmetrical power relations. On the contrary, Bogason and Musso (2006, p. 7), claim that 'structural power differentials and conflicts' is one of the main issues of network governance. Arguably, the general distribution of power in society is reflected in networks, which can be criticized for contributing to maintaining status quo and existing power imbalances (Fischer, 2006).

How does network governance relate to the discussion of input and output legitimacy in Chapter 2? Input legitimacy refers to the democratic prospects of network governance, while output legitimacy concerns institutional effectiveness and environmental outcomes. First, we should note that networks are primarily geared towards the resolution of collective policy problems. As Aars and Fimreite (2005, p. 244) write: 'Networks are predominantly legitimised on the basis of the results they achieve, not the processes through which they are reached. Thus, it can be argued that (network) governance means a shift from input to output legitimation.' While networks are organizational forms geared towards collective problem-solving, a critical question is what type of policy outcomes networks indeed produce. The interdependency between actors suggests that it is difficult for policy-makers to use networks as an implementation mechanism. Instead policy implementation is carried out through a process of bargaining where actors implement measures only to the extent that they perceive that it is beneficial to their own interests. The challenge for policy-makers in network governance is thus to persuade actors to implement the policy measures aligned with the common good.

There is a lively academic debate on whether networks pose a risk to, or can enhance, the democratic qualities of decision-making. Critics argue that networks lack many of the formal attributes necessary for achieving a democratic process (Aars and Fimreite, 2005). Others see network governance as an unavoidable attribute of modern politics and argue that traditional liberal accounts of democracy fail to assess its democratic potentials (Meadowcroft, 2007; Bogason and Musso, 2006; Sørensen, 2002). Clearly, networks challenge the authority of elected representatives and question traditional forms of legitimacy. The three dimensions of input legitimacy that were presented in Chapter 2 (participation, accountability and deliberative quality) will be discussed in the following.

For participation and deliberation the effects of network governance are mixed. First, the participants in networks are seldom selected through a process of democratic representation. New groups can be included in the decision-making process, which can be conducive to deliberation and consensus seeking. However, there is also a risk that powerful groups will take control and that deliberation deteriorates into bargaining and power abuse. A particular problem regarding control and accountability is that networks consist of both formal and informal interactions and dependencies. Informal deliberations between participants often take place outside democratic control and public scrutiny. Thus, political leadership is essential to make sure that accountability is maintained. For this reason Bell and Park (2006) argue for the need to 'bring government back in' when analysing network governance. Metagovernance has been suggested as an important strategy (Bell and Park, 2006; Sørensen, 2006; Aars and Fimreite, 2005). However, empirical research shows that politicians are often reluctant or unable to assume such a role (Bell and Park, 2006; Sorensen, 2006; Aars and Fimreite, 2005). Hence, it remains uncertain to what extent it is possible to metagovern networks democratically, particularly since a fundamental characteristic is that they elude steering of any one actor.

MUNICIPALITIES, CLIMATE MITIGATION AND NETWORK GOVERNANCE

Since the early 1990s, municipalities have been active in local climate mitigation efforts, and climate change is now gaining ground as a central policy issue in many cities around the world (Betsill and Bulkeley, 2007; Bulkeley and Betsill, 2003; Collier, 1997). Municipalities have responsibilities in many sectors that are important for the emission of greenhouse gases, such as energy, transportation, land use planning, housing and waste handling (Khan, 2007; Coenen and Menkveld, 2002; Collier, 1997). Some municipalities can be regarded as forerunners, for example, if they are characterized by an early engagement in climate change, have ambitious policy goals and are implementing mitigation measures (Forsberg, 2007; Allman et al., 2004; Bulkeley and Betsill, 2003).

Municipalities engaged in climate change, however, face difficult policy challenges. Betsill and Bulkeley (2007) argue that municipalities are crucially dependent on other actors in order to carry out their policy aims. Multi-level governance relations are important, particularly those toward central government (Aall et al., 2007; Forsberg, 2007). The implementation capacity of municipalities hinges on governments and other administrative levels, in terms of legislation, resource allocation and the institutional framework. The political context for municipal climate mitigation differs between states, varying from being hostile, as in the US under the Bush administration (Byrne et al., 2007; Bulkeley and Betsill, 2003), to a supportive political environment, with Sweden and the Netherlands as examples (Granberg and Elander, 2007; Lundqvist and Biel, 2007; Montin, 2007; Coenen and Menkveld, 2002).

Municipalities are also increasingly dependent on local actors. On the one hand, there is a need to find a broad consensus for ambitious climate policy goals and support from different parts of the public administration and major stakeholders. On the other hand, municipalities have to find new ways to implement policy measures since they lack full implementation capacity and the authority to enforce compliance with policies in areas such as transportation, energy efficiency, housing and energy. As a consequence, municipalities have been experimenting with institutional innovations where network governance is instrumental (Kern and Bulkeley, 2009; Gustavsson et al., 2008; Granberg and Elander, 2007). There is no coherent pattern in network governance in municipalities around the world. Local climate governance takes different forms due to local and national contextual factors. Examples of network governance are formalized interactions between public and private actors such as public–private partnerships and multi-stakeholder decision processes, and informal networks based on personal relations between individuals from public and private organizations.

In this chapter four main types of local network, with different functions and organizational forms, are distinguished (see Table 11.1). City-to-city networks and intra-municipal networks are formed between and within public organizations. Networks in policy formation and implementation networks, by contrast, consist of interactions between public and private actors. In the following section, these four network types will be discussed from the perspective of policy formation and implementation.

City-to-city Networks

Since the early 1990s there has been a proliferation of national and transnational networks between cities with the aim of supporting local climate mitigation. The three largest transnational networks, the Cities for Climate Protection (CCP) campaign, the Climate Alliance and Energie Cités, formed

Table 11.1   Networks in municipal climate governance

Type of network	Actors in the network	Organizational forms	Function of network	Dominating rationalities
1. City-to-city network	– Municipalities – Politicians and civil servants	– National and transnational city networks	– Information sharing – Building legitimacy	– Administrative – Deliberative
2. Internal network in municipal administration	– Municipal departments – Civil servants	– Informal contacts between civil servants – Working groups, action groups	– Engaging municipal administration – Enhancing internal cooperation	– Administrative – Deliberative
3. Policy formation network	– Politicians and civil servants – NGOs – Business – Environmental consultants – Researchers	– Working groups – Stakeholder participation	– Developing local climate policy – Building support for climate policies	– Deliberative (– Administrative)
4. Policy implementation network	– Politicians and civil servants – Business – Other actors (farmers, consumers, households, (NGOs)	– Implementation projects – Informal contacts between actors	– Implementing climate policy measures	– Deliberative – Economic

in the early 1990s, today involve approximately 3000 local governments in Europe, North America and Australia (Kern and Bulkeley, 2009; Lindseth, 2004; Bulkeley and Betsill, 2003). City-to-city networks have steering boards with representatives from member cities. The aims are to encourage municipalities to implement mitigation measures and to function as an arena for diffusion of knowledge, tools and best practice examples (Kern and Bulkeley, 2009). Other motivations for municipalities to join these networks are to gain access to funding and to add credibility to local mitigation efforts. Interaction between cities occurs mainly in the form of study visits, participation in workshops and informal contacts between civil servants. The purpose of membership in climate networks and the degree of activity varies considerably between individual municipalities (Kern and Bulkeley, 2009). In a study of five cities in the UK, the US and Australia, that are members of the CCP campaign, Bulkeley and Betsill (2003) found that the membership only had modest effects on the climate policies of the municipalities.

Internal Municipal Networks

Networks within the municipal administration are important ways to find broad support for the climate strategy through the involvement of various administrative sectors. A typical municipal organization relies on hierarchical forms of governance and administrative rationality. Climate policy goals are drawn up by elected representatives and implemented by the different parts of the municipal administration. In practice implementation is not smooth and policies are frequently blocked or transformed in the process. Turning to the city of Växjö in Sweden, there was awareness of this problem (Khan, 2008). The climate strategy group was placed right under the political leadership and had a clear strategy to create engagement for climate action within the municipal administration. Civil servants from the climate strategy group worked through personal contacts in a proactive way by focusing on those sectors with already engaged individuals while simultaneously trying to persuade sceptics to join. As one civil servant expressed it:

> We have had a general strategy, when there was an area that was a little slow we have tried to start a project, an EU-project or a national project, to get some economic space to really look at the issue. Then when a project plan exists it has to be implemented. It is a way to start a discussion and to move things forward (Interview 1, 2007).

In Växjö, the soft approach of the climate strategy group has meant that the municipal climate policy is not coherent, being strong in some sectors (heating, biofuels, housing) and weak in others (transport, land use planning) where civil servants are less engaged (Khan, 2008).

Policy Formation Networks

Municipalities are experimenting with decision processes that differ from the traditional representative democratic model. In these networks municipal actors cooperate with major stakeholders in order to find a consensus on ambitious climate policy goals. The formation of working groups, consisting of civil servants, politicians, NGOs, university staff and business organizations, is a common way to organize the planning process. Finding consensus on climate policies and developing new knowledge of the problem are important functions of these policy formation networks, which make learning and deliberation key elements. In Växjö, the city council set a goal in 1996 to become a fossil fuel-free municipality. This decision was a result of a partnership between the municipality and the largest environmental NGO in Sweden, the Swedish Society for Nature Conservation (SSNC). The cooperation between the municipality and the SSNC meant that people with very different backgrounds and world-views came together in deliberations in different working groups. This constituted a learning process for all involved as in the words of the previous mayor of Växjö:

> In the daily work it was mainly municipal officers who worked together with staff from the environmental NGO. Our senior officers are older men with long experience. Very professional but a bit old. The NGO had younger academics, between 25 and 30, many of which were women. This contributed to a creative dialogue and from this process the idea came that we should strive to become fossil fuel free (Interview 2, 2008).

Kinney et al. (2007) describe a similar process in the city of Boulder, US, where a working group consisting of civil servants, politicians, university staff and environmental consultants came together to develop and suggest policy measures for the municipality. Bulkeley and Kern (2006) also refer to deliberative policy processes in their study of local climate governance in Germany and the UK.

Working groups are normally initiated by the municipality as a complement to the traditional planning process. However, private actors are not passive recipients in this process. They promote their own agendas and independently take policy initiatives. In the city of Kristiansand in Norway, a local environmental NGO pushed ahead of the municipality and demanded that a local climate plan should be developed. They received a planning grant and made a draft version of a climate plan, which led to the development of a formal municipal plan (Hepsø, 2009). The municipality is thus not the sole, or even the main, driver in policy formation networks. Instead these networks can be perceived as deliberative practices where actors within and outside the municipality form alliances to develop and promote climate mitigation policies.

Although important for policy formation, the networks are not decision-making arenas. They provide input to traditional representative decision-making but do not replace it. There are no cases in the literature where working groups or other types of stakeholder processes have been given formal authority to make policy decisions. Thus, network governance and deliberation function as a complement to hierarchy and administrative rationality, which at the end of the day is the predominant form of governance.

Policy Implementation Networks

Network governance is even more pronounced in the implementation of climate policy measures. In a study of local climate governance in the UK and Germany, Bulkeley and Kern (2006) found that hierarchical forms of governance are becoming increasingly difficult for municipalities to employ. 'Self-governing' (municipalities implement climate measures in their internal activities) has been instrumental in many municipalities, but only amounts to a small proportion of local emissions. 'Governing by provision' (municipalities implement policies in their role as service provider) is more difficult since municipalities have increasingly less service provision in sectors such as energy, transportation and waste.[2] 'Governing by authority' (municipalities use regulation to enforce implementation by other actors) is problematic because municipalities have few areas where they have regulative authority and they are reluctant to propose tough requirements on private firms and citizens. Finding that hierarchical steering is not enough, Bulkeley and Kern highlight 'governing through enabling', which is when municipalities promote climate policy measures of other actors by employing soft and voluntary policy instruments such as information, economic incentives, guidance and partnerships. Governing through enabling is very similar to the concept of network governance as it is based on soft policy measures and on an extensive cooperation with other actors.

Policy implementation networks are typically formed around specific projects (often financed by national or international funds) with the aim of developing a technology or building a facility. In these projects the municipality engages with private actors either as partners or project facilitators. In the city of Växjö projects have been implemented in areas such as bioenergy, biofuel production and energy efficiency in buildings, with the participation of municipal departments and business organizations (Khan, 2008). While participation in policy formation networks involves a wide array of stakeholders, implementation networks are mainly made up of civil servants, municipal companies and private enterprises. Business plays a key role while NGOs are less visible, as business actors are responsible for a large part of the local emissions. A deliberate strategy by municipalities is to focus on policy measures that give co-benefits to the local economy, such as in the CCP campaign where the opportunities for local economic gains were an important argument to motivate cities to engage in mitigation efforts (Lindseth, 2004; Bulkeley and Betsill, 2003).

In policy implementation networks different rationalities are at play at the same time. Deliberative rationality is present in the development of joint projects and solutions. Economic rationality is manifested by the involvement of business, which aims for profitable solutions. For individual cities a common strategy is to focus on areas where local business has a competitive advantage. Växjö is situated in a forest region with a strong tradition in small-scale forest-related industries. Climate policies therefore revolve around using the biomass resources of the region (Gustavsson et al., 2008). In order to establish a secure supply of biomass fuel, there is a close cooperation between the municipal energy company, the regional forest industry and forest owners. In the nearby city of Kristianstad climate engagement started as a cooperation between the municipality, farmers and the local food industry with the construction of a biogas plant for biodigestion of organic material (Hepsø, 2009). In Denmark, with its world-leading wind power industry, supporting local private ownership of wind turbines is an important strategy in the climate policies of municipalities.

THE LEGITIMACY OF NETWORK GOVERNANCE

What can be said about the input and output legitimacy of network governance in municipal climate policies? First, output legitimacy will be analysed since it is the main promise that has been attributed to network governance. Arguably, network governance is the main option available for municipalities if they want to implement policies that go beyond self-governing, governing by provision and governing by authority. Progressive or leading climate municipalities are thus compelled to turn to network governance. This said, the question still remains of how effective network governance is in achieving tangible policy outcomes. Two observations suggest that networks indeed increase policy performance.

First, we can see that many cities actually manage to reach ambitious policy goals. Attributes such as 'Fossil fuel-free', '100 per cent renewable' and 'Carbon-neutral' are common among climate active cities. These long-term goals are combined with more concrete goals on emission reductions in the short to medium term. The policy goals also have the backing of major stake-holders, which is shown by the frequent participation of civil society and business organizations in policy formation. Second, policy implementation can be successful when the municipality manages to build implementation networks with key stakeholders such as energy companies, farmers and local business actors. Measures that the municipality would not have been able to undertake alone and that private actors would be unlikely to initiate can be carried through.

However, engaging private actors is far from easy. In a study of the willingness of local actors to engage in climate action in the Gothenburg region in Sweden, it was found that business actors are in general reluctant to cooperate, since they view resources as scarce and do not regard climate activities as central to their organizations (von Borgstede et al., 2007, p. 88). One implication is the importance of access to resources. Several studies conclude that financial support to municipalities is crucial in order to start joint projects with business actors (Granberg and Elander, 2007; Bulkeley and Kern, 2006). However, financial support may not be enough. This finding is underlined by a Swedish subsidy scheme to municipalities for local climate mitigation investments and measures (KLIMP), which aimed to generate cooperation between the municipality and private actors. While the scheme led to the implementation of many climate projects, private sector involvement was limited (Naturvårdsverket, 2008).

For genuine and effective cooperation to take place it is essential that private actors feel that they have something to gain and that climate action becomes central to the aims of the organization. The examples of successful cases, such as Växjö and Kristianstad in Sweden, clearly display these features. Municipal climate policies where network governance is important therefore tend to focus on technical solutions and on areas where business opportunities exist. Measures with no clear win–win situation that run counter to the interest of powerful actors (for example reduction in transport volumes and car traffic) are much more difficult to implement.

The analysis of input legitimacy is based on the three dimensions that were outlined in Chapter 2 (this volume). Participation in policy formation relies on organized stakeholders, such as NGOs, university staff and business organizations. Citizen participation in local climate networks is less common and is organized in a fairly traditional way in the form of information and consultation. According to Meadowcroft (2007), participation of major stakeholders can be seen as legitimate to the extent that they represent a broad range of societal interests. In the policy formation this seems to be the case, but in policy implementation the situation is more problematic. In the latter case there is a clear domination of business interests, which has influenced the type of measures that are implemented. With regard to accountability, an important feature of local climate governance is that decisions are still made in the local council. Accountability through electoral democracy remains important, but is to various degrees influenced by networked forms of governance and deliberative rationality.

However, the lack of decision-making powers of networks is not without problems since actors influence policy-making in a non-transparent way. The deliberative quality of the municipal climate governance processes is not easy to evaluate. Nevertheless, it is clear that they fail to meet the high standards of deliberative democratic theory as outlined by Lövbrand and Khan in Chapter 3 (this volume). The deliberative elements have not been introduced primarily for enhancing the democratic qualities of the policy process but for pragmatic reasons, such as mobilizing initiatives from external actors and finding support for climate policies. However, these pragmatic reasons have in some cases led to decision processes that have clear deliberative qualities such as in Växjö and Boulder.

As noted previously in this chapter, discussions of the democratic legitimacy of network governance have centred on the ability of politicians and civil servants to metagovern networks. In the case of local climate policies both politicians and civil servants have a clear presence, and network governance does not seem to erode the authority of local governments. However, politicians and civil servants primarily aim to use networks to increase policy effectiveness rather than to safeguard the democratic aspects. Network governance becomes a way to overcome the deficiencies of hierarchical steering where low policy effectiveness is the main problem.

In sum, we can see that the effects of network governance are mixed when it comes to both output and input legitimacy. Ambitious policy decisions are reached and many examples can be found of effective implementation networks. However, the dependence on business actors contributes to a one-sided focus on win–win policies and technological solutions. Network governance does not undermine the democratic legitimacy of the decision process since it involves a fairly broad range of stakeholders and decisions are made by the elected representatives. However, neither does it strengthen input legitimacy since the deliberative elements are quite weak and there is a clear lack of citizen participation.

IS NETWORK GOVERNANCE STATUS QUO IN DISGUISE?

In an important article from 2005, Bulkeley and Betsill seek to explain the gap between policy rhetoric and implementation in the climate policies of the two cities of Newcastle and Cambridge in the UK, which is a good starting point for a critical interpretation of network governance. By connecting urban politics to political and economic processes at the global and national levels, they demonstrate how municipalities are constrained in what they can achieve even when a strong rhetoric on climate action exists (Bulkeley and Betsill, 2005).

Economic goals tend to gain priority over sustainability goals and it becomes difficult to break with business-as-usual. As discussed in Chapter 3 (this volume), there is a strong trend of marketization of contemporary environmental governance, which consolidates certain interpretations of how environmental problems should be handled (O'Neill, 2007). Environmental protection and economic growth are seen as compatible and market actors are viewed as the best providers of environmental solutions, given the right incentives. The dominance of market forms has led critical observers to be sceptical of environmental governance arrangements that emphasize cooperation and partnerships between public and private actors (Whitman, 2008). Dryzek et al. (2003) add fuel to this critique by arguing that there is a risk of mainstreaming and co-optation if there is too close link a between environmental NGOs and the state. In a study of four countries, they found that in countries where the state deliberately engages in close cooperation with environmental organizations, a de-radicalization of the green public sphere occurs (Dryzek et al., 2003).

In the previous section it was argued that, while network governance has problems, it can contribute to effective policy implementation and remain democratically legitimate. However, caution should be taken about how progressive municipalities are in tackling climate change. The dominance of market environmentalism confines climate change policies to the marketplace, while the critique by Dryzek questions the motivations of public bodies to invite civil society actors in deliberations to reach consensus on policy objectives. From this vantage point the policy innovations examined in the previous section do not reflect more democratic decision-making or a genuine concern for the environment. Instead, local climate politics and the emergence of network governance can be interpreted as a strategy for local political and economic elites to take control of an emerging policy issue that threatens the legitimacy of the established order, and to define what the problem and the appropriate solutions are. Does this critical interpretation find support in the empirical observations?

When it comes to policy formation, climate municipalities have an impressive record, and are tied to long-term policy goals captured by positive notions such as 'carbon neutrality'. Rhetorically, this is a goal that everyone can agree upon and that helps to create a sense of unity among major stakeholders. However, in practice policy goals of this kind tend to mask underlying conflicts that need to be resolved if the high ambitions are to be realized. For instance, what does carbon neutrality imply for the transport sector and the use of the car? How will consumption patterns be affected? Which current planning practices are in conflict with the aim to become carbon-neutral? Since visionary policy goals of this kind are seldom accompanied by concrete policies, these pressing issues are seldom addressed.

Critics of network governance also draw attention to the actors participating in the policy process. A recurring claim is that actors who adopt the dominant agenda will be invited to the policy process, while radical organizations will become marginalized (Dryzek et al., 2003). This claim is confirmed by empirical examples. Organizations involved in network governance tend to be moderate environmental NGOs, environmental consultants and university staff (Khan, 2008; Kinney et al., 2007). In Sweden, as in other countries, there has been a general decline in citizen participation in local environmental politics. During the 1990s there was experimentation with participatory policy processes in the Agenda 21 process. However, the concrete results of these experiments were modest (see Chapter 8, this volume) and currently municipalities are more action oriented and focused on technological and market-based arrangements. Such arrangements primarily engage business and established NGOs, while citizen participation is more marginal.

In the previous section we found that the participation of business actors in policy implementation was successful when climate goals were linked up with commercial goals. From a critical perspective this finding confirms that network governance has become captured by the ideology of market environmentalism and has thereby lost its radical potential. The focus of the CCP campaign on local benefits and economic gains is an additional indication that local climate action has been co-opted (Slocum, 2004). While advancements are made and substantial emission reductions can be achieved, these advancements are arguably mainly cosmetic as the main societal trends point in the wrong direction. As discussed in the introduction of this chapter, interdependency is an essential feature of network governance. This is most pronounced in implementation networks where the municipality is crucially dependent on the goodwill of business actors in order to implement measures. As a consequence, there is a bargaining imbalance between the municipality and business actors.

In Denver in the US, Bulkeley and Betsill (2003) found that there was strong opposition from local business interests to climate action (due to the strong position of the coal industry), which led to a weakened municipal strategy that focused mainly on in-house measures. In Kristianstad in Sweden, Hepsø (2009) found that the municipality has worked constructively with the local meat industry in building a biogas plant. However, at the same time the importance of the meat industry meant that a more profound debate on the role of meat consumption in relation to climate change became taboo (Hepsø, 2009, p. 66). There are examples of how local climate policies in the transport sector become undermined due to dominant perceptions of the need for increased mobility and economic growth, which legitimizes the supply of new transport infrastructure (Pettersson, 2009; Forsberg, 2007; Bulkeley and Betsill, 2005). Network governance tends to reinforce these patterns since it favours strongly organized interests (food industry, farmers, business, car owners) over those less organized (green consumers, vegetarians, commuters).

CONCLUSIONS

This chapter has analysed network governance in the formation and implementation of local climate policies. It has been shown that municipalities clearly are important political actors in climate governance and that they often have more ambitious policies than those of national governments and international organizations. While network governance implies an increased reliance on a deliberative and economic rationality, this chapter has shown that hierarchy and administrative rationality remain important, particularly in policy formation. Thus the move towards a 'new' mode of governance does not mean the retreat of the old, only a new role for it.

The chapter has provided an ambivalent account of the virtues of network governance. On the one hand, network governance can be seen as an adequate response to the climate challenge. Network governance, though imperfect, offers clear possibilities for municipalities to take on a leading role in mitigation efforts, together with other actors at the local level. Network governance can be democratically legitimate, and may thus increase input legitimacy. On the other hand, critics have argued that municipalities are fundamentally restricted by the pressures of global political and economic forces. Network governance is seen as an elitist endeavour and reflects the dominance of market environmentalism.

A benign interpretation of these contrasting perspectives is that municipal climate policies are going through different phases. In a first phase, the municipality focuses on in-house measures, greening its own facilities and activities. In a second phase, the municipality engages with other actors in order to implement measures that can generate local benefits. In a third phase, when climate action has gained public acceptance, the municipality can tackle more difficult questions that challenge predominant behaviours and interests. However, it remains to be seen if municipalities can assume the progressive role that is implied by the last phase. Empirical experience does not yet support this view.

NOTES

1. The case study of Växjö municipality included eight interviews with politicians, civil servants and representatives of business and other organizations, as well as the use of written documentation.
2. This is of course different from country to country. In Sweden, for example, municipalities still maintain a fairly large ownership of services such as district heating, waste handling and public transportation, which means that service provision remains important.

REFERENCES

Aall, Carlo, Kyrre Groven and Gard Lindseth (2007), 'The scope of action for local climate policy: the case of Norway', *Global Environmental Politics*, **7**(2), 83–100.

Aars, Jacob and Anne Lise Fimreite (2005), 'Local government and governance in Norway: stretched accountability in network politics', *Scandinavian Political Studies*, **28**(3), 239–56.

Allman, Lee, Paul Fleming and Andrew Wallace (2004), 'The progress of English and Welsh local authorities in addressing climate change', *Local Environment*, **9**(3), 271–83.

Bell, Stephen and Alex Park (2006), 'The problematic metagovernance of networks: water reform in New South Wales', *Journal of Public Policy*, **26**(1), 63–83.

Betsill, Michelle and Harriet Bulkeley (2007), 'Looking back and thinking ahead: a decade of cities and climate change research', *Local Environment*, **12**(5), 447–56.

Bogason, Peter and Juliet A. Musso (2006), 'The democratic prospects of network governance', *American Review of Public Administration*, **36**(1), 3–18.

Bulkeley, Harriet and Michelle Betsill (2003), *Cities and Climate Change*, London: Routledge.

Bulkeley, Harriet and Michelle Betsill (2005), 'Rethinking sustainable cities: multi-level governance and the "urban" politics of climate change', *Environmental Politics*, **14**(1), 42–63.

Bulkeley, Harriet and Kristine Kern (2006), 'Local government and the governing of climate change in Germany and the UK', *Urban Studies*, **43**(12), 2237–59.

Byrne, John, Kristen Hughes, Wilson Rickerson and Lado Kurgelashvili (2007), 'American policy conflict in the greenhouse: divergent trends in federal, regional, state and local green energy and climate change policy', *Energy Policy*, **35**, 4555–73.

Coenen, Frans and Marijke Menkveld (2002), 'The role of local authorities in a transition to a climate neutral society', in Marcel Kok, Walter Vermeulen, André Faaij and David de Jager (eds), *Global Warming and Social Innovation: The Challenge of a Climate Neutral Society*, London: Earthscan.

Collier, Ute (1997), 'Local authorities and climate protection in the EU: putting subsidiarity into practice?', *Local Environment*, **2**(1), 39–57.

De Rynck, Filip and Joris Voets (2006), 'Democracy in area-based policy networks: the case of Ghent', *American Review of Public Administration*, **36**(1), 58–78.

Dryzek, John, David Downes, Christian Hunold, David Schlossberg and Hans-Kristian Hernes (2003), *Green States and Social Movements*, Oxford: Oxford University Press.

Fischer, Frank (2006), 'Participatory governance as deliberate empowerment: cultural politics and the facilitation of discursive space', *American Review of Public Administration*, **36**(1), 19–40.

Forsberg, Björn (2007), *Med sikte på Klimatmålet Lokalt? [Aiming at the Climate Goal Locally?]*, Stockholm: Naturvårdsverket.

Granberg, Mikael (2006), 'Alla talar om vädret: Svenska kommuner, klimatförändringar och samverkan' ['Everyone talks about the weather: Swedish municipalities, climate change and cooperation'], *Kommunal Ekonomi Och Politik*, **10**(1), 9–35.

Granberg, Mikael and Ingemar Elander (2007), 'Local governance and climate change: reflections on the Swedish experience', *Local Environment*, **12**(5), 537–48.

Gustavsson, Eva, Ingemar Elander and Mats Lundmark (2008), 'Multilevel governance, networking cities, and the geography of climate-change mitigation: two Swedish examples', *Environment and Planning C*, **27**(1), 59–74.

Hepsø, Marit (2009), *Lokal Klimatpolitikk: Utslipp, Makt og Ansvar* [*Local Climate Politics: Emissions, Power and Accountability*], Master's thesis, Oslo: University of Oslo.

Kern, Kristine and Harriet Bulkeley (2009), 'Cities, Europeanization and multi-level governance: governing climate change through transnational municipal networks', *Journal of Common Market Studies*, **47**(2), 309–32.

Khan, Jamil (2007), 'Local climate governance: the example of Swedish municipalities', paper presented at the 8th Nordic Environmental Social Science Research Conference (NESS), 18–20 June, Oslo.

Khan, Jamil (2008), 'Climate governance in Växjö: deliberation, networks and marketing', paper presented at the workshop Climate Governance Beyond Rhetoric, 29 May, Lund, Sweden.

Kinney, Larry, Mark Ruzzin, Sarah van Pelt and Elizabeth Vasatka (2007), 'Bolder Boulder: a city's quest to meet Kyoto when federal policies fail', paper presented at The ECEEE Summer Study, 4–9 June, La Colle sur Loup, France.

Koimann, Jan (2003), *Governing as Governance*, London: Sage Publications.

Lindseth, Gard (2004), 'The cities for climate protection campaign (CCPC) and the framing of local climate policy', *Local Environment*, **9**(4), 325–36.

Lundqvist, Lennart J. and Anders Biel (2007), 'From Kyoto to the town hall: transforming national strategies into local and individual action', in Lennart J. Lundqvist and Anders Biel (eds), *From Kyoto to the Town Hall*, London: Earthscan, pp. 1–12.

Meadowcroft, James (2007), 'Democracy and accountability: the challenge for crosssectoral partnerships', in Frank Biermann and Arthur Mol (eds), *Partnerships, Governance and Sustainable Development: Reflections on Theory and Practice*, Cheltenham, UK and Northampton, MA, USA: Edward Elgar, pp. 194–212.

Montin, Stig (2007), 'Kommunerna och klimatpolitiken: ett exempel på tredje generationens politikområden' ['Municipalities and climate change: an example of a third generation political area'], *Statsvetenskaplig Tidskrift*, **109**(4), 37–57.

Naturvårdsverket (2008), *Styrmedel i klimatpolitiken* [*Policy Instruments in Climate Politics*], Stockholm: Naturvårdsverket.

Næss, Lars Otto, Guri Bang, Siri Eriksen and Jonas Vevante (2005), 'Institutional adaptation to climate change: flood responses at the municipal level in Norway', *Global Environmental Change*, **15**, 125–38.

O'Neill, John (2007), *Markets, Deliberation and Environment*, London: Routledge.

Pettersson, Fredrik (2009), 'Infrastructure planning in Scania: a discourse theoretical approach to the concepts of regional development and sustainability in the planning process', paper presented at ICURPT 2009, 24–26 June, Paris.

Pierre, Jon and B. Guy Peters (2000), *Governance, Politics and the State*, New York: St. Martin's Press.

Slocum, Rachel (2004), 'Consumer citizens and the Cities for Climate Protection campaign', *Environment and Planning A*, **36**, 763–82.

Sørensen, Eva (2002), 'Democratic theory and network governance', *Administrative Theory and Praxis*, **24**, 693–720.

Sørensen, Eva (2006), 'Metagovernance: the changing role of politicians in the processes of democratic governance', *American Review of Public Administration*, **36**(1), 98–114.

Storbjörk, Sofie (2007), 'Governing climate adaptation in the local arena: challenges of risk management and planning in Sweden', *Local Environment*, **12**(5), 457–69.

von Borgstede, Chris, Mathias Zannakis and Lennart J. Lundqvist (2007),

'Organizational culture, professional norms and local implementation of national climate policy', in Lennart J. Lundqvist and Anders Biel (eds), *From Kyoto to the Town Hall*, London: Earthscan, pp. 77–92.

Whitman, Darell (2006), '"Stakeholders" and the politics of environmental policy-making', in Jacob Park, Ken Conca and Mathias Finger (eds), *The Crisis of Global Environmental Governance: Towards a New Political Economy of Sustainability*, London and New York: Routledge.

Interviews

Interview 1: Planning Officer, Climate Strategy Group, Municipality of Växjö, conducted 17 September 2007.

Interview 2: Mayor of Växjö (1995–2006), conducted 10 March 2008.

PART IV

Conclusions

12. Environmental politics after the deliberative turn

Karin Bäckstrand, Jamil Khan, Annica Kronsell and Eva Lövbrand

In this book we have combined theoretical inquiry with empirical investigations in order to answer the question: *can new modes of governance ensure effective environmental policy performance as well as deliberative and participatory quality?* This overarching research question was inspired by a general observation that the study and practice of environmental politics has taken a deliberative turn in recent years. We have found evidence of such a turn in the increased attention paid to procedural qualities of the policy process, such as participation, dialogue, transparency and accountability. In this book we have approached the recent proliferation of new modes of environmental governance as our case in point. While typically associated with less hierarchical and 'softer' forms of steering, we have argued that governance arrangements such as stakeholder dialogues, citizen juries, network governance, and public–private partnerships also rest upon a normative agenda to open up politics and make environmental decision-making more inclusive, transparent, accountable, reflexive and effective. By involving public and private actors in collective decision-making, new modes of environmental governance hold the promise to bring about both more legitimate and effective policy outcomes.

A central aim of this book has been to critically scrutinize this promise. In order to do so in a theoretically informed way, the chapters in Part I traced the deliberative turn and the promise of new modes of governance in scholarly work such as green political theory, international relations, science and technology studies and governance studies. In this broad and diverse literature we found a recurrent commitment to participatory and deliberative forms of governance that involve public and private actors in collective decision-making. While far from uniform, these theoretical traditions all seem to share the assumption that inclusive and deliberative decision procedures will increase the legitimacy and improve the performance of environmental policies. In Part I, we linked this assumption to a governance tradition that prescribes good governance ideals. Such ideals resonate with the environmental policy rhetoric following the Rio summit on Environment and Development in 1992 and promote the participation of lay and stakeholder groups in deliberative and market-oriented governance arrangements.

In Parts II and III we introduced eight case studies of governance arrangements in policy areas such as sustainable development, climate change, forestry, water and food safety in order to assess how these ideals play out in practice. While situated in different institutional contexts, and informed by a diversity of disciplinary perspectives, these eight chapters shared a critical-empirical ambition to scrutinize the normative assumptions underpinning the deliberative turn by means of in-depth analysis of concrete environmental governance practices. In order to evaluate the high expectations tied to new modes of environmental governance, most chapters were informed by a normative conception of legitimacy outlined in Chapter 2 (this volume). Aligned with a scholarly tradition that sees democratic or procedural legitimacy as only one source of legitimacy for non-electoral governance arrangements beyond the nation-state (Scharpf, 1999; 2006; Börzel and Risse, 2005), our normative framework stipulates criteria for both procedural qualities (input legitimacy) and environmental effectiveness (output legitimacy). From this vantage point, the legitimacy of new governance arrangements cannot rely on procedural values such as participation and accountability alone. When assessing if the promise of new modes holds, policy effectiveness and performance play an equally central role.

In this final chapter, we draw upon the findings in our eight case studies in order to return to the main research question of the book. In three steps we address whether new modes of governance can ensure effective environmental policy performance as well as deliberative and participatory quality. The first section builds on the theoretical framework developed in Chapter 2 and examines how rationalities (administrative, economic, deliberative) and forms (hierarchy, network, market) of governance play out in the various case studies. By focusing on dominant rationalities and forms of steering, we here move beyond the distinction between 'old' and 'new' modes of governance. We also seek to transcend governance scholars' preoccupation with the *loci* and actors of governance. In the second section, we return to the three lines of critique against participatory and deliberative modes of governance outlined in Chapter 1: (i) are new governance arrangements really win–win mechanisms that can strengthen both input and output legitimacy, (ii) are new modes of governance compromised by market environmentalism, and (iii) does the deliberative ideal underestimate the degree of conflict in political life and therefore prove ill-equipped to deal with environmental challenges? In the final section we sum up the arguments of the book and give our view on the promise of new modes of environmental governance.

RATIONALITIES AND FORMS OF GOVERNANCE

Debates on new modes of governance have been prolific in the social sciences. Schemes and conceptualizations have emerged to differentiate the old from the new, the legitimate from the illegitimate, hierarchies from networks, and the public from the private, just to name a few examples. This mapping exercise has been worthwhile and scholars are now much better equipped to make sense of the evolving ideas and practices of environmental governance. However, the emphasis on differences has sometimes overshadowed the similarities. In this book we have thus not sought to advance yet another definition of what new modes of governance are (and are not). Instead we have developed a framework that explores how forms and rationalities of governance play out in contemporary environmental politics. Although our analysis focuses on governance forms typically associated with new modes (for example public–private partnerships, networks, stakeholder deliberations), a large section of the book also draws attention to how hierarchy, often in the form of traditional state governance, has been influenced by the deliberative turn. Accordingly, the chapters in Part III examine Sweden as a pioneering green state at the forefront of experimentation with deliberative, participatory and market-based mechanisms. Our study of these participatory innovations prompts us to return to the role and conception of the state in the contemporary governance landscape.

Wither Hierarchy and Administrative Rationality?

As discussed in Chapter 1 (this volume), studies of global governance often emphasize the changing role and power of the state in a time of globalization (Rosenau and Czempiel, 1992). The increased participation of non-state actors in world affairs is often interpreted as a challenge to the state as the obvious centre of political action, and as a sign of dispersed sovereignty (Sending and Newmann, 2006). The assumed relocation of authority from public to quasi-public, or even private, actors is partly reiterated in this book. Many of our case studies suggest that there has been a shift from hierarchy towards market and networks in environmental governance. Hierarchical governance forms combined with administrative rationality, which have been the dominant type of governance of states and supranational institutions, have gradually been accompanied or replaced by more decentralized governance forms informed by economic and deliberative rationalities. However, instead of interpreting this trend as an example of eroded state authority in favour of new actors and spheres of governance, our empirical cases call for a more nuanced view.

First, the historical case studies of Swedish forest and food safety governance suggest that the shift to decentralized forms and deliberative rationalities of governance is not necessarily a new phenomenon. Instead of a deliberative turn, we can in some cases talk of a deliberative *return*. As Schlyter and Stjernquist argue in Chapter 10, in the early twentieth century, long before the adoption of the Swedish forestry legislation in the 1990s prompting participatory approaches, there was a tradition of stakeholder deliberation and consultation in forest governance. Investigatory commissions and multi-stakeholder consultations in the extensive public comment and review processes on legislative proposals, represent a deeply entrenched deliberative tradition in Swedish state governance. These early examples of deliberation in Swedish forest politics resonate with Holmberg's analysis in Chapter 9. The governance of frozen food technology in the post-war Swedish welfare state indicates that 'new' modes of governance were present long before the term was coined. These historical examples tell us to be careful to assume a clear trajectory of democratization in governance. In contrast to a presumed linear evolution of environmental governance from old to new, leading to increasingly legitimate and effective modes, our empirical findings reiterate the importance of context in the analysis of governance processes (Treib et al., 2007). In line with Richardson et al. (1982), we note that governance traditions of different countries and institutions may vary, for example, along the line of conflictual/consensual styles of policy-making.

A second and related finding of this book is that states and hierarchical forms of steering remain central in environmental politics. Most case studies suggest that new modes of environmental governance occur in 'the shadow of hierarchy'. Participatory and deliberative mechanisms often require the state to take an active role as coordinator, facilitator and mediator. In Chapter 6 on EU food safety and GMO governance, Bengtsson and Klintman found that deliberative interactions took place within or close to core political institutions and legislative bodies. Thus, stakeholder deliberations were mainly exercised within a hierarchical governance form. Hagberg's analysis of the EU Water Directive in Chapter 7 (this volume) also highlighted the central role of the state as facilitator and enabler of participatory governance processes. Given the complexity of the directive and the time constraints of affected actors, few stakeholder processes would have come about without administrative support from public officials. Along the same lines, Hildingsson illustrated in Chapter 8 (this volume) how local Agenda 21 processes in the post-Rio context were initiated by the Swedish state and facilitated by national authorities and local governments, rather than through authentic grass-roots or community initiatives. In the case of network governance for local climate mitigation (Chapter 11, this volume) Khan noted that, although deliberations on climate policies occurred between public and private actors, decision-making remained with elected representatives in the city council.

All these findings tap into writings on neoliberal forms of governmentality (cf. Barry et al., 1996). Rather than interpreting the rise of new modes of environmental governance as a trend that weakens the state in favour of new actors, governmentality studies encourage us to rethink the role of the state in environmental politics. Informed by economic and deliberative rationalities of governance, governments no longer seem to regulate environmental affairs in a top-down fashion and through the threat of sanctions. Acting as a facilitator of public–private partnerships and stakeholder dialogues, governmentality scholars would instead say that the state is engaged in a process of 'responsibilization' (Burchell, 1996; Shamir, 2008) that calls upon civic and private actors to actively undertake self-governing tasks either through the market or civic networks. From this vantage point the deliberative turn in environmental politics does not signify a retreat of government. Instead it can be seen as an expression of a changed logic or rationality of government that redefines statehood in environmental affairs.

While our empirical cases indeed show evidence of a decline in administrative rationality across several policy fields, the predominance of deliberative rationality seems to vary in relation to the policy cycle. Innovations in new modes of governance have primarily gained ground in agenda setting, policy initiation and implementation. While these stages in the policy process seem open to deliberation, decision-making often remains reserved for elected representatives. Hence, a useful avenue for future research would be to explore in further depth how forms and rationalities inform various stages in environmental policy-making. Where in the policy cycle does deliberative rationality prevail and what space for social change does it produce? The observation that hierarchical forms of governance are informed by deliberative rationality only at selected times and contexts, does indeed question the deliberative turn as a fundamental shift in the way that environmental politics is exercised. The proliferation of deliberative innovations could, on the one hand, be seen as a sign of increased state reflexiveness and a potential source of input and output legitimacy (see Chapter 8, this volume). On the other hand, it could just as well be interpreted as a way for the state to keep control through symbolic or cosmetic initiatives that include citizens, while retaining the power to take decisions (Leach et al., 2007).

In either case, our observations give support to arguments about the need to 'bring the state back in' to scholarly work. Authors with a base in green political theory (Barry and Eckersley, 2005) discuss the role of the state in these terms, but with few links to environmental policy practice. Also, governance scholars argue that the state may no longer be the supreme authority in terms of traditional forms of hierarchical steering, but can still play a central role as manager, coordinator and facilitator of governance processes (Pierre and Peters, 2000). In his most recent book on Climate Politics (2009), Anthony Giddens talks about the ensuring state that acts as a facilitator and enabler.

Such a state has to enable different societal groups to drive policy onwards as well as to ensure environmental outcomes. A task for future research is to connect work on environmental governance, legitimacy and deliberative democracy with the studies on the role of the state. A pertinent question could be: what is the role of hierarchical forms of governance after the deliberative turn?

Hybrid Modes of Governance

Another interesting theme emerging from this book is how governance forms and rationalities relate to each other. Although all authors in Parts II and III found the distinction between rationalities and forms of governance useful, the empirical cases also show that this distinction tends to break down in practice. To reiterate the conceptual framework in Chapter 2, rationalities refer to the ways of thinking or the underlying logic of governance that frame the choices open to individuals and thereby determine the prospects for social change. In this sense rationalities take priority over forms of governance that merely refer to the 'hardware' or the organizational aspect of governance. As Stripple argues in Chapter 4 (this volume), governance studies often fail to highlight the central role played by rationalities of governance. Rationalities offer different understandings of the prospects and avenues for social change. Administrative rationality relies on the delegation of political authority to expertise and civil servants who govern for the common good. Economic rationality emphasizes the possibilities of economic incentives and sanctions to produce desired outcomes. Deliberative rationality, in turn, highlights legitimacy and processes of inclusion, dialogue and participation among multiple actors.

The governance of environmental policy problems seems to take place in a continuum of governance rationalities and forms. Many of the case studies in this book display hybrid modes. Common hybrids are those that combine market forms with administrative rationality, like the Kyoto Protocol's Clean Development Mechanism (CDM) or the Johannesburg partnerships discussed in Chapters 4 and 5. Although the market form is characterized by self-regulation, both the CDM and Johannesburg partnerships are examples of governance modes that operate in the shadow of hierarchy. In Chapter 4, Stripple highlights how carbon market governance is informed by an administrative rationality, irrespective of which form of governance is in place. The procedures, codes, standards and 'technologies' of the CDM become established as legitimate regardless of the type of agency that supervises and controls them. The Johannesburg partnerships, which are examined in Chapter 5 by Bäckstrand, also represent a hybrid mode of governance initiated in the shadow of hierarchy in the UN system. While authority is delegated by sovereign states, the partnerships rely on the good intentions of involved actors to enact the partnerships through deliberative as well as economic rationality.

While hybrid modes of governance rely on an understanding that it is possible to combine different rationalities and forms to achieve their combined strengths (legitimate and effective governance), our cases raise the question whether rationalities and forms really are that easily combined. Are the underlying rationalities necessarily complementary or can they perhaps be contradictory or even conflicting? In Chapter 3 (this volume), Lövbrand and Khan talked about tensions between deliberative and economic rationalities of governance in a time of market environmentalism. This finding is underlined by Stripple's and Bäckstrand's analyses of the global carbon market in Chapters 4 and 5 (this volume). Although carbon market governance includes a number of entry points for stakeholders, the ultimate aim of the CDM is not to democratize climate governance but to increase its cost-effectiveness. Economic rationality takes priority. Also the analysis of forest governance in Chapter 10 underlined such a tension. In contexts when economic rationality dominated Swedish forest politics, Schlyter and Stjernquist illustrate how deliberative processes included only those actors who favoured timber productivity as the most important goals for forestry.

This finding brings us to another, and equally contentious, hybrid form, namely, deliberative rationality applied in hierarchical forms of governance. As discussed above, various modes that call for participation, consultation and deliberation with the public and with stakeholders are actually initiated, sponsored and run through hierarchical forms of governance. Obviously, hierarchy then also controls the deliberative process and decides which actors to include and when. Deliberation takes place at the mercy of hierarchy. The different chapters addressing Swedish environmental governance (Chapters 8–11, this volume) show how the control over deliberation was enacted and also changed over time.

Several chapters also examine the network as a third hybrid governance form. In the governance literature the network form is often praised as a way to accommodate both deliberative ideals and effective policies. As argued in Chapter 2 (this volume), networks rely on the interdependency of individuals or organizations and thus sidestep hierarchy and formal structures. Networks are governance forms dependent on communication, information sharing and deliberative rationality as important assets and conditions for successful interaction. Much hope is invested in the promise of networks to deliver legitimate and effective environmental policies, and in this way networks typify the deliberative turn. Chapters 9 and 11 (this volume) make an important contribution here.

In these two cases Holmberg and Khan differentiate networks according to the rationalities that influence them. They thereby end up with a more nuanced and mixed picture of the promise of networks for environmental governance. In the Swedish governance of food technologies in the 1950s (Chapter 9, this volume), Holmberg illustrates the role of networks under the logic of administrative rationality. Here the interplay between hierarchy and networks is apparent, as are the different rationalities at work. Deliberation occurs mainly between different experts, who also develop network links with the potential to deliver effective outcomes. However, a critical challenge to this established network is not possible since the deliberations are guided by administrative rationality and thus include only expertise, while being closed to outside actors and the general public. In the analysis of networks of local climate politics (Chapter 11, this volume), Khan also finds that these networks were highly influenced by administrative rationality. It was shown that local networks were mainly perceived as a tool to strengthen environmental performance. In this case, improving the deliberative quality was secondary.

Hence, although the modes of governance examined in this book combine different forms and rationalities of governance to reach multiple ends, some ends seem to take priority over others. This finding suggests that different governance rationalities may not be combined so easily. Although the deliberative turn may be enacted through multiple forms of governance, in different sites and institutional contexts, deliberative rationality does not necessarily go hand-in-hand with administrative or economic understandings of environmental governance. If environmental politics is still largely informed by administrative and economic rationalities, what does this tell us about the (deliberative) promise of new modes of environmental governance? In the following section we return to the critical perspectives discussed in Chapter 1 (this volume) in order to address this question.

REVISITING THE CRITICS OF NEW MODES OF GOVERNANCE

In Chapter 1 we introduced three main lines of critique that challenged deliberative governance arrangements from empirical, structural and ontological angles. In this section we return to this critique in light of the empirical observations in our case studies. Does the critique still hold? And, if so, what does it mean for the prospects of new modes of governance?

Does the Promise Hold? Returning to the Tension Between Process and Outcome

The core research question guiding this book is whether new modes of governance along the public–private frontier can reduce the prevailing governance, implementation and legitimacy deficits in environmental politics as illustrated in Figure 1.1 in Chapter 1 (this volume). Not surprisingly, our study of environmental policy practice confirms that there are central tensions or trade-offs between the ambition to increase democratic engagement and to promote effective environmental problem-solving. Despite the win–win promise of new modes of environmental governance, actors involved in environmental policy practice have trouble meeting the multiple expectations embedded in the deliberative turn. In line with critics of deliberative models of democracy, this finding suggests that there is no guarantee that deliberative governance arrangements will deliver green outcomes. The long-standing tension in green political theory between process and outcomes, input and output legitimacy, remains valid. In the following we revisit this tension in light of our empirical cases.

First of all, our study suggests that the deliberative turn in environmental politics seems to be geared toward output legitimacy and effectiveness rather than democratic procedure. Public or multi-stakeholder deliberation is frequently advocated as an instrument to reach policy outcomes, rather than a goal in itself. The promise of the EU Water Directive (Chapter 7, this volume) is to secure an effective implementation process through a broad participatory process of stakeholders. Similarly, by pooling together resources and expertise from business, civil society and government sectors, the primary aim of public–private partnerships such as the CDM or the Johannesburg partnerships is to contribute to the implementation of the Kyoto Protocol or Agenda 21 respectively (Chapters 4 and 5, this volume). Network governance in local climate politics follows the same logic (Chapter 11, this volume). The aim of local climate networks is to reduce greenhouse gas emissions effectively, not to democratize environmental politics. This overarching focus on effective outcomes is perhaps not surprising. To a large extent, the legitimacy of environmental politics rests upon the effective management of urgent environmental threats. However, in some cases dimensions of input legitimacy (wider representation of stakeholders, strengthened deliberative processes and transparency) have followed as a side-effect.

The stakeholder consultations analysed in Chapters 6 and 7 (this volume) indeed demonstrate a better record of procedural values such as deliberation, participation and accountability in the EU governance of food safety and water. In fact, the only clear exception to the priority of policy effectiveness in this book is found in Bengtsson and Klintman's study of the EU stakeholder deliberations on food safety and GMOs. Designed with the aim to restore public trust after a series of European food scandals in the 1990s, these stakeholder consultations were typically strong with respect to transparency and inclusion. Stakeholders, too, seemed satisfied with the organizational set-up. However, the deliberative quality varied across the various consultations examined. The closer to the scientific risk assessment processes such as GMO authorization, the more symbolic the consultations. Some even displayed symptoms of 'empty proceduralism'. Hence, although this case illustrates clear efforts to reduce the legitimacy deficit in the European Union through strengthened democratic procedures, it resonates poorly with the deliberative ideals of legitimacy discussed in Chapter 3 (this volume).

Secondly, if the deliberative turn is geared towards environmental ends, we still need to find out whether new modes of governance actually generate more effective environmental policy performance compared to other forms, like traditional regulation. Local climate governance is a case in point here. As illustrated by Khan in Chapter 11 (this volume), local climate policies do show signs of effective implementation through policy formation and implementation networks. Climate municipalities have adopted ambitious and well-supported policy goals, and many concrete measures have been implemented through cooperation between public and private actors. However, while local policy goals were met, it is less clear to what extent they have successfully contributed to a lasting reduction of the climate impact of the involved municipalities. While some emissions have been reduced due to specific measures, overall emissions often tend to increase due to political decisions that go against climate mitigation. Stripple and Bäckstrand's analyses of carbon market governance point in a similar direction (Chapters 4 and 5, this volume).

Through mechanisms for accountability, transparency and the monitoring of performance, the CDM has indeed created a framework for institutional effectiveness. The environmental effectiveness of the CDM is, however, more contested. As discussed previously, the CDM is a hybrid mode that combines administrative and economic rationality in a market form. The price mechanism means that it is easily evaluated and followed up. Yet the limits of economic rationality are clear, as discussed particularly in Chapter 5 (this volume). The CDM displays difficulties when it comes to fulfilling its sustainability criteria. The CDM has not generated sustainability development values, partly because sustainability is not easily priced and therefore cannot be included within the logic of economic rationality, and partly because the CDM project cycle offers little room for meaningful deliberation among affected actors. Thus, although the CDM may lead to effective policy outcomes, such outcomes are primarily based on economic rather than democratic processes.

While we cannot assess the performance of new modes of environmental governance on the basis of a limited number of case studies, our attention to output legitimacy does raise methodological questions of a more general kind. First, what baseline is used to assess policy performance? Or more specifically, related to Chapter 11 (this volume), what emissions could be expected from cities and municipalities such as Växjö if there were no climate action networks put in place? While new modes of governance may reach their goals effectively, it is important to critically discuss how ambitious these goals are compared to business-as-usual scenarios as well as the gravity and urgency of environmental problems. Second, how do we evaluate the environmental effectiveness of different governance modes when goals are poorly specified? Here the Johannesburg partnerships emerge as a case in point (see Chapter 5, this volume). Compared with the CDM, the Johannesburg partnerships lack governance structures and monitoring mechanisms for evaluating policy and environmental performance. As a consequence, their environmental performance is inherently difficult to assess. In general, we observe that the use of market-based, voluntary and deliberative policy instruments tends to move environmental governance away from stringent policies to more blurry, ambiguous policy objectives. The rise of voluntary and soft governance modes may therefore limit the possibility of measuring environmental outcomes.

Are New Modes of Governance Compromised by Market Environmentalism?

In Chapters 1 and 3 of this book, concerns were raised that new modes of environmental governance are dominated by a market norm that transforms environmental goods and services to commodities subject to monetary exchange. When recast in the language of capital, new governance arrangements such as emissions trading or product labelling schemes are typically said to deliver environmental improvements without compromising economic growth (Newell, 2008). Linked to a neoliberal order that shifts power from the political to the economic sphere, the deliberative turn thereby runs the risk of defusing the radical potential of civic critique and instead functioning as a legitimizing strategy of global capital (cf. Paterson, 2008). Following an economic rationality, critics also argue that market arrangements promote decisions guided by narrow economic interests rather than public dialogue and reason-giving (O'Neill, 2007). As such, they are unlikely to deliver the reflexive green results envisioned by green deliberative scholars. To what extent do our empirical cases give support to this structural critique?

As outlined above, some of our cases do point to a tension between economic and deliberative rationalities of governance. The CDM emerges as the most prominent example in this context. Designed to channel low carbon investments to the developing world, Bäckstrand notes (Chapter 5, this volume) that the CDM primarily functions as a market that identifies the cheapest alternatives for greenhouse gas emission reductions. Although this project-based mechanism does include several entry points for stakeholders, its deliberative potential has time and again been compromised by the economic incentives of carbon producers and consumers. While the CDM hereby appears as a case in point for the structural critique advanced by critical political economists, its hybrid form impels us to paint a more complex picture. As outlined in detail by Stripple in Chapter 4 (this volume), the CDM represents a highly administrated market. In order to turn emission reductions into tradable commodities, the CDM draws upon a complex series of monitoring and verification practices regulated and supervised by the CDM Executive Board, an international organization to which states have delegated authority. In this carbon marketplace, unconstrained deliberation may indeed be circumscribed. However, so is the clout of global capital.

Since the CDM is the only market-based governance arrangement examined in this book, it does not allow us to draw any general conclusions. However, in this particular case the deliberative turn seems to have little to do with actual practices of deliberation. The collaboration between public and private actors is instead guided by a mix of economic and administrative rationalities that gives priority to economic incentives and expert practices at the expense of inclusive public reason-giving. Although clearly guided by a market norm, the CDM does not, however, point to an opposition between the state and the market. Nor does it signify a relocation of power from the political to the economic sphere. Rather, drawing upon studies of neoliberal forms of governmentality (Rose, 1996), carbon market governance can be said to represent a reconfiguration of political power that shifts responsibility for corrective actions from central governments to free and rational-economic actors. Mediated through auditing, accounting and management schemes that enable a 'market' for public goods and services, government itself turns into a kind of enterprise that mobilizes consumers and producers to take responsibility for their actions (Burchell, 1996).

In Chapter 8 (this volume), Hildingsson explores how such 'degovernmentalisation of state' is enacted in Swedish sustainability governance. Through Local Agenda 21 schemes, local investment programmes for ecological sustainability, and the introduction of environmental quality objectives, a range of stakeholders have over the past decades been mobilized to take responsibility for the implementation of Swedish environmental policies. Although the scope for unconstrained public deliberation has been limited, the Swedish enactment of the Rio agenda has effectively turned into 'everyone's responsibility'. Also in Chapter 11 (this volume), Khan examined how Swedish municipalities have 'governed by enabling' private actors to take on voluntary climate mitigation targets and measures. By introducing 'soft' policy instruments such as information campaigns, economic incentives and partnerships, political authorities have acted upon the moral agency of 'the responsibilized corporation' (cf. Shamir, 2008) to implement the long-term goal of carbon neutrality.

When interpreting the deliberative turn from this perspective, new modes of environmental governance are not compromised by the market norm.

Rather, the rise of 'softer' forms of steering such as performance indicators, auditing schemes, and codes of conduct all embody the imagery of a competitive market as the very blueprint for action. Instead of securing the performance of environmental policies through traditional forms of steering (for example command-and-control, the treat of sanctions), these novel 'techniques of accountability' delegate responsibility for environmental performance to various 'partners' such as business, NGOs, and individual consumers (cf. Rose, 1996). Although this interpretation of the deliberative turn recasts the structural critique advanced by critical political economists, its prospects for social change may still deviate from the deliberative ideal advanced by green political thinkers. This is the issue to which we turn next.

The Unattainable Deliberative Ideal?

Compared to deliberative ideals of democracy found in (green) political theory, all the governance processes studied in this book fall far short. Not surprisingly, we have found that the deliberative and participatory quality of new modes of governance is seldom upheld, and accountability mechanisms are often lacking. In fact there are clear shortcomings in all our empirical cases. However, the assessment of these shortcomings depends on the reference point used in the analysis. Inherently, policy practice will always deviate from theoretical ideals. As a consequence, Eckersley (2004) has suggested that we need to see the deliberative ideal as a critical vantage point from which policy practice can be evaluated. Along the same lines Dryzek (2007, p. 250) asks us to approach deliberative democracy not as a hypothesis that can be falsified, but as 'a project, to which theorists, researchers, citizens and activists alike can contribute'. Even if we accept this more modest starting point, the findings in this book run the risk of disappointing anyone who expects the deliberative turn in environmental politics to epitomize such a project.

In the light of our empirical case studies we will now return to the ontological critique against the deliberative ideal advanced by scholars attuned to the politics of difference. Firstly, it was argued that practices of deliberation tend to privilege the agendas of dominant actors and, as a result, maintain inequalities of power and voice in political life (Young, 2003; Mouffe, 2000). To some extent, our cases give support to this claim. Deliberation on highly technical and expert-driven matters, such as the governance of GM food (Chapter 6, this volume) or the reform of the CDM in the context of the global carbon market, indeed seem to privilege certain voices over others. In these two examples, the scientific community, the biotech industry and carbon market actors enjoyed privileged access due to their expertise. In other cases public deliberation and consultation processes took place downstream in the decision process.

Although participatory processes have been introduced in the decision-making phase of the policy cycle, several of our cases suggest that public participation more often is encouraged in the implementation phase. The Johannesburg partnerships (Chapter 5, this volume), which were launched as participatory implementation mechanisms, reflect this trend. Established groups such as industrialized states, business and Northern NGOs have dominated the public–private partnerships at the expense of more marginal groups, such as women, indigenous people and Southern NGOs. Another example is the Water Framework Directive discussed in Chapter 7 (this volume), where the effectiveness of activities regarding diffuse source pollution such as forest operations required the active support of practitioners in order to be realized. There is nothing wrong per se with deliberation in the implementation phase, and it can often be valuable. However, if deliberation is exclusively used downstream in the policy process, it can be symbolic and used by elites as a tool for co-optation and to legitimatize decisions already made.

Secondly, and closely related to the first concern, is the claim that so-called deliberative governance arrangements easily collapse into corporatism and competitive interest group politics, with the risk of strategic bargaining between the most powerful societal groups rather than deliberation and 'arguing' (Risse, 2004). With the exception of public and citizen involvement in local Agenda 21 in Swedish municipalities (Chapter 8, this volume), all the case studies have indeed exclusively involved group-based stakeholder deliberation and consultation in the EU, global and municipal context. For example, in the governance of GMOs in the EU, as well as in the food safety domain in general, policy-makers use a deliberative logic in relation to societal stakeholders, whereas the public is, per definition, excluded from the concept of 'stakeholders'. Although many (green) deliberative theorists seem to favour deliberations that involve citizens, ready to transform their preferences in line with the common good, Meadowcroft (2004) argues that group-based deliberation holds the promise of more results-based environmental governance. Deliberation at the state–society interface, or where organized interests of state, economy and civil society interact (Meadowcroft, 2004, p. 183), are more likely to pool together resources and expertise from different domains and generate effective policy implementation (Fiorini, 2006).

Finally, some of our cases speak to the concern that deliberative governance arrangements are only conducive to policy issues with low stakes, leaving matters of greater political importance to traditional decision-making elites. Chapter 6 on EU food safety governance, for instance, illustrated that the closer stakeholders came to the scientific core, the less stakeholder deliberation there was. Moreover, Bengtsson and Klintman found a gap between high ministerial deliberations and stakeholder dialogues. High-stake decisions (such as GMO authorization) were mainly discussed outside the realm of stakeholder dialogues. Stakeholders deliberated on procedural issues with no particular relevance for food safety or GMO. This finding suggests that policy issues that deal with questions of high risks and survival, and where there is a need to take urgent action, often remain 'outside' the democratic process.

This tendency is perhaps best illustrated by security issues or 'high' politics. Such high-stake issues often demand urgency, secrecy or diplomacy and are therefore seldom subject to broad public scrutiny, participation and deliberation. This debate is a major topic of scholarly work in the 'environmental security' field (Dalby, 2009) and is not included in our study. However, an interesting input to this critical debate is offered by Schlyter and Stjernquist in their analysis of Swedish forest politics (Chapter 10, this volume). Building upon a historical overview of different governance forms and rationalities, they propose that forest governance in Sweden has been more influenced by the ways in which the function and role of the forestry sector has been understood, than by ideas on optimal modes of governance. Hence, in times when increased timber production has been a major concern, the scope for stakeholder consultation and deliberation has been low.

In sum, these findings do suggest that new modes of environmental governance in many respects fail to live up to the deliberative ideal as articulated in (green) political theory. However, we leave it up to the reader to determine whether these practical challenges are so fundamental that they undermine the deliberative ideal itself. Deliberative theorists may indeed underestimate the struggles for power and the conflictual dimensions of political life in their quest for rational consensus on the common good (Mouffe, 2000). However, our study does not allow us to draw any final conclusions about the 'nature' of environmental politics. By focusing on shifting rationalities and forms of governance, this book has instead highlighted the instability of categories and schemes that seek to establish a clear-cut trajectory for environmental politics after the deliberative turn.

ENVIRONMENTAL POLITICS AFTER THE DELIBERATIVE TURN

This book has systematically examined the promise of new modes of environmental governance through eight case studies in policy fields such as climate, water, food safety, forestry and sustainable development. The most significant and obvious finding is that the win–win rhetoric of new modes fails to translate into practice. Not surprisingly, the promise to deliver more legitimate and effective environmental policies seems too ambitious. While many of the governance arrangements analysed in this book have indeed increased the participation of new actors in environmental politics, the procedural qualities of these new modes are secondary to the quest for improved policy performance. At the same time there is no conclusive evidence that the governance arrangements actually generate more effective environmental problem-solving. Even in cases where environmental policy innovations, such as the Kyoto Protocol's Clean Development Mechanism, have established an institutional structure for the monitoring of performance, the environmental effectiveness remains uncertain. The extent to which new modes of environmental governance will in fact lead to marked improvement of the natural resource base or decreased pollution levels, therefore remains an open question.

Another central conclusion of this book is that the concept of 'new' modes is misleading. The shadow of hierarchy, which is the catchword for the continued influence of states, intergovernmental organization and supranational organizations in environmental politics, is prevalent in all of the governance arrangements examined in this book. The state and international organizations often initiate, broker and facilitate new modes of governance that can garner public legitimacy. This finding does not, however, challenge the claim that environmental politics has taken a deliberative turn in recent decades. It merely questions the assumption that such a turn is enacted in the absence of government. In general we have found evidence of a governance trend towards increased public participation, openness and dialogue. Although the deliberative turn primarily seems to engage organized societal groups in collaborative decision-making, some of our cases also indicate that the 'softer' forms of steering can enable more inclusive reason-giving among a diversity of actors. Encouraging examples are to be found in the implementation of the EU Water Directive and deliberations around GMOs in the EU. While far from the ideal model of deliberative democracy, these deliberative encounters emerge as an important, albeit piecemeal, complement to representative democracy that may add legitimacy to decision-making processes.

To conclude, we suggest that new modes of governance should be measured against other forms of decision-making in the environmental policy domain, not only against normative ideals of deliberative democracy. Even if deliberative encounters fail to meet the high standards of green political theory, they can be a considerable improvement compared to business-as-usual. Given the unavoidable realities of interest group politics, agenda setting and power struggles, we argue that the modes of governance studied in this book have, on the whole, strengthened procedural values of representation and deliberation in environmental politics.

REFERENCES

Barry, Andrew, Thomas Osborne and Nicolas Rose (eds) (1996), *Foucault and*

Political Reason: Liberalism, Neo-Liberalism and Rationalities of Government, Chicago, IL: The University of Chicago Press.

Barry, John and Robyn Eckersley (eds) (2005), *The State and the Global Ecological Crisis*, Cambridge, MA: MIT Press.

Börzel, Tanja and Tomas Risse (2005), 'Public private partnerships: effective and legitimate tools for transnational governance?', in Edgar Grande and Louis W. Pauly (eds), *Complex Sovereignty: Reconstituting Political Authority in the Twentyfirst Century*, Toronto: University of Toronto Press.

Boström, Magnus and Mikael Klintman (2008), *Eco-Standards, Product Labelling and Green Consumerism*, Basingstoke: Palgrave Macmillan.

Burchell, Graham (1996), 'Liberal government and techniques of the self', in Andrew Barry, Thomas Osborne and Nicolas Rose (eds), *Foucault and Political Reason: Liberalism, Neo-Liberalism and Rationalities of Government*, Chicago, IL: The University of Chicago Press.

Dalby, Simon (2009), *Security and Environmental Change*, Cambridge: Polity Press.

Dryzek, John (2007), 'Theory, evidence and tasks of deliberation', in Shawn W. Rosenburg (ed.), *Can the People Govern? Deliberation, Participation and Democracy*, Houndmills and New York: Palgrave Macmillan.

Eckersley, Robyn (2004), *The Green State*, Cambridge, MA: The MIT Press.

Fiorini, Daniel (2006), *The New Environmental Regulation*, Cambridge, MA: The MIT Press.

Fishkin, James and Peter Laslett (eds) (2006), *Debating Deliberative Democracy*, Malden, MA, Oxford and Melbourne, VIC: Blackwell Publishing.

Giddens, Anthony (2009), *The Politics of Climate Change*, Cambridge: Polity Press.

Jordan, Andrew and Duncan Liefferink (eds) (2004), *Environmental Policy in Europe: The Europeanization of National Environmental Policy*, London: Routledge.

Leach, Melissa, Ian Scoones and Brian Wynne (eds) (2007), *Science and Citizens: Globalization and the Challenges of Engagement*, London: Zed Books.

Meadowcroft, James (2004), 'Deliberative democracy', in Robert Durant, Daniel Fiorini and Rosemary O'Leary (eds), *Environmental Governance Reconsidered: Challenges, Choices and Opportunities*, Cambridge, MA: MIT Press, pp. 183–217.

Mouffe, Chantal (2000), *The Democratic Paradox*, London and New York: Verso.

Newell, Peter (2008), 'The marketization of environmental governance: manifestations and implications', in Jacob Park, Ken Conca and Mathias Finger (eds), *The Crisis of Global Environmental Governance: Towards a New Political Economy of Sustainability*, London and New York: Routledge, pp. 77–95.

O'Neill, John (2007), *Markets, Deliberation and Environment*, London: Routledge.

Paterson, Matthew (2008), 'Sustainable consumption? Legitimation, regulation and environmental governance', in Jacob Park, Ken Conca and Mathias Finger (eds), *The Crisis of Global Environmental Governance: Towards a New Political Economy of Sustainability*, London and New York, Routledge, pp. 110–31.

Pierre, Jon and B. Guy Peters (2000), *Governance, Politics and the State*, London: Macmillan and New York: St. Martin's Press.

Richardson, Jeremy, Gunnel Gustafsson and Grant Jordan (1982), 'The concept of policy style', in Jeremy Richardson (ed.), *Policy Styles in Western Europe*, London: George Allen and Unwin, pp. 1–16.

Risse, Tomas (2004), 'Global governance and communicative action', *Government and Opposition*, **39**(2), 288–13.

Rose, Nicolas (1996), 'Governing "advanced" liberal democracies', in Andrew Barry, Thomas Osborne and Nicolas Rose (eds), *Foucault and Political Reason:*

Liberalism, Neo-Liberalism and Rationalities of Government, Chicago, IL: The University of Chicago Press.

Rosenau, James and E. Czempiel (eds) (1992), *Governance without Government: Order and Change in World Politics*, Cambridge: Cambridge University Press.

Scharpf, Fritz W. (1999), *Governing in Europe: Effective and Democratic?*, Oxford: Oxford University Press.

Scharpf, Fritz W. (2006), *Problem Solving Effectiveness and Democratic Accountability in the European Union*, Political Science Series, Vienna: Institute for Advanced Studies.

Sending, Ole Jacob and Iver B. Neumann (2006), 'Governance to governmentality: analyzing NGOs, states and power', *International Studies Quarterly*, **50**, 651–72.

Shamir, Ronen (2008), 'The age of responsibilization: on market-embedded morality', *Economy and Society*, **37**(1), 1–19.

Treib, Oliver, Holger Bähr and Gerda Falkner (2007), 'Modes of governance: towards a conceptual clarification', *Journal of European Environmental Policy*, **14**(1), 1–20.

Young, Marion Iris (2003), 'Activist challenges to deliberative democracy', in James Fishkin and Peter Laslett (eds), *Debating Deliberative Democracy*, Malden, MA, Oxford and Melbourne: Blackwell Publishing, pp. 102–20.

Index